THIS BODY OF DEATH

THIS BODY OF DEATH

FORM AND DECAY IN EARLY MODERN LYRIC

EILEEN SPERRY

CORNELL UNIVERSITY PRESS
Ithaca and London

Ada Limón's "The End of Poetry" from *The Hurting Kind*. Originally in *The New Yorker* (May 4, 2020). Copyright © 2020, 2022 by Ada Limón. Reprinted in North America with the permission of The Permissions Company, LLC, on behalf of Milkweed Editions, www.milkweed.org. Reprinted in the UK and Commonwealth with the permission of Little Brown Book Group Ltd. through PLSclear.

Copyright © 2025 by Eileen Sperry

All rights reserved. Except for brief quotations in a review, this book, or parts thereof, must not be reproduced in any form without permission in writing from the publisher. For information, address Cornell University Press, Sage House, 512 East State Street, Ithaca, New York 14850. Visit our website at cornellpress.cornell.edu.

First published 2025 by Cornell University Press

Library of Congress Cataloging-in-Publication Data

Names: Sperry, Eileen author
Title: This body of death : form and decay in early modern lyric / Eileen Sperry.
Description: Ithaca : Cornell University Press, [2025] | Includes bibliographical references and index.
Identifiers: LCCN 2025016455 (print) | LCCN 2025016456 (ebook) | ISBN 9781501784316 hardcover | ISBN 9781501784309 paperback | ISBN 9781501784293 pdf | ISBN 9781501784323 epub
Subjects: LCSH: Lyric poetry—History and criticism | English poetry—Early modern, 1500–1700—History and criticism | Death in literature
Classification: LCC PN1356 .S65 2025 (print) | LCC PN1356 (ebook)
LC record available at https://lccn.loc.gov/2025016455
LC ebook record available at https://lccn.loc.gov/2025016456

Contents

Acknowledgments vii

Introduction: World Enough and Time   1
1. Dying Well   29
2. Lyric Prosthesis   61
3. Time of Death   97
4. Intimacies of Decay   130

   Epilogue: Not Alone   161

Notes 171
Bibliography 193
Index 205

Acknowledgments

When Donne found himself thinking about death, his main revelation was about the value of community: No one, he realized, is an island. Writing about death and dying over the last few years has led me to the same conclusion.

Work on this book was supported by Faculty Development and Dean's Office grants from Skidmore College and by fellowship support from The Folger Shakespeare Library. Portions of chapter 4, "Intimacies of Decay," first appeared as "Decay, Intimacy, and the Lyric Metaphor in Donne" in *Studies in English Literature 1500–1900* 59, no. 1 (Winter 2019): 45–66, published by Johns Hopkins University Press. A portion of the introduction, "World Enough and Time," first appeared as "'As Thou Art, I Once Was': Death and the Bodies in *2 Henry IV*" in *The Shakespearean Death Arts: Hamlet Among the Tombs,* edited by William Engel and Grant Williams (New York: Palgrave Macmillan, 2022). My gratitude to both presses for permission to shared revised versions of that work here.

In addition to fellowship support, the Folger Shakespeare Library has offered numerous and invaluable opportunities for intellectual community throughout this project. In particular, the 2019 "Rethinking Lyric Histories" seminar provided me the space to think through many of the core questions of this project in conversation with an incredible group of scholars: DeVan Ard, Gabriel Bloomfield, Emily Barth, Megan Heffernan, Lindsey Larre, Shannon McHugh, Jeremy Specland, and especially Ayesha Ramachandran, who has always been both the toughest and most generous reader one could ask for. The gift of this group cannot be overstated, and I hope you all can hear the joys of that seminar room still echoing here. Particular thanks to Ashley Buchanan, Kathleen Lynch, and Owen Williams, without whom none of these opportunities would have been possible.

The seeds of this work have been carefully nurtured by a lifetime of dedicated teachers. Dustin Griffin's Milton seminar at NYU suggested to me that I could happily spend a lifetime studying early modern poetry, and Jean-Pierre Mileur's seminars at Binghamton confirmed it. Ben Robinson and Doug Pfeiffer were careful, encouraging, and supportive mentors; I'm grateful for their ability to see potential in this project, often when I could not. They, along with Rachel Eisendrath, offered early feedback that shaped the long trajectory of this work for the better.

Several Shakespeare Association of America seminars allowed me to workshop early versions of this work and, more importantly, helped to foster the communities that sustained its writing. Thanks to Genevieve Love, Kat Williams, and members of Early Modern Disability Methodologies (2019); William Engel, Grant Williams, and members of Shakespearean Death Arts (2020); and Bellee Jones-Pierce, Lindsey Row-Heyveld, and members of Shakespeare's Other Disability Plays (2022). I am also grateful for the enthusiastic welcome I received from *The Pulter Project* editors, especially Leah Knight, Elizabeth Kolkovich, and Wendy Wall, who modeled what collaborative scholarship can look like at its best. Deserving of additional thanks are Holly Dugan, Penny Geng, Matthew Harrison, Dyani Taff, Rebecca Totaro, Maggie Vinter; and, of course, the decacephalic Letty Garcia, Yasmine Hachimi, Jess Hamlet, Sawyer Kemp, Lauren Eriks Kline, Emily Lathrop, Emer McHugh, Richard O'Brian, Aley O'Mara, Sydnee Wagner, Rho Chung, Nora Williams, and Robbie Hand.

I'm indebted to members of English department at the College of Saint Rose for their support and friendship, especially Nicole Cosentino, Eurie Dahn, Kathryn Fore, Jennifer Marlow, Daniel Nester, David Rice, and Brian Sweeney. These colleagues walked with me and one another through the college's decline and eventual closure in 2024. I am forever grateful for the generosity of spirit I witnessed in them throughout that experience; they helped me become a better scholar, teacher, and colleague, a debt I cannot repay. I am also appreciative to colleagues at Skidmore College in the English department and throughout the College: Kim Frederick, Maggie Greaves, Ruth McAdams, Susannah Mintz, Peter Murray, Kristi Peterson, beloved members of the NTT Organizing and Negotiating committees, and especially the many iterations of Scholarly and Creative Endeavors working groups who helped me see my way through the writing and revision process, week by laborious week. I owe a debt of gratitude to the tireless Interlibrary Loan teams at both schools, who made research possible when not much else was, and to Marta Brunner at Skidmore for help navigating the bureaucracies of publication.

Thanks to the team at Cornell University Press for all their incredible work bringing this book to life. Mahinder Kingra has been a fierce advocate and careful reader from the outset and this project is all the better for his guidance; additional gratitude to Susan Specter, Kristen Ashley Gregg, Karen

Hwa, and Carol McGillivray. Finally, I'm thankful for my incredible student research assistants, Kit Simpson and Sam Vesey, whose help with the final stages of revisions and (more importantly) infectious joy was nothing short of a gift.

Laura James, Daniel Lee, Katharine Perko, and Connor Pitetti read the earliest inchoate versions of these ideas, and it's my hope that their fingerprints are still visible. The lessons I learned with them about the joy of writing in community still inform my practices today, for which I am continually grateful.

The most dedicated readers throughout this process have been the Capital District Early Modernists: Andrew Bozio, David Morrow, Ineke Murakami, Christi Spain-Savage, and Pattie Wareh. For many dinners, for reading innumerable drafts, for being incredible colleagues and mentors and friends: thank you.

Thanks to Emily, who helped me remember to take a break. I am so proud of the person you are becoming. Thank you for being my favorite kid—I love you.

Finally, to Drew, for everything: for talking with me through these ideas, for patiently answering my questions about theology, for walking with me through the hardest parts, for seeing the way forward when I couldn't, and for being my partner. I love you.

THIS BODY OF DEATH

Introduction
World Enough and Time

Death is, above all else, a problem of time.
The carpe diem poets knew this best. As part of their seduction rhetoric, their lyrics offer their subjects the fantasy of timelessness, a space where the poets and their beloveds could stand outside the endless destruction of time to luxuriate in the pleasure of one another. Take, for instance, Andrew Marvell's "To His Coy Mistress."[1] Here, the poet opens by imagining what might happen "had we but world enough and time." Absent the pressures of time, the beloved's body remains in a state of perfection, adored piece by piece.

> A hundred years should go to praise
> Thine eyes, and on thy forehead gaze.
> Two hundred to adore each breast:
> But thirty thousand to the rest.
> An age at least to every part,
> And the last age should show your heart:
> For, lady, you deserve this state;
> Nor would I love at lower rate. (13–20)

In the hermetic world of the poem, both poet and lover have the opportunity for infinite leisure and infinite pleasure—an age to every part. Christopher Marlowe's shepherd makes the same offer, promising his love "a thousand fragrant posies" (10), "all the pleasures" (2), a world of limitless enjoyment.[2] John Donne, too, retreats to the safety of lyric: "We'll build in sonnets pretty roomes" (32) he promises, a withdrawal both in time and space that guarantees perpetual intimacy.[3] In these fantasies, there is no threat of ever running out of pleasure; there is always world enough and time.

"But," Marvell then turns to tell us, such a fantasy is always fleeting. Almost in the same breath they propose these fantasies, these lyrics remind us that escape is, of course, impossible. In the world outside the poem, time never stops. Walter Raleigh's nymph, in a moment revealing the form's conceit, rebukes Marlowe's shepherd.[4] She reminds him that those posies "soon break, soon wither," and are "soon forgotten" (15). Even Marvell's speaker admits that time always seems to catch up.

> But at my back I always hear
> Time's winged chariot hurrying near:
> And yonder all before us lie
> Deserts of vast eternity.
> Thy beauty shall no more be found;
> Nor, in thy marble vault, shall sound
> My echoing song: then worms shall try
> That long-preserved virginity:
> And your quaint honour turn to dust;
> And into ashes all my lust. (21–30)

That same body that fills the world of the lyric, that would spill its pleasures over into eternity, is, by virtue of its materiality, fundamentally incapable of doing so. Eventually, the poets remind us, time triumphs, and the poem ends; the body eventually dies. While these lyrics suggest that there is a kind of timeless pleasure available inside the poems, they simultaneously acknowledge that the bodies that are the source of such pleasure are inevitably bound up in the passage of time. Carpe diem lyrics, writes Wendy Beth Hyman, "are like all lyrics, only more so. . . . They not only enact a dread of time and work formally to constrain it. They also make the aspirations and limits of poetry's parallel temporal universe their subject."[5] Lyrics last, these poets remind us; bodies do not.

These poems do not, as we might expect, draw our attention away from the dying body. The body, after all, is at the heart of the pleasure, intimacy, and desire that drives these texts; abandoning the body would mean abandoning all the good that comes with it. But in order to make their case for consummation, these poets also need to underscore the ephemerality of that same body. The coy mistress is not worms and dust—not just yet. For the poem's argument to take hold, the bodies at its center must always be moving toward eradication; death is unavoidable but also continually deferred in the face of the present opportunity for pleasure. And for these poets, the form of lyric itself makes that paradox possible. As the speakers of these poems explicitly acknowledge, their writing cannot stop time. Timelessness is a fantasy and, in the logic of the carpe diem form, a particularly undesirable one: Lose time, and you lose death; lose death, and you lose the argument for urgency. Instead, the lyrics seem to offer the promise of a moment in the balance. The space of the lyric allows these poets a relationship with time that acknowledges the inescapability of its progress while also stepping outside that movement, if only temporarily. Time's winged chariot is always hurrying near in these poems—always hurrying and never nearer. For these carpe diem poems to succeed, as several centuries of readers suggest that they have, the bodies of their subjects must stand poised at this collision point of dissolution and permanence.

This book is about precisely that collision point. In the chapters that follow, I argue that lyric and other nonnarrative forms can sustain the kind of complex relationship between temporality and embodiment described here and, in doing so, provide alternate models for thinking about what it means to be mortal. Previous studies of death in early modern literature have tended to focus on narrative representations and have, unsurprisingly, reflected narrative models of mortality—linear or sequential temporalities that emphasize death as the culminating event or end point toward which all of time moves. But when we turn to lyric forms, I argue, mortality begins to look less like a moment in time and more like a quality of embodiment. These representations foreground decay, the ephemerality so essential to the carpe diem lyrics. Decay is, in short, the material instability of the body in the here and now, the immanence of mortality in all moments, not just the last; it is the recognition that the body is made of fragile stuff but that that fragility can be separable from a moment of future rupture. This claim is about the way time functions in lyric, and in making it, I am also advocating for more nuanced models of lyric time than previous critical models have provided. For instance, my argument here is not that lyric is a form in which nothing ever happens—though it is to claim, echoing W. H. Auden, that lyric can make nothing happen. Likewise, I push back against authors' own claims of lyric's timelessness, showing that such promises were almost always broken before they were made. As the carpe diem poems included earlier suggest, and as the discussion in the chapters to follow detail, while poems will often offer the fantasy of timelessness, the texts themselves frequently undermine that very promise, articulating a relationship with time that moves beyond the binary of temporary/timeless. Lyric time, as I argue throughout this book, is defined not by a single temporality but by its ability to engage in multiple temporalities, to move in multiple directions simultaneously. If time is a river, running ever forward, then lyric is an eddy in the current, flowing forward and backward, everywhere and nowhere all at once.

I use *decay* as the overarching term for the model of mortality that emerges in lyric for several reasons. First, while it had signified a general sense of decline in English since the late fifteenth century, the term took on more material, bodily overtones in the early modern period.[6] By 1600, *decay* had come to suggest "wasting or wearing away, disintegration," "decline of the vital energy or faculties," and "destructive decomposition or wasting of organic tissue; rotting."[7] This new set of bodily connotations suggests that the period's evolving attitudes about embodiment were beginning to require fresh vocabularies. Evidence of these new senses appears throughout the works of the authors I examine. William Shakespeare, for instance, uses *decay* frequently throughout *The Sonnets*, accounting for a third of the total uses recorded across all his works.[8] Perhaps no instance there better captures the term than Sonnet 11.[9]

> As fast as thou shalt wane, so fast thou grow'st
> in one of thine, from that which thou departest,
> and that fresh blood which youngly thou bestow'st
> thou mayst call thine, when thou from youth convertest.
> Herein lives wisdom, beauty, and increase;
> without this, folly, age, and cold decay.
> If all were minded so the times should cease,
> and threescore year would make the world away. (1–8)

Decay here serves as the negative parallel to *increase* and is aligned with old age. It is not death, precisely, but rather the antithesis of reproduction and growth. Decay also presses back against time's forward march—if all were to decay as the young man decays, growing older and refusing reproduction, "the times should cease," and the world would end. The guarantee of not just the future but *any* future—the idea that time might continue to move forward—is threatened by the presence of decay. A half century later, Hester Pulter frequently returns to *decay* as a byword for the instability of her own body. In "Made When I Was Not Well," Pulter reflects on the impact of illness and age. She bemoans her former beauty and health, noting how life has worn down every aspect of her body. Finally, at the poem's culmination, she exclaims

> Then why, my soul, art thou so fond to stay,
> seeing all that's lovely in me doth decay?
> For shame! Pack up thy virtues, and away.[10]

Like Shakespeare, Pulter offers decay as a contrast to youthfulness and health, a decline brought about by time and written on the body. Aging and ailing here blend together: Pulter notes her failing eyesight, her gray hair, and the loss of her "sportive wit and mirth" in her grief. While, as these examples suggest, there are areas of significant semantic overlap, there are also areas of significant divergence, indicative of the wide range of possibilities for the term in the period. I am not suggesting that *decay* was the period's only—or even primary—term for the qualities of embodiment central to this book. I am, however, arguing that its emergence during the early modern period, coupled with what are clear attempts in its early use history to begin to capture some of those qualities, make it an effective term to capture lyric's particular view on mortality.

Moreover, decay helps to distinguish the particular dimension of mortality captured in lyric. "Death" is the narrative reality of mortality, a discrete event fixed in time either before us or behind us, a point we are moving toward or away from (though, as I discuss in the chapters to come, the subject of time becomes significantly more complicated after death). To think only through this term means sorting bodies into alive and dead, with no overlap between the two; such a binary often results in the insistence that death has no place among the living, leading to mortality's repression. Decay, on the other hand, shifts our focus from an event in time to a material quality of the body. Decay is the quality of entropy that inheres in the body's materiality, the tendency of flesh to fail. In the chapters that follow, the texts I examine feature a range of experiences, including aging, dying, decomposing, grieving, and resurrecting. While none of these are death, all of them are decay: All capture the body's vulnerability and ephemerality, and all are physical manifestations of mortality that occur not as a single event but as experiences across time. For some, the term *decay* might at first evoke the same kind of end-driven structure suggested by a narrative account of mortality. That is, it is easy to imagine decline or dissolution as necessarily directed to a particular, fixed end point: One decays until one is gone and then no more. But I want to insist that we can—and that the lyric and other nonnarrative forms examined here in fact require us to—

distinguish the transformation from the destination. Like Marvell's chariot, always hurrying and never arriving, decay asks us to imagine that state of perpetual change as separable from any state to which it might arrive. And, for early modern readers, that destination was entirely unclear. As the discussion in chapters 3 and 4 of Donne and Pulter's works on resurrection explore in more detail, those who believed in bodily resurrection saw physical transformation as an inevitable condition of existing in time. The body aged, died, decayed, decomposed, recomposed, reanimated, changed ceaselessly until the moment of revelation, at which point time itself would cease. Bodies in time, therefore, are necessarily bodies in decay, and the only end point toward which they might move is the complete elimination of time itself.

Finally, the term *decay* echoes my focus on the embodied realities of mortality. As decades of scholarship confirm, mortality is a site on which nearly every aspect of our lives in some way converges. How we die, for instance, involves definitions of identity and selfhood, theology and systems of belief, ritual and social behaviors, medical and scientific discourse, or political ideologies, to name only a few.[11] In short, the way we die is a reflection of the way we live. The chapters that follow touch on many of these dimensions—for instance, the relationship between body and soul, or the shifting theologies of salvation and resurrection during the Reformation. But my primary focus is on the physical reality of the body's decline, the embodied experience of mortality. Because of this focus, this book engages deeply with contemporary disability theory, a theoretical vocabulary that has been previously neglected by studies of death, to their detriment. As I discuss in more detail later in this introduction, disability studies has devoted more careful attention to the relationship between literary form and embodiment than any other field. Consequently, scholars of early modern disability such as Elizabeth Bearden have challenged critics "to consider how pertinent early modern and contemporary theoretical models [of disability] can be mutually informative."[12] Decay, as a category, allows me to begin to bridge the divide between these two disparate fields and identify areas of common ground. To think through the lens of decay is to blur the lines between future and past, self and other; this is a way of thinking about mortality that recognizes that there is, perhaps, no clear distinction between the dead and the living and that all share in the condition of being mortal. I turn to *decay* to signal the shift lyric and other nonnarrative forms invite in our thinking: to consider our mortality not as a singular moment in time but as a feature of our embodiment.

Form and the Body

In this book, I approach form primarily as a verb rather than a noun—not as a static description of literary structure but instead as the structuring force that shapes representation in any given literary work. By emphasizing this dynamic element of form, I join other new formalist scholars in reading for the activity of form: of *forming*, shaping, of the ability of aesthetic conventions to mold the political, social, phenomenological possibilities of the world. Ellen Rooney, for instance, in her call for a return to form, invites literary scholars to read for "the work that form does."[13] We should understand form as "the enabling condition and the product of reading," she argues, "the force that permits the text to emerge as ideology's or theory's interlocutor, rather than as its example."[14] This approach focuses on a form's affordances, the possibilities inherent in a given structure. "Forms matter," Caroline Levine writes, "because they shape what it is possible to think, say, and do in a given context."[15] While Levine's definition suggests absolute states of possibility or impossibility, I contend that it might be more useful, particularly in literary form, to approach the affordances of a work as dynamic forces of give and resistance—not limitations, per se, but pressure. (It is worth noting that while Levine and the many other literary scholars who take up the language of affordance note its origin in design theory, the term also has a rich history in disability activism, where it is used to describe the accessibility of a given environment—a history that often goes unacknowledged.) I am not arguing, for instance, that lyric and other nonnarrative forms exclude death as an event entirely or that they can only represent a small slice of what it means to be mortal. But lyric's affordances are not those of narrative, or drama, or any other literary form, and those differences necessarily impact the model of mortality that emerges in these works.

Focusing on the activity of forms rather than on just their structure is particularly useful for sorting out the relationship among the many forms that guide any particular text. A number of the texts I explore in this book comprise multiple overlapping forms, the affordances of which often run contrary or counter to one another. Levine describes such moments as collisions. When two forms collide, Levine writes, "Which will organize the other? It is not always predictable. New encounters may activate latent affordances or foreclose otherwise dominant ones. Forms will often fail to impose their order when they run up against other forms that disrupt their logic and frustrate their organizing ends, producing aleatory and sometimes contradictory effects."[16] While Levine's project explores collisions at the level of ideology—the collision of aesthetic, social, and political forms—I borrow this term here to explore the relationship between aesthetic forms within texts, collections, or authorial careers. Despite the difference in scale, collision remains a useful framework because it highlights the active quality of these intersections. In particular, I focus on the collision of lyric and narrative forms across texts. I look to works such as Edmund Spenser's *The Faerie Queene* or Shakespeare's *Sonnets*, for instance, constructed of both lyric and narrative elements, or to authors such as Donne or Pulter, who theorize their relationship with time and the body through both lyric and narrative frameworks. These collisions help reveal most clearly the affordances of lyric, demonstrating how the differences in form shape the model of mortality that emerges. In choosing collision, I am also intentionally avoiding the term *hybrid* in discussing these texts. Heather Dubrow argues that this term is an inaccurate description of early modern multiform texts. "A concept used too readily and loosely in contemporary parlance," she writes, *hybrid* "is sometimes but certainly not always the most apt description . . . narrative and lyric variously supersede one another, suppress one another, and coexist."[17] *Collision* answers Dubrow's call for a vocabulary that better captures the dynamism and instability of these relationships. Unlike hybridization, which can suggest static unity and a settled final creation, and unlike the dialectic, which suggests direct competition and perhaps unresolvable tension, collision encompasses a range of dynamic and unpredictable relationships. Multiple forms can be, variously and simultaneously, contradicting, amplifying, refracting, and reflecting one another.

There are several particular narrative forms that shape the period's attitudes about embodiment with which these lyric and other forms collide. The vast majority of previous studies of early modern death and dying have focused on Elizabethan and Jacobean tragedy.[18] Michael Neill, most notably, has argued that "tragedy was among the principal instruments by which the culture of early modern England reinvented death."[19] Early modern tragedy highlighted "the dying person's ability to make death the consummation of a life conducted according to immaculately theatrical precepts," Neill writes, calling the form "profoundly teleological" and with a "fiercely end-driven narrative design."[20] David Bevington observes that in the late sixteenth century, death moved into the final act of the period's morality plays, creating the genre he terms the "homiletic tragedy."[21] There, once again, the narrative structure of the play works to place damnation, rather than salvation, as the climactic action; death becomes, once again, the end to which both the narrative and moral arc of the play bend. Maggie Vinter highlights the common ground between the period's dramatic works and the robust *ars moriendi* tradition.²² Both, she notes, emphasize the active role participants played in bringing about the actions of the stage or deathbed, with this action serving to underscore death (ideally, a good death) as the appropriate goal of this work. As these various descriptions suggest, these narrative forms afford an understanding of death as event, as terminus, and as culmination. Placed at the height of the play's action, death becomes a moment of meaning making, the resolution of all the action that has been directed toward this singular moment.

But perhaps more surprisingly, one of the other most influential narrative forms that shaped early modern mortality—and one that has been generally neglected in studies of mortality—emerged not from prose or drama but primarily within the early modern lyric tradition. Neoplatonism offered one of the most common vocabularies and structuring systems of belief for how to think about, among other things, the body's relationship with the soul and with divinity. In its broadest and most general sense, Neoplatonism offered a framework for thinking about the hierarchy of creation, sorted from the lowest (the material, the real) to the highest (the spiritual, the ideal) order. However, because of the sheer breadth of its influence in the early modern period, Neoplatonism is almost impossible to discuss as a singular or unified philosophical framework. "The Neoplatonist pattern hardly ever presents itself in complete and unadulterated form," Verena Lobsien notes.²³ Rather, Neoplatonism is more legible, both then and now, where it joins with other existing discourses. One of the most influential of these was Petrarchism, the predominant lyric mode through the end of the Elizabethan period and arguably the tradition that exerted the most influence on all early modern lyric in general. The union of Petrarchism and Neoplatonism is a strange one because, as Gordon Braden points out, Neoplatonism as such would have been "inaccessible to Petrarch himself," not crystallizing until later in the Italian Renaissance.²⁴ It was not Francesco Petrarch but his readers and his readers' readers who saw in the *Rime sparse*'s narrative structure a deep compatibility with Neoplatonism: The poet's gaze turns slowly from his earthly desire for Laura to his spiritual devotion to the divine, redirecting his attention from the material to the ideal.²⁵

This narrative structure, in turn, fosters attitudes about embodiment that come to define the Petrarchan mode and its inheritors, even its detractors. Take, for example, Baldassare Castiglione's *The Book of the Courtier*, one of the primary texts that Braden argues worked to fit Petrarchan themes with Neoplatonic values. When the figure of Bembo is asked about the relationship between sense and reason, he responds by describing the danger of desire. The ideal courtier, he argues, must "first consider that the body, where that beauty shyneth, is not the fountain from whence beauty springeth, but rather because beauty is bodiless and (as we have said) a heavenly shining beauty, she loseth much of her honor when she is coupled with that vile subject and full of corruption, because the less she is partner thereof, the more perfect she is, and clean sundered from it, the most perfect."[26] Bembo's advice captures perhaps the main feature that came to define Petrarchism's Neoplatonic legacy. Castiglione emphasizes that the body and its pleasures and beauty are valuable only when we understand them through the appropriate narrative framework. The lover who considers beauty only in the body thus interprets the physical as the narrative and apotheotic apex of being; the body is the goal, the end of the journey. Bembo is careful not to reject the body (or the courtier's desire for physical love) entirely; he repeatedly assures his fellow interlocutors that these desires have their place. But, he stresses, the body must take its true place as rising action. It belongs not in act 5 but in act 3, pointing the way forward to the true conclusion. "The body is a most diverse thing from beauty," Bembo cautions, "and not only not increaseth, but diminisheth the perfection of it."[27] The body, vile and full of corruption as it is (in Castiglione's original, *"vile e corruttibile"*), is not ideal but real and therefore cannot function as the end point of all desire. Here, the role of mortality becomes clear: The beloved's place on the Platonic ladder of being is revealed by her vulnerability to decay. The realization that she might die, might rot, signals that the value of the body resides in its transformative, redirecting potential, its role in moving the action forward. The end of the story, under this Neoplatonic framework, must be the eventual shedding of the body and its limitations.

The model of embodiment afforded by this narrative form helps to enforce what Tobin Siebers describes as the "ideology of ability," in which ability—health but also wholeness, beauty, and/or the capacity to work—becomes the prime indicator of individual worth. Like Neoplatonism, this ideology deploys various and sometimes contradictory narrative structures that attempt to move our attention past the body, especially the mortal body, toward some future ideal. Siebers notes that "the briefest look at history reveals that human beings are fragile. Human life confronts the overwhelming reality of sickness, injury, disfigurement, enfeeblement, old age, and death . . . whatever our destiny as a species, we are as individuals feeble and finite."[28] And yet, despite the unavoidable fact of our mortality, "the vision of the future to which we often hold promises an existence that bears little or no resemblance to our history. The future obeys an entirely different imperative, one that commands our triumph over death," promising utopian fantasies like eternal life, perfect health, and the absence of disease.[29] The ideology of ability, in Siebers's account, is built on narratives of progress, like Neoplatonism, that aspire to move past the body's mortality toward some future ideal free of decay. The effect of this narrative is that bodily impairment becomes a symbol of corruption, a legible sign of an individual body's distance from the ideal of ability. The drive to move those individual bodies closer to that ideal then manifests itself in what Alison Kafer describes as the "curative imaginary," the expectation that all disabled bodies should progress steadily toward perfect health (and thus toward the erasure of disability entirely).[30] "If disability is conceptualized as a terrible unending tragedy, then any future that includes disability can only be a future to avoid," Kafer writes. "A better future, in other words, is one that excludes disability and disabled bodies," whether via cure or systemic eradication; "indeed, it is the very *absence* of disability that signals this better future."[31] Like Siebers, Kafer recognizes the extensive normalizing pressure exerted by these narrative models of ability. The curative imaginary offers a clear narrative arc—from sick to well, suffering to peace—and then works to exclude bodies and persons whose experiences cannot or will not conform to that trajectory.

Building on Jack Halberstam's theory of queer temporality, Kafer then argues that we can resist the eugenic logic of these narrative structures by looking to crip temporalities, orientations toward time that resist the totalizing eradication of the curative imaginary that I discuss in more detail in chapter 3. Siebers, too, calls for what he terms a model of complex embodiment that resists the pressure exerted by the ideology of ability. Siebers argues that "embodiment seen complexly understands disability as an epistemology that rejects the temptation to value the body as anything other than what it was and that embraces what the body has become."[32] In other words, a complex model of embodiment—a model shaped by acknowledging, rather than rejecting, disability—resists the imperative to always progress to some imagined future, choosing instead to dwell with the body in the present; such a model rejects the temptations to erase or inflate the pain and transience of embodiment. While Siebers and Kafer do not describe their work in these terms, the acts of resistance they describe are, at their core, a resistance to narrative. Both recognize that these ideologies of able-bodiedness are built on the foundation of teleologic narratives, and both suggest that upending these ideologies requires finding new forms through which to imagine our embodiment.

The recognition that literary form is inherently tied to the value we assign to various bodies has long been a core tenet of disability theory, which has argued that narrative and narrative forms in particular often afford ableist ideology. Lennard Davis, for instance, argues that "the novel form, that proliferator of ideology, is intricately connected with concepts of the norm. From the typicality of the central character, to the normalizing devices of plot to bring deviant characters back into the norms of society, to the normalizing coda of ending," these narrative forms engage in the disciplinary work of norming, of defining clearly the boundaries between normal and abnormal.[33] In narrative, "disability looms before the writer as a *memento mori*," Davis argues; "normality has to protect itself by looking into the maw of disability and then recovering from that glance."[34] Likewise, David T. Mitchell and Sharon L. Snyder contend that narratives often attempt to prostheticize their disabled subjects, working to erase or explain away disability (which often occurs not as reality but as a metaphor for difference or Otherness), thus reinscribing an ideology of wholeness by the narrative's conclusion. These formal structures enact Kafer's curative imaginary, linking narrative development with progressively more able embodiment. Their culmination, as Davis, Mitchell, Snyder, and others suggest, is the elimination of disability and of complex embodiment; slowly but surely, the narrative moves the body through time to its own erasure.

More recently, work in early modern disability studies has continued this focus, exploring how the affordances of early modern forms shaped that period's attitudes about ability, disability, and embodiment. Some have noted, in line with contemporary disability theory, that the period's narratives are already at work responding to the disruptions posed by disability. Bearden, for instance, asserts that the prevalence of "experimental narrative forms such as those of the chivalric romance" in the early modern period reveals the period's fascination with disabled and deformed bodies.[35] These texts present "narrative chronologies and topographies that 'crip' or transgressively disable ableist concepts of timeliness, productivity, and mobility," she writes, noting that these wandering texts allowed authors to find ways to push back against normative temporalities, a resistance I trace in Spenser's contribution to the genre in chapter 2.[36] Lindsey Row-Heyveld, likewise, examines the narrative function of disability on the early modern stage, particularly when that disability is perceived to be fraudulent or exaggerated. Counterfeit disability became a common narrative device, she argues, one that encouraged the development of the audience's (and the period's) "suspicion about the non-standard body."[37] Others focus on how the embodied medium of performance allowed actors and authors to explore new dimensions of disability. "In a form that thinks through the medium of an actor's body," Katherine Schaap Williams observes, "disability is not an abstraction."[38] Instead, she notes, it becomes realized in its specific inherence in specific bodies. "On the stage, disability does not neatly metaphorize because the medium of the actor's body is never fixed enough to limit the transfer of meaning."[39] Genevieve Love looks at the way that disabled characters on stage become figures for the theater's representational capacity, allowing audiences to meditate on both the capacities and limitations of the theater as a mimetic form.[40] As these studies demonstrate, formalism remains a productive vocabulary for early modern disability studies, providing a framework for thinking about how the wide variety of texts, modes, and genres of the period shape ideologies of ability and embodiment.

But despite the widespread acknowledgment that literary form so profoundly shapes our understanding of disability and embodiment, early modern disability studies and early modern lyric studies have been slow to come into contact.[41] This may be in part because the initial goals of the subfield were explicitly to recover as much as possible of the lived reality of disability in the early modern period. In response to Davis's claim that disability as we understand it did not exist in the period, work by Allison P. Hobgood, David Houston Wood, and others focuses on unearthing previously silenced or ignored representations of disabled lives.[42] Without the real bodies of performers or the mimetic representation of individual characters, lyric forms represent disability, in large part, through metaphor; as Hobgood and Wood note, their goal, in the first movements of early modern disability studies, was "the diminishment of disability framed merely as metaphor."[43] When disability is only metaphorical, they write, or when we only attend to the metaphorical value of disability, the reality of disability's lived experience—and the persons who live it—is pushed further from view. But, as Williams notes, we may have simply missed the representative capacity of lyric if our only standard for representation is that of strict mimesis. "Early modern texts," she writes, "are not easily identified through the literary conventions of realism of the first-person memoir. Figuring monstrosity as extravagant bodily difference, marking lines with 'limping' meter, and inventing lyric poems about deformed mistresses, sixteenth- and seventeenth-century English literature brims with unfamiliar registers of disability representation."[44] Representation can take many forms, Williams observes, including those that complicate the metaphorical/literal binary. Scholars who have begun to work on the connections between lyric and disability argue, as I do here, that lyric's primary representational language is that of form—the forms of lines, images, genres, meter, rhyme, temporality, and voice, to name only a few.[45]

In this book, I aim to do just that—explore what lyric forms of decay, an unfamiliar register of disability representation, can offer our understanding of embodiment, both early modern and contemporary. I want to underscore that my argument is not that early modern readers understood mortality and disability as entirely overlapping categories. While it is the case that all bodies are mortal, it is not equally true that all bodies share in the experience of being disabled. My work is informed by the social model of disability, which recognizes that disability is, in part, a culturally and socially constructed reality created by the systems and infrastructure of the world we have chosen to build. I also recognize, following the work of Tom Shakespeare, Kafer, and others, that an exclusively social model may downplay the reality of life with impairment, minimizing some of the lived experience of pain that may accompany disability.[46] An important area of divergence between decay and disability lies in the relationship between these experiences and the social systems in which individuals are rooted. As the other studies of early modern disability cited earlier attest, disability was present throughout the period as an identifiable and functional identity category that, while not identical to contemporary definitions of disability, nonetheless shaped the experience of individuals as they interacted with their parishes, neighbors, and families. Decay, on the other hand, is an accommodated experience; aging and dying, for instance, generally fall within the range of "acceptable" bodily difference and do not provoke systematic exclusion.[47] Recognizing this distinction is crucial, especially as disabled individuals and allies continue to advocate for accessibility and accommodation. We all are privy to the experience of being mortal; we do not all face the real, material exclusion endured by disabled persons. I am also conscious of the long history of destructive conflations between disability and death—namely, that eugenic logic often describes death as a preferable alternative to disability. The futures of many disabled individuals are often foreclosed from public imagination, seen only as lifetimes of possible pain and suffering; ideologies of compulsory able-bodiedness result in many disabled individuals being regarded as good as dead already.[48] My argument in this book, emphatically, is not that disability is a death sentence. As many scholars and activists have shown, passionately and persuasively, life with disability can be full of advantage, joy, pleasure, and, most importantly, vitality.[49]

However, while it is false to claim that death and disability are one and the same, it is equally untrue to suggest that mortality and disability share no common ground. One of my central arguments in this book is that death studies' failure to listen to and learn from disability studies has been to its great detriment and is past due for correction. This common ground becomes more recognizable to us as we turn our gaze away from death as a moment or category of being and toward decay as a quality of embodiment. This turn is enabled by turning away from narrative forms and exploring the affordances of nonnarrative forms like lyric that offer alternate temporal models. By resisting or refusing narrative temporality, we can reject the eugenicist and curative teleologies that conflate disability with an absence of life and focus instead on complex embodiment in the present. Decay describes the material ephemerality of the body, its refusal to remain whole or stable across time. We might hear in this an echo, for instance, of the familiar figure in disability studies of the temporarily able body, which serves as a reminder that disability is not a fixed identity but rather a state in which all bodies may, at some point, find themselves. The temporarily able body exists in two times simultaneously: the future of possible disability and the contingent present of ability. The figure of the temporarily able body also underscores another major advantage of turning to decay: Disability, unlike race or culture, is a transient identity category, one that individuals may add or shed at various points in life.

Recognizing this widespread impact, disability studies has begun to expand its areas of inquiry into some of the various aspects of decay I explore in this book. For instance, several of the chapters that follow explore the experience of aging and the resistance authors and readers demonstrated to getting old. Kafer, in a dialogue essay with Ruth Bartlett, a scholar of aging and dementia, notes that "the logics of ableism and ageism perpetuate each other and are embedded in each other," informing social values around productivity, personhood, value, and quality of life.[50] Likewise, disability studies offers valuable frameworks for resisting or reframing futurist narratives that imagine not only the elimination of disability but, often, the delay or elimination of death itself. For early modern writers, the most common utopian futurist fantasy was that of the resurrection: the promise of eternal life in utter happiness and, often, a perfected body. In chapters 3 and 4, I explore how Donne and Pulter trouble these narratives, instead turning to versions of resurrection that question the nature of this future and the role the body might play there. As these examples suggest, disability theory offers an important vocabulary not just for disability but for bodies across time and identity. Much like queer theory provides an essential framework not just for queerness but for sexuality of all kinds and degrees, disability theory provides a rich vocabulary for thinking about ideologies of embodiment in general. By bringing together disability studies and death studies, I aim not only to deepen our understanding of how early modern literature engages with mortality but also to suggest new areas, archives, and methods that might be enriched by a disability-informed approach.

This Body of Death pulls together these critical vocabularies of new formalism, lyric studies, disability theory, and death studies to discover ways of thinking about what it means to live in a dying body. Through this work, I join others who have called for our field's return to form with an eye toward social and cultural ideologies. Michelle Dowd, calling for literary studies to once again take up more formalist methods, notes that such a return is contingent on scholars' readiness to embrace the political and social dimensions of the act of criticism. "New formalism can become a truly significant force in early modern studies, one that pushes the field to make space for presentist as well as historicist analyses of early modern texts, that brings a renewed attention to form while keeping contemporary critical concerns squarely in the frame," she writes. "But it can only do so if it joins forces not only with traditional historicisms, but with feminism, critical race studies, disability studies, and ecocriticism, among other modes of inquiry."[51] If formalism is to avoid its past mistakes, Dowd notes, it must seriously engage with the work of scholars examining the intersections of early modern literature with contemporary social concerns. A turn to form should not and cannot be a turn from the world in which we read and teach; we should regard it instead as an opportunity to dive deeper into it. To add to Dowd's call, there is a need for lyric scholars—who, as in previous generations, have been some of the earliest adopters of formalist methodology—to incorporate engaged, activist methods like disability studies into their critical vocabulary. This book aims, in some small way, to explore what it might look like to do just that.

Early Modern Forms of Decay

I turn now to another early modern example to illustrate just how closely linked these questions of form and decay were. In the sixteenth and seventeenth centuries, England was awash in *ars moriendi* treatises, popular literature about how to die well. As David W. Atkinson notes, while *artes moriendi* originally developed out of medieval Catholicism, they were easily adopted into England's new spiritual landscape; Protestants "retained what was valuable of the established tradition and adapted it to a theological framework" more suited to the new orthodoxy.[52] Vinter, likewise, discusses the remarkable flexibility of this genre, describing it as "doctrinally diverse, reflecting confessional outlooks from Catholicism to radical puritanism."[53] But despite the variety of their theological approaches, many of the *artes moriendi* to emerge in England in the early seventeenth century shared a common goal: to encourage active engagement with the process of dying. For early modern readers, "death is not something you suffer," Vinter writes, "but something you do."[54] *Ars moriendi* texts of the period emphasized complex "models of action" that underscored the agency both of the dying and the communities in which they died, encouraging all to approach death as a sophisticated ritual requiring active engagement.⁵⁵ These texts, wildly popular with early modern readers, offer concrete evidence that early modern readers were eagerly and voraciously working to understand their own mortality.

This work was accomplished largely through what we might describe as formal thinking. These *artes moriendi* offered their readers templates, scripts, patterns of thought and behavior into which they might fit their own experiences. They were encouraged to seek out forms of prayer, devotion, and belief to help draw meaning out of the chaos of decay. To contemplate death in this period necessarily meant to think formally, to consider the possible models available for making sense of one's own mortality. As William Engel and Grant Williams observe, early modern death was defined in and by its many formal manifestations—*ars moriendi* literature, memento mori motifs, the rich tradition of devotional writing surrounding death and dying, to name only a few. There was, they argue, a "pluralization of knowledge and practice around dying, death, and the dead in the period."⁵⁶ They continue, "With its affiliations to artifice and techne, the premodern conception of art also highlights the artisanal dimension of this robust cultural activity. For Shakespeare's age, death was not just a knowing, but a doing and a making."⁵⁷ These *artes moriendi* are yet another reminder that mortality does not exist outside the forms in which it is represented.

I want to offer one example that illustrates some of the ways forms—particularly the collision of narrative and nonnarrative forms—helped guide readers as they contemplated their own mortality. Christopher Sutton's treatise, *Disce Mori, Learne to Die*, was first published in England in 1600. For Sutton, clergy of the Church of England and devoted Protestant, a good death meant a lifetime of spiritual discipline: studying scripture, living righteously, and praying regularly. *Disce Mori* shows its readers "howe behooveful it is for every Christian man, soberly to meditate of his end" and "that we need not fear Death, much less to meditate thereof."⁵⁸ Like many *artes moriendi*, *Disce Mori* proved immediately popular with English readers. A thick duodecimo of twenty-two gatherings, the treatise went through eleven editions by four different printers between 1600 and 1662.⁵⁹ In addition to these stand-alone editions, the text was bound with Sutton's 1602 follow-up, *Disce Vivere*, in three subsequent printings by three different printers. This kind of popularity was not entirely unusual for an *ars moriendi* treatise. Thomas Becon's 1558 *Sick Mans Salve*, another popular example, went through "between twenty-nine and thirty-one known editions (more if one counts those contained in the larger collections of Becon's works) and remained in demand for six decades after his death."⁶⁰ Even so, Sutton's lengthy run puts *Disce Mori* potentially among the most widely read texts of the early seventeenth century.

As was conventional for the genre, Sutton's text features a number of illustrations. Images were prominent beginning with the first English *ars moriendi*, William Caxton's vividly illustrated 1491 translation of *The Art and Craft to know well to die*, a popular continental treatise. In the centuries of *artes moriendi* that followed, authors included detailed illustrations to reinforce the form's spiritual directives. Nigel Llewelyn notes that these "devotional exercises were assisted by an extraordinary range of visual artefacts of the *memento mori* type, together with moralizing texts such as *the Dance of Death* and descendants of medieval poems such as 'Erthe upon Erthe.' All this prepared the sinner for the afterlife and helped the bereaved make more sense of the loss of an individual by turning the experience of death into a didactic *tableau*."[61] The images of the *ars moriendi* tradition, including Sutton's, provided visual echoes of the textual instructions of these treatises and were often a portable and frequently consulted iconographic reminder of the works' central moral lessons for dying. The last image of Sutton's opening paratexts echoes this tradition, depicting what appears to be a conventional early modern deathbed scene (see fig. 1). An older man lies in bed, pointing admonishingly at the young man standing by his side. The dying man's warning is spelled out across the top of the frame: "As thou art, I once was," he says. "As I am, thou shalt be." This message, which sometimes appears in its original Latin—*tu fui, ego eris*—is a conventional one, a familiar trope of memento mori iconography. The old man's primary audience is the other figure present in the image: a young soldier, dressed in full armor and holding a lance. This young man stands next to the bed, but his body is angled away; with one hand on his hip, he looks backward over his shoulder in a clear sign of disdain. The young man's answer is clear: No, I will not.

This image, and the *tu fui* form in general, relies on a set of internal binaries. First, it necessarily involves two people: a dead—or, in this case, dying—speaker and a young, healthy listener. These provide the *I* and *thou* of the statement, the self/other. The *tu fui* also asks the reader to balance a number of temporal paradoxes, creating a constellation of past/present and present/future relationships. The dying man insists that his past correlates to the young man's present and his own present to the young man's future. The young soldier, on the other hand, refuses this equation, implicitly insisting that the present differences between the two men must lead, necessarily, to different futures. In all of this, the moment of death itself is deferred. D. Vance Smith notes that in medieval English literature, death possessed a kind of representational impossibility. "The state of death cannot be signified," he writes. "The naked souls we see in art and literature are either living a life after death or still in the process of losing being."[62] That is, if death

FIGURE 1. Christopher Sutton, *Disce Mori* (London, 1662), sig. A11v. STC 23490. Folger Shakespeare Library.

is a moment, that point must always be an absent one; it is the moment when experience—and therefore representation—ceases. To these medieval writers, Smith notes, "death can never be a predicate of the human; it is false to say that a man 'is dead' (*est mortuus*), false to say that being can be a predicate of nonbeing. We can talk only about the duration of dying itself: *homo moritur, homo moriebatur*. . . . Death takes us out of time and beyond language. Only dying can be linguistically analyzed, because it is still a movement toward something, an aspect of the unfolding of time."[63]

Death's resistance to representation is a result of its unique relationship with time; because of its phenomenological nature, death can never exist in the present. It must always be somewhere—or rather, sometime—else. This deferral is realized in the paradoxes central to the *tu fui* form. For both self/other, then/now, the objects must be utterly identical, totally the same: *I* and *thou* are subject to the same conditions of humanity, the same fragile materiality, and the same eventual death. The things that happened in the past are happening in the present and will happen again in the future. The form makes the claim that every living body is also a corpse in waiting and that any apparent difference between the two is superficial; all bodies are identical, and all bodies must die. At the same time, the *tu fui* also insists on total difference. The living and the dead, the present and the future, these are represented—grammatically, dramatically, visually, logically—as distinct from one another. There is the speaker who knows death and the listener who refuses to recognize it; a present where death is only a vague threat and a future where it is an unavoidable certainty.

This tension between now and then, self and other, is a fundamental affordance of memento mori iconography, inviting the viewer into what Rose Marie San Juan describes as a troubled sense of identification. Looking at another commonplace of the memento mori tradition, the de-fleshed skull, San Juan describes how that icon creates a kind of empathy between viewer and object. Viewers impose a face and thus a persona on the bones, creating in effect a mirror of themselves. But, like the *tu fui*, the relationship between the two is simultaneously encouraged and resisted. "The skull's undeniable ability to forge a connection between the dead and the living is highly ambiguous," she writes, "charged as it is by its transitory status in which presence and absence, visibility and invisibility, can never be fully extricated from each other. The skull thus becomes a key transit point in life and death, both the furthest point before complete material disappearance and oblivion, and the closest point from which one might imagine being looked at from the other side."[64] The skull, while inviting the viewer to project a face and thus an identity, also resists that projection; it is both a reminder of personhood and a denial of that same quality. The viewer thus sees in it both a future version of themselves—the fate of their own face—and something utterly foreign to their current lived reality.

Such is the paradox of Sutton's deathbed image. The dying man's gesture emphasizes similarity and identification; he tries to impress on the young man that they are fundamentally the same. But, as is evident from the young man's response, this claim fails to take hold. The young man's refusal to acknowledge his inevitable death conveys the major moral flaw Sutton's treatise is intended to address in its readers. Individual sinfulness, Sutton argues, is a result of the failure to recognize one's own mortality. Sutton dedicates a chapter early on in *Disce Mori* to "the causes why men so seldom enter into a serious remembrance of their end."[65] The neglect of our own deaths, he continues, is an extension of Satan's Edenic deception. "To induce the sons of men lightly and loosely to pass over a religious remembrance of this their end," he writes, "is the sleight of him, whose business was, and is, at, and since the fall of Adam, to slay souls, *Nequaquam morienmini*; Tush, saith he, you shall not die at all."⁶⁶ And while the evidence of the fallen world should lay bare that deception, Sutton notes, humanity seems to cling desperately to the temptation of exceptionalism. "It is a marvel above marvels that in a battle where so many before our eyes go to the ground, paying the debt to nature daily, our remiss hearts can take no warning to enter into some remembrance of our state," he writes. "The neighbor's fire cannot but give warning of approaching flames. *Mihi heri, tibi hodie*: Yesterday to me, today to thee, saith the wise man: whose turn is next, God only knows."⁶⁷ Even when death is clearly visible, he notes, our human tendency is toward denial: Others may die, but not I.

The reader enters Sutton's treatise, therefore, on this visual reminder of the unresolved paradoxes of mortality and in a state of plausible deniability. Death is inevitable, yet occupies a future that never seems to arrive. Everyone must die, yet our own deaths seem always elsewhere. Rather than insisting that time moves sequentially—that the past must predate the present, which must anticipate its own future—the memento mori disrupts that linear organization, making time more vertical than horizontal. This is the same strategy, exemplary of a nonnarrative approach to mortality, shared by the carpe diem poets. Take, for instance, the last stanza of Robert Herrick's "Corinna's Going A-Maying," where the speaker begins to wrestle with the collapse of future and present.⁶⁸

> Come, let us go, while we are in our prime,
> And take the harmless folly of the time.
> > We shall grow old apace, and die
> > Before we know our liberty.
> > Our life is short; and our days run
> > As fast away as does the sun;
> And as a vapor, or a drop of rain
> Once lost, can ne'er be found again:
> > So when or you or I are made
> > A fable, song, or fleeting shade,
> > All love, all liking, all delight
> > Lies drowned with us in endless night.
> Then while time serves, and we are but decaying,
> Come, my Corinna, come, let's go a-Maying. (57–70)

Herrick's speaker, like the dying man of Sutton's illustration, insists that his audience must understand that they are living in narrative time. "We shall grow old apace, and die," he reminds Corinna. The world in which they live is one hurtling always toward death. This movement, the speaker insists, is irreversible; that which is "once lost, can ne'er be found again." These conventional warnings project the speaker and his beloved far into the future, into the time of their deaths. Like the deathbed woodcut, the speaker calls our attention forth to a future inevitable end.

But Herrick's future projection is layered on top of several other competing temporalities. In his future, the speaker imagines, the current present moment—the spring morning on which Corinna is being urged to get out of bed—will be transformed into a cautionary past. In this future, the two lovers are dead, drowned in the endless night of their own mortality. Once they are dead, when (not if) they are memorialized "in fable, [or] song," their deaths will be perceived by other future lovers, who might similarly refuse to recognize the inevitability of their own mortality. The speaker imagines a future in which his past overlaps with the readers' present and in which his present presages the readers' future. That is, the singular linearity of narrative mortality—youth, aging, dying—is replaced with a tangled pileup in which all futures and pasts become present. And like Marvell, Herrick concludes his poem not by escaping narrative mortality but by acknowledging the poem's ability to exist alongside that future. "Then while time serves," he offers, "let's go a-maying." That conditional—"while time serves"—reveals the temporality of lyric.[69] Cleanth Brooks notes that "'while time serves' means loosely 'while there is yet time,' but in the full context of the poem it also means 'while time serves us.'"[70] Rather than time guiding the lovers forward, it now follows their lead. No longer is narrative sequentially an irresistible impulse; time, in the world of the poem, waits for them. Ramie Targoff argues that the poem's sudden final reversal should be read as a kind of nihilistic shrug. The final urge to go a-Maying "becomes eerily dissonant once it is paired with so different a message from the earlier stanzas. To 'go a-Maying' hardly seems an adequate response" to the threat of decay.[71] But to read the poem's return to its seduction rhetoric only as a surrender misses the mark. The poem is comprised almost entirely of imperative verbs like the *come* and *let's go* of the final lines. Targoff's reading, like many others, positions these as future instructions: Here is what we will do next, here is how we must act going forward, given what we know now. But these imperative verb forms are nearly indistinguishable from the second-person present tense that fills the poem and blur the lines between the commandment to do something and the description of present action. Lines like "Come, my Corinna, come; and coming, mark / how each field turns a street" (29–30) invoke not just a narrative future but a lyric present—the lines themselves enact the pair's wandering, with each commandment creating the very actions it invites. It is not that the poem surrenders to sequential temporality; rather, it creates a space that exists separate from and concurrent with that possibility. Like Sutton's memento mori, Herrick's closing carpe diem sentiment therefore offers both an acknowledgment of the narrative temporality of death and, simultaneously, a representational form through which that temporality can be interrupted.

It is not until the appearance of a subsequent woodcut in Sutton's treatise, first printed in the 1601 edition, that the temporal paradoxes of the *tu fui* image begin to dissolve.[72] Several hundred pages later, after the end of the body of the text but before a number of closing paratexts, is a second image, the other half of the pair (see fig. 2). The young man is now dead on the battlefield, broken lance in one hand. Standing above him is a skeleton, wearing a sash and waving a flag victoriously. The skeleton has one foot planted squarely on the fallen soldier's chest, demonstrating his conquest. The paradox of the initial *tu fui*—the notion that while the soldier, like the dying man, is subject to the inevitability of death, perhaps he (like the reader) might also somehow be different—collapses in this second image. Death the great leveler finally wins out. This pair of images and the journey between them, I argue, frame the readers' experience of mortality in Sutton's treatise. The opening deathbed scene establishes a nonnarrative relationship to time to facilitate its internal paradox. The memento mori iconography there insists that all time is present and that past and future are only illusions of difference, a message reinforced by the visual medium. As a snapshot, the image may gesture toward a future or past but can itself contain only a perpetual present, only a single moment captured outside the flow of time. This allows the dying man's message to remain unresolved: In a mode comprised only of present, a claim that one's past is another's future—as I am, thou shalt be—cannot be proven or unproven. The *tu fui*, in this way, is as much an escape from mortality as it is a reflection on it. At the very same time the form insists on the inevitability of death, it also takes the reader out of the entropic flow of time that leads to that future.

The second woodcut at the other end of Sutton's treatise, however, shifts the reader from a nonnarrative to a narrative experience. With the addition of a second image—establishing a beginning and an ending—we move from the vertical structure of the *tu fui* into the linear orientation of narrative time. The young man, who could initially sustain the claims of death being both unavoidable and totally foreign, is now forced to recognize his own mortality. The readers, too, are reminded that they cannot avoid death, try as they might. The soldier exists within time rather than outside it. With the deathbed image now past, the victory woodcut becomes his future, a future

FIGURE 2. Christopher Sutton, *Disce Mori* (London, 1662), sig. A12v. STC 23490. Folger Shakespeare Library.

that ends (as it must) in death. The two images together impose a narrative arc on Sutton's treatise, echoing the reader's passage from denial to acceptance, from youthful resistance to inevitable defeat. However, the placement of these images on either end of the text embeds Sutton's entire argument within the frame of their collision; *Disce Mori* is surrounded by and enmeshed in the negotiation between these two forms of mortality. While the argument within the text confirms, over and over again, that the young man's belief that his future will be different is in error, the very existence of the book belies the psychological and rhetorical hold of that belief on the readers' thinking. Even if readers can easily acknowledge that *of course* the young man will die, they may be much less likely to embrace that truth about themselves. So even while Sutton's text, on its face, argues that we must accept the inevitability of our own deaths, the openness of the initial deathbed image and the fact that that openness is sustained for the entirety of the text until the emergence of this second image allow, even subconsciously, for some measure of resistance. They create a space for a nonnarrative approach to mortality, even as the treatise itself calls for a narrative understanding of death.

But this arrangement of the images—one on either end of Sutton's treatise—does not last long. After the text's first few decades in print, the second image, the victory woodcut, drifts toward the front of the text. By the 1634 and 1662 editions, this image appears on the page immediately following its paired deathbed woodcut. The initial distance of several hundred pages between the two is ultimately reduced to a single page turn. Indeed, in the 1634 edition, both images are printed on the verso side of two subsequent pages. The result is that when this edition is held open to the deathbed image, the second, the victory woodcut, is partially visible through the adjacent page. Now, rather than the image of the young man's resistance, the last image a reader would encounter before reading Sutton's advice on dying would be death's ultimate victory. Rather than sustaining the claims of the deathbed scene over the entire treatise, in other words, readers would now encounter both claim and refutation in virtually the same moment, prior to reading the treatise itself. These late editions of *Disce Mori* begin not on a note of denial and resistance—a refusal to die—but with a stark reminder of death's inevitability. The paradoxes of the *tu fui* are immediately replaced by the narrativization of mortality.

There are a number of reasons why later printers might have decided to rearrange *Disce Mori's* woodcuts. Several of the treatise's images and other paratexts were replaced or rearranged over its long print run, as was the norm for texts that shuttled from printer to printer. But I am less interested here in the reasons why the images move than in the effect that moving them has on the treatise's argument about how to die. *Disce Mori* offers us a prime example of the friction produced through the collision of forms—here, narrative impulse and the nonnarrative orientation of the memento mori. Like Marvell's poet noticing the forward impulse of time's winged chariot, Sutton's treatise hears the call of the dying man to recognize death's inevitability, time's linear impulse. And yet, both also offer the opportunity to step outside that trajectory, to shift into nonnarrative temporalities that reorient the speaker or reader's relationship with their own mortality. For Sutton and Herrick, and the many other authors and texts I examine in the chapters to come, it is ultimately the collision of these forms—of narrative death and lyric decay—that shapes the account of mortality that emerges.

This Body of Death

Neither narrative, nor lyric, nor any literary form exists in a vacuum. These forms collide in various ways and in various places, refracting, contradicting, and compounding one another. The chapters that follow engage with texts or authors whose work highlights these collision points, particularly the collision between narrative and lyric, demonstrating how these interactions shape the understanding of mortality that emerges. I begin with texts in which those collisions are most explicitly oppositional, in which the affordances of narrative crash up against the lyric and other nonnarrative forms of the works. These texts overtly theorize the conflicting accounts of mortality that emerge from these respective forms, exploring the models of embodiment that result. The first chapter focuses on the allegory of temperance in Spenser's *Faerie Queene*. Guyon's journey must be understood not just as a quest for temperance, I want to suggest, but specifically as a quest for a temperate form of decay, a virtue that is revealed to be fundamentally incompatible with narrative accounts of dying. Spenser takes up two predominant nonnarrative forms that I have already introduced here: carpe diem lyric and memento mori iconography. The first corpses Guyon encounters in his journey, Amavia and Mortdant, are presented in the familiar language of memento mori iconography, while the last, Verdant's lifeless body in the Bower of Bliss, is framed by the garden's infamous carpe diem song. The structure of Spenser's quest highlights the difficulty of finding a middle way, neither entirely denouncing the body's materiality nor fully embracing its pleasures but rather defining a model of temperance and a poetics in which embodied existence coexists with spiritual health. The difficulty of navigating extremes in moralities of decay is compounded by the narrative form of the quest itself. Reading Spenser's epic narrative alongside Sutton's *Disce Mori* and other early modern *artes moriendi*, I argue that early modern temperate dying resisted narrative linearity, instead opting for forms that captured the concurrent sense of motion and stasis inherent in that virtue. Ultimately, Spenser's choice to place these two nonnarrative moments at opposite ends of the book, thus turning the reader inward against the flow of narrative, reveals the insufficiency of narrative forms such as epic to fully embody a temperate death.

From Spenser's romance epic, I then turn to the sonnet sequence, a genre that highlights perhaps better than any other the constant negotiation between narrative and lyric forms. The second chapter argues that Shakespeare's *Sonnets* offer what I term the *prostheticizing* model of lyric, supplementing the declining life of the fair youth's body through lyric extension. Previous Petrarchan sonneteers compensated for their beloved's mortality through memorialization, preserving their memory in verse. This impulse, I argue, is bound up in the Neoplatonic narrative structure common to lyric sequences. This Petrarchan model enacts a narrative movement up and away from the body and toward a disembodied ideal of immortality. Responding to this tradition, Shakespeare instead explores a model of lyric immortality that prioritizes bodily existence, even in its decay. The prosthetic lyric Shakespeare develops in this sequence is most legible in the sequence's formal structures, particularly its interest in fraught sites of connection. The relationship between couplet and quatrains and the link between the fair youth and dark lady sonnets provide formal counterparts for the relationship the poet imagines between his verse and his aging beloved. Ultimately rejecting the traditional Neoplatonic model of immortality, Shakespeare explores both the sonnet and the sonnet sequence's capacity (and failures) to augment decay through a prosthetic model of lyric immortality, one that centers decay not as anathema to lyric but as an essential feature of its preservative ability.

After these examples, I then turn to texts and authors that foreground the many possibilities within lyric itself, exploring how this form builds on or differs from narrative models of embodiment. The third chapter looks at Pulter's lyric works, which show a sustained interest in the way decay disrupts linear models of time. Pulter's speakers return repeatedly to the subjects of grief, decay, and resurrection and, in doing so, find themselves pulled out of objective, sequential time. These experiences instead reveal time to be subjective, recursive, and disordered—a far cry from expectations that grief might resolve slowly but steadily into hope and wholeness. As a way of expressing the disrupted temporalities of decay, Pulter turns to the language of forms, both literary and conceptual. She offers two models for time: the circle, an expression of time as constant but unchanging activity, and the speck, the absence of motion and the erasure of time. Her lyrics find decay's temporality in the collision of these two forms, a constant negotiation between circle and speck, between always and never. This dynamic temporal model is best read, I argue, as an expression of crip time, rooted in the body's decay and in its refusal of linearity. Through these alternate models of time, Pulter's work offers a new model for lyric time, one that better captures the multiple temporalities available through lyric forms and the complex temporality of embodiment.

Finally, in the book's last chapter, I turn to Donne and the work of the metaphysical conceit. Donne's early lyrics often turn to decomposition as a conceit for intimacy. Decay eradicates the boundaries between individual bodies to allow for hyperbolic physical contact between lovers, creating a more intense sexual and emotional union. This conceit later shapes Donne's preaching on resurrection, illustrating the degree to which lyric thinking shaped Donne's later theological work. Responding to early modern debates about the possibilities for bodily resurrection, Donne presents the body's physical destruction after death as a necessary material condition of resurrection and connection with the divine. It is only by decomposing, Donne preaches, that the body can be reformed in perfect union with God. Donne's theology offers some of the hallmarks of what we might now describe as disability theology, a theology of the body in which its imperfections and tendency toward decay are foregrounded rather than condemned.

As I have argued here in the introduction, nonnarrative forms like lyric offered early modern readers and authors a way of understanding their own mortality that allowed them to access the kinds of complex models of embodiment that contemporary disability theorists like Siebers and Kafer propose. In the epilogue, I look at the ways lyric forms continue to offer the possibility of reimagining what it means to die—and, in particular, what it means to die well. As of April 2025, the World Health Organization (WHO) has recorded more than seven million total deaths from COVID-19, with most of those occurring between January 2020 and April 2022.[73] The images that haunted early modern readers—individuals on their deathbeds, plagued by demons and doubt, tempted into renouncing their faith—have been replaced with images reflecting new fears during the height of the COVID-19 pandemic: the infected dying alone, attended by family only via video chat or, worse, by no one at all. In this final section, I trace some of the ways that the main question of this book—how form shapes our understanding of what it means to be mortal—remains pressing today. I explore how lyric, against a backdrop of quarantine, isolation, and loneliness, has and can continue to serve as *techne* for dying well, a way of creating presence and connection otherwise impossible in a world of lockdowns and restrictions. The pandemic and its lasting effects make clear that there is still a need—perhaps more urgent than ever—to interrogate the values and frameworks through which we define our mortality. The forms through which we understand our bodies and our deaths matter. They create and reinforce the value we assign to individual bodies, to their suffering, to their illness; they shape the boundaries by which we define ourselves and our community. And by turning to this new archive of decay, we can uncover models of mortality that foreground the community and continuity between living and dead, models that insist on the shared materiality of all bodies.

Chapter 1

Dying Well

> The association of the body with human mortality and fragility, however, forces a general distrust of the knowledge embodied in it. It is easier to imagine the body as a garment, vehicle, or burden than as a complex system that defines our humanity, any knowledge we might possess, and our individual and collective futures.
>
> —Tobin Siebers, *Disability Theory*

The first question that early modern readers encountered when thinking about what it meant to die was, at least on its surface, not about death at all. For these individuals, a good death was predicated on having a good life—on having lived virtuously and, by doing so, developing the moral values and practices necessary for facing the ultimate challenge of death when the time came.[1] Christopher Sutton makes this very argument in *Disce Mori*'s opening epistle to the readers: "It is both an old saying and a true saying, *bene vive & bene morieris*, live well, and die well."[2] But, as Sutton emphasizes, these were not simply parallel goals. Living and dying were a Möbius strip, bound together and inextricable; it was not just that living well prepared one to die well, but that living well *was* dying well. The opposite was also true: As Sutton and others frequently reminded their readers, in order to live well, one must always have a virtuous death in mind. "To guide the ship along the seas, it is no doubt a good skill; but at the very entrance to the haven, then to avoid the dangerous rocks and to cast anchor in a safe road is the chiefest skill of all," Sutton writes; "to run the race in good order is the part of a stout champion, but to run towards the end of his race, that he might obtain the crown, is the very perfection of all his pains."[3] The virtues developed during one's lifetime had to be oriented not just toward right living but to a good death. One must live with decay always at the foreground, knowing that the body's time is limited.

As these discussions suggest, debates about the correct morality of embodiment were far from settled in the late medieval and early modern period. At one extreme were the period's Christian ascetic movements, which declared the body to be a burden on the true self of the soul. England's late medieval anchorites, mystics like Julian of Norwich, were emblematic of this orthodoxy. After taking a vow of permanent enclosure, these devotees were sealed into their cells and embarked on a life defined by constant prayer and little to no food. These individuals represent an ethos of embodiment, described by Siebers in the epigraph to this chapter, in which the body and its needs are viewed suspiciously "as a garment, vehicle, or burden" to be thrown off as quickly as possible. As a way of symbolizing this, anchoritic enclosure rites included portions of the Offices of the Dead, framing the transition into isolation as an act both of physical death and spiritual release.[4] At the other end of the spectrum, England's mortalist thinkers argued that the body—not just, but *especially* its decay—was the only pathway to virtue.[5] Unlike asceticism, with its dualist approach to body and soul, mortalism—and especially annihilationist strains that viewed death as the complete cessation of being—almost inevitably entailed monism, an approach to body and soul much like what disability theorists like Sami Schalk have termed the *bodymind*, "the enmeshment of the mind and body."[6] Mortalism viewed the death of the body as the termination of all virtue, rather than its culmination—a loss, rather than the goal. While ascetics instrumentalized death as a necessary step toward perfection, mortalists saw death as the end of possibility, not its beginning. Caring for the body *was* caring for the soul—indeed, for the whole self—and thus carried with it an enormous burden of responsibility and expectation of virtue. While the ascetics argued that embodied life was rendered unimportant by decay, mortalists argued that decay was what infused it with meaning.

While these two extreme positions—asceticism and mortalism, spiritualism and materialism—illustrate the wide range of possible moralities of decay, the reality was that most early modern Christians fell somewhere in the middle. For most, death was neither the beginning of life nor the end of the self but instead a subtle and unknowable transformation; while temporary, the body was also very present in ways that made its management a crucial aspect of everyday life. The role of temperance was to guide that balance, constructing a moral framework for the day-to-day needs, wants, and pleasures of a dying body; death should be neither wished for nor avoided but simply acknowledged. This is the position revealed in most early modern English *ars moriendi* treatises, and this is also precisely the middle ground that Spenser sets out to establish in book 2 of *The Faerie Queene*. In order to develop the correct moral framework for their own decay, early modern readers turned to temperance. This was the virtue, both classical and Christian, that most explicitly addressed the uncertainty that came with living in a dying body. To be temperate meant learning to avoid extremes, particularly as they related to bodily appetites and affects; it meant caring for the body while not indulging it or being overcome by its desires. In addressing these concerns, *The Faerie Queene* shares an ethical and methodological core with the *ars moriendi* tradition: shaping its readers' habitual virtues and fostering ongoing spiritual discipline throughout their lives—and, as I argue in this chapter, their deaths. While I am not arguing for a specific line of influence between Spenser and any particular *ars moriendi* text, I am suggesting that, by writing on the subject of temperance in the late 1590s, Spenser could not have avoided participating in this broader shared conversation around embodiment and virtue—and, moreover, that the same readers who might have turned to *The Faerie Queene* for virtuous instruction may very well have been reading the poem alongside texts like Sutton's or William Perkins's, both of which are first published in the same decade as Spenser's epic. Spenser famously declared in his letter to Sir Walter Raleigh that "the generall end therefore of all the booke is to fashion a gentleman or noble person in vertuous and gentle discipline."[7] This instructive goal was, in part, a feature of all early modern literature. As Jeff Dolven has argued, early modern poets were constantly aware of the expectation that their work should be didactic; "poets *were* teachers, or thought they had to be. Instruction was the better half, the justifying half," of the poet's labor, whether they liked it or not.[8] And so, in some ways, that *The Faerie Queene* strives to teach its readers goes without saying. But Spenser also echoes specific lessons of the *ars moriendi* tradition here in book 2, focusing on the moral dilemma of temperance: how to live virtuously in a dying body. Since living well and dying well are inseparable, and since one must be temperate to live well, then one must also be temperate in their decay.

In this chapter, I argue that Spenser structures book 2 of *The Faerie Queene*, Guyon's quest for temperance, around the very same warnings that appear in many of the period's *artes moriendi*: In order to die temperately, one must avoid extreme moralities of decay, neither caring too much nor too little for the body and its pleasures. Spenser offers this lesson through the literal form of Guyon's quest, using the twinned scenes of Amavia's death and the Bower of Bliss in cantos 1 and 12, respectively, to allegorize each of these dangers. Confronting the problem of Amavia's and Mortdant's corpses in canto 1, the Palmer suggests to Guyon that death is something to be wished for, a goal to be pursued; the body, correspondingly, should be rejected. Later, in the

Bower of Bliss, decay fulfills an antithetical role, serving in Acrasia's argument as a reason to postpone death and instead embrace the pleasures of living. The Bower and its residents celebrate the body, drawing it closer, even in its decay. These instructive moments, representative of *The Faerie Queene*'s sustained interest in instruction and hermeneutic strategies, also illustrate the work's concern with literary forms and their relationship with the virtues at the heart of the text. In each of these moments of moral instruction, Spenser turns to nonnarrative forms closely associated with decay. Guyon's encounter with Amavia and Mortdant is framed in the language of memento mori iconography, drawing the readers' attention to imagery and contemplation and urging them to reject the body and its pleasures. Later, in the Bower, the epic turns to lyric, and Spenser centers a carpe diem poem that reframes decay as an argument in favor of bodily pleasure. In both scenes, Guyon is presented with the temptation of a moral extreme in the language of nonnarrative form and seems nearly ready to accept this lesson. But in both cases, Guyon refuses extreme morality in favor of moderation—of temperance. Mortdant's body is buried, and the Bower is destroyed. Through these actions, Guyon chooses a middle path, a temperate approach to decay.

As the resonance between *The Faerie Queene* and these *ars moriendi* texts suggests, the early modern period experienced a widespread interest in temperance. However, as many have pointed out, these cultural conversations were sometimes difficult to trace because of the variety of terms and vocabulary for this virtue and its development. Michael Schoenfeldt notes that, throughout book 2, Spenser conflates two related Aristotelian virtues, temperance and continence, under the single term *temperance*. "Where temperance is literally a static virtue, a physiological and psychological *state*, achieved through proper humoral balance," Schoenfeldt writes, "continence is a perpetually active virtue, a dynamic and ethical program demanding unending vigilance to exercise damage control over the eternally burning 'fire of greedy desire.'"[9] Kasey Evans identifies Spenser's terminological choice of *temperance* over *continence* as part of a broad early modern project of renaming and redefining the virtue at the heart of Spenser's allegory. Temperance was nudged away from its classical roots toward more explicitly Christian aims, Evans notes: "In assimilating classical ethics to Christian ideology, Renaissance Christian humanists wrest Aristotle's terms away from their original significations in order to valorize Christian suffering, and to recommend an ethics of restlessness and ambition."[10] Spenser errs on the side of simplicity, housing several dimensions of temperate living under a single lexical roof, thereby contributing to the broadening of the term. In contrast to Spenser, neither Sutton nor Perkins use the term *temperance* in their respective treatises; in fact, both *temperance* and *continence* are rare across the period's *artes moriendi*. And yet, while these authors might eschew the term, Sutton, Perkins, and the early modern *ars moriendi* tradition more broadly are actively participating in the period's conversations about temperance and in fact offer an essential and previously unexamined element of the virtue's development. These authors frequently wrote about the need for temperance in life to prepare for a good death in good time. Perkins, in *A Salve for A Sicke Man* (1595), notes that while the divinely ordained lifespan of man "can not be lengthened by any skill of man . . . it may easily be shortened, by intemperance in diet, by drunkenness, and by violent diseases," emphasizing the relationship between temperance and bodily appetite.[11] Sutton is more metaphorical, discussing the difficulty of navigating the mean between material body and spiritual self in his characteristically imagistic language. "Our bodies walk on earth," he writes, "but our souls should be in heaven, by our heavenly desires; and we should frame our affections in the form of a ship, that is close downward, but open upward, in a hearty desire of a superior condition."[12] For Sutton, the goal of the virtuous Christian is to stay just there, at the water's surface, neither sinking nor departing but instead remaining poised at the border between earthly and divine.

As these examples demonstrate, early modern temperance was intimately tied up with the concepts of time and temporality. Evans notes that temperance comes to suggest "two possible forms of temporal activity: the ability either to delay gratification of desire *over time*—i.e., patience or temporization; and/or temperance as the control of time *itself*, the virtuous subjection of time to heroic subdual."[13] This question of temporal control is at the heart of how *ars moriendi* authors developed moral frameworks for decay. These texts asked their readers to balance the timelines of their spiritual and physical selves, weighing physical health (their present mortal bodies, existing within time) against spiritual righteousness (the eternity of the soul and their infinite future existence). For Spenser, that question of temporality is manifest through book 2's strategic use of literary form. *The Faerie Queene* is an epic—a romance epic, but an epic nonetheless—centered on the narrative teleology of the quest. As David Quint notes, "While the narrative romances that we are most familiar with, including the *Odyssey* itself, contain seemingly aimless episodes of wandering and digression—*adventures*—they also characteristically are organized by a quest that, however much it may be deferred by adventure, will finally achieve its goal."[14] Such a form, in Spenser's use of it, centers the trajectory of narrative in its approach to virtue. Goal-oriented, the journey moves constantly forward, however errantly, to its eventual end. For Guyon, that means a movement from the dying Amavia to the Bower of Bliss. It is this narrative form, I would like to suggest, that affords moralities like those Siebers warns of in the epigraph to this chapter; it assigns a narrative ethos, a desire for closure, to the body's decay, positioning bodily death—throwing off the garment of the body—as the inevitable goal of temperance. But rather than strictly adhering to this narrative ethos, Spenser frames his quest within two major nonnarrative forms, intimately linked with temperance. In both canto 1 and 12, the reader is drawn out of narrative time into the world of nonnarrative form. Drawing on recognizable moral frameworks from these popular texts, Spenser uses the body's decay in each of these scenes as an instructive tool to develop virtue in the reader, fostering an understanding of temperance that accommodates mortality without elevating or rejecting death. But in addition, the positions of these parallel nonnarrative moments at the beginning and end of the quest highlight the friction between temperance and narrative linearity. Ultimately, I argue, Spenser rejects narrative as a form for temperance, exploring its inability to achieve the idealized balance at the heart of this virtue and instead creating structures that begin to examine nonnarrative affordances of time and decay. *The Faerie Queene*, in these moments, offers its readers not only a model of temperance that accommodates decay but also a way of thinking further about the relationship between embodiment and literary form.

Ars Moriendi and Temperate Decay

The sheer popularity of early modern English *ars moriendi* literature speaks to the wide influence of texts in the late sixteenth and early seventeenth centuries. As discussed in the introduction, works by Sutton and Thomas Becon ran for a staggering fourteen and thirty editions, respectively. Another, Perkins's *A Salve for a Sicke Man* (1595), was "one of the most popular works on dying well written in English," printed on its own at least six times in addition to copies included in collected volumes of Perkins's works.[15] On the whole, these texts reflect a profound anxiety around how readers might allocate their attention between their body and soul. Perkins's treatise, for instance, begins by arguing, like many other *artes moriendi*, that a good death (and the subsequent eternal life) was better by far than any joy afforded in life. Even so, Perkins writes, so many readers find themselves horrified by the disconnect between the fate of the body and the fate of the soul. Though "in death the souls of men enter into heaven," Perkins writes, "yet their bodies, though they have been tenderly kept for meat, drink, and apparel, and have slept many a night in beds of down, must lie in dark and loathsome graves and there be wasted and consumed by worms."[16] While this image is, at least in part, an argument against worldly pleasure—what use are down beds, if we are all only going to end up as worm food in the end?—Perkins's comparison is also just as much an expression of the real tension inherent in embodiment. The body is and has been a thing tenderly cared for—fed, clothed, and kept—not only as a source of pleasure but as a locus of selfhood. Perkins seems to acknowledge that, having spent an entire lifetime caring for the needs of the body, readers might be understandably reluctant to abandon it to decay. As a way of responding to this difficulty, *ars moriendi* authors stressed the importance of temperance, cautioning their readers to find a way of existing as virtuous, embodied, mortal beings. To do this, they argued, readers should steer clear of two major pitfalls.

First, the faithful should not care too much about their bodies. Bodies were temporary, and so too were the pleasures they offered. In *Disce Mori*, Sutton notes that transient worldly pleasures, while tempting, were a pale substitute for permanent spiritual rewards. By way of illustration, Sutton invokes the story of the tribes of Reuben and Gad. As Moses and the rest of the Israelites suffered the long journey through the desert to the promise of the holy land, these two tribes, seeing that the land on the east side of the Jordan River was arable, asked to remain there and establish farms rather than accompanying the rest of the tribes across the river to conquer Canaan. Just so, Sutton writes, "Are there not some in the World, not far unlike these children of *Reuben* and *Gad*, who desire to make their stay here, and would go no further, for that they esteem the pleasures and profits of a life temporal, more than they do the incomprehensible joys in that life eternal?"[17] Sutton continues that those who resist death are "not unlike those guests, who being invited to a great supper, feed so long upon coarser dishes, that when they come to the banquet, they have no appetite; they are so satisfied with earthly things, that when they should come to the best or desire of heavenly [things] they have no desire at all."[18] This desire to prematurely settle for immediate-but-temporary comfort, rather than eventual-but-permanent spiritual fulfillment (who among us, he asks, has not regretted filling up on bread?), is a failure of patience and of foresight. The pleasures of embodiment are real and present and in that way offer immediate satisfaction. Spiritual pleasure, on the other hand, involves the difficult work of delayed gratification. No small wonder then, Sutton writes, that "regenerate man, whom God hath made by grace, a contemplative creature, and by glory equaled unto the fate of Angels, should be so delighted in the affairs of this uncomfortable world, so enchanted with the Harlot-like allurements of sin, so carried away from himself, by the sway of sensual security, as utterly to cast away all remembrance of this their end."[19] To be intemperate, Sutton and Perkins both argue, is to mistake temporary pleasure for everlasting good.

But while readers were cautioned against too much care for their bodies, they were also regularly warned not to neglect their bodies entirely. The devoted Christian also needed to act temperately to forestall premature death, itself an equally bad way of dying. Readers should care for their earthly body to keep it healthy and well until God willed otherwise. Failing to do so means they risked falling into another sort of intemperance: the intemperance of neglect. This was, of course, a tricky distinction to navigate. These *artes moriendi* were concerned primarily with helping readers overcome their fear of dying, and so anything that seemed to suggest that death was something to forestall or avoid might run counter to that goal. But accepting decay, these authors argued, was not synonymous with completely neglecting the body. Perkins, for instance, dedicates a lengthy section to advising his readers to seek medical care for illness. He is careful to note that, while the body needs care, any act of healing should address a patient's physical and spiritual needs. "He that is to take physic," Perkins writes, "must not only prepare his body, as physicians do prescribe; but he must also prepare his soul by humbling himself under the hand of God in his sickness for his sins, and make earnest prayer to God for the pardon of them before any medicine come in his body."[20] But even with this caveat, Perkins never suggests anything approaching neglect or asceticism. In fact, he urges his readers to avail themselves of all possible care, tending to their bodies' needs for rest and nourishment—not as a way of avoiding death but of coming into it honestly. "We must carry in mind the right and proper end of physic," he writes, "lest we deceive ourselves . . . that physic serves to prevent old age or death."[21] The purpose of caring for the body, Perkins argues, is to live in accordance with a divinely ordained sense of time. "The true end of physic is to continue and lengthen the life of man to his natural period, which is when nature, that hath been long preserved by all possible means, is now wholly spent. . . . care must be had to avoid all such evils, that the little lamp of corporal life may burn till it go out of itself."[22] Overindulgence of the body's capacity for pleasure is clearly intemperate, Perkins reminds his readers, but so too is neglecting its need for care. Only after pursuing "all possible means" of preservation can one be assured that the body's natural lifespan has been reached and God's will for a good death honored.

As Perkins's argument here suggests, failing to care for the body was viewed as a comparable sin to overindulging its appetites. In fact, in *Disce Mori*, Sutton goes so far as to equate a neglect for the body's needs with self-destruction and suicidality. Urging his readers to accept the inevitability of their death, Sutton writes

> True it is, that our abode here in this world, is an ordinance established of God, and may also in this respect be acceptable to man. To procure the continuance of life, by means ordained, is allowable: to avoid things hurtful to the preservation thereof, is behovefull. Willfully to hinder our own health is not only against the course of nature, but a way to tempt the very God of Nature. To will either to be gone soon, or to stay longer in this earthly station, when it shall seem good unto him, by whose appointment we all stand, is a part (saith one) of great ingratitude.[23]

Like Perkins, Sutton emphasizes the readers' need to accept God's "ordinance" for the duration of their life. Willfully hindering our own health, he argues, is tantamount to rejecting God's plan; attempting either to die too soon or to avoid death both represent an equal neglect of care. Procuring the continuance of life, he argues, means engaging in appropriate acts of care for the body: avoiding hurtful things, extending life by any "means ordained." In this regard, Sutton shows less confidence in the work of the physicians than Perkins. "When sickness beginneth sharply to touch us, we are careful (as I said) in seeking and sending to procure the health of the body," he writes, "when [we] should have rather sent . . . [for] some spiritual receipt for [our] sick soul."[24] But all the same, Sutton urges temperate care for the body's health. "The time therefore allotted to us to walk in, we may accept, until God calls us away with thankful hearts, using that space to serve him in holiness and righteousness . . . to be content to stay our dissolution, to be helpful to others: in which respect we may accept of and wish (so it stand with the good pleasure of God) yet some farther continuance of ourselves and others."[25] Sutton's description underscores the role of time in these conversations: Caring for the body, responding to decay, means being content to stay and content to go. It means, for Sutton, accepting the time allotted.

These *artes moriendi* remind their readers that to live temperately in an inevitably dying body entails constantly negotiating between these two extremes of embodiment. Do not run from death, but do not embrace it either; do not indulge the body's pleasures, but do not wallow in its sicknesses. Be temperate; care just enough. The best way to do this, according to Perkins, is "to exercise and inure ourselves in dying by little and little so long as we live here upon earth, before we come to die indeed. And as men that are appointed to run a race, exercise themselves before in running, that they may get the victory: so should we begin to die now while we are living, that we might die well in the end."[26] Sutton writes, "Wherefore to grow more and more out of love and liking with these transitory delights, to break off by little and little from this wearisome world to hie homeward, disposing himself for the day of his departure, is a course most beseeming every wise Christian."[27] Both Sutton and Perkins invoke a sense of not only temperance but tempering—of mortality introduced little by little, moving the body ever closer to death. Temperance, in the framework of these *ars moriendi*, regards decay as a morally neutral experience. The faithful are reminded to care for the body to keep it alive and healthy while also acknowledging, even embracing, the futility of that labor—futile not in the sense of not being useful but in the sense that that work is destined for failure. The model of temperance that emerges from these treatises emphasizes the difficult dynamism of the virtue: Temperance requires both remaining still and steady while also accepting the inevitable disabling of the body that will ultimately lead to death. This is, these authors acknowledge, a difficult balance to strike.

Spenser's Memento Mori

This same advice on how to die temperately—avoid asceticism but also overindulgence—serves as the main structuring principle for Guyon's own quest for temperance in book 2 of Spenser's *Faerie Queene*. The danger of caring too little for the body is the first obstacle Guyon must overcome in his journey. Amavia's first words in the text—and the impetus for the book's long journey to the Bower of Bliss—contrast the pain of life against the consolations of death.

> But if that carelesse heuens (quoth she) despise
>   The doome of iust reuenge, and take delight
>   To see sad pageaunts of mens miseries,
>   As bownd by them to liue in liues despight,
>   Yet can they not warne death from wretched wight.
>   Come then, come soone, come sweetest death to me,
>   And take away this long lent loathed light:
>   Sharpe be thy wounds, but sweete the medicines be,
> That long captiued soules from weary thraldome free. (2.1.36)

The world is a place of despair, Amavia warns; the "sad pageaunts of mens miseries" demonstrate that injustice prevails and that suffering is inevitable. But while "iust reuenge" seems out of reach, there is still one comfort left: death. Amavia's cries paint death as both inevitable and desirable. Even the "careless heuens" cannot keep mortality at bay, and so death emerges as the preferable alternative to the pain of the world. Faced with her own immense suffering, a state of both emotional and physical pain, Amavia begs for an end. Death is doubly "sweete," a medicine against the physical agony of Acrasia's poison and an end to her "long lent loathed" existence. As some have noted, her message—that lived existence is suffering and that death provides a welcome respite—echoes Stoic philosophies of self-killing, which enjoyed widespread visibility in the Senecan revenge tragedies of the early modern period. As Michael Neill argues, this philosophy approached death as a structuring force in the midst of chaos. "To shape one's own end," he notes, "is to render oneself immune to the unshaping hand of death."[28] Amavia's despair invokes this classical model of virtue, recalling Spenser's debt to the classical tradition.

But *The Faerie Queene* is not only a classical but a Christian epic. Consequently, Spenser layers on top of this Roman death scene a newer, more theologically appropriate form for moralizing decay: the memento mori. Amavia's cries here are best understood in the broader context of this moral and artistic tradition, which frequently centered decay as an instructive tool useful for developing individual virtue. As discussed in the introduction, this form presents readers or viewers with an image of decay as a way of inviting self-reflection. Seeing the loss of another, we remember our own. Thomas Browne, in *Religio Medici*, reflects on the development of the memento mori across the period, focusing on its moral function in Christianity. While Browne's writing is later than Spenser's, his text is one of the few to overtly theorize the memento mori within the early modern period itself and so provides an important perspective on the morality of decay in the form. Because this iconographic language was so familiar, so naturalized, throughout medieval and early modern England, few writers ever explicitly discuss the tradition as an ideological tool; for most, memento mori were simply part of the vocabulary of decay. But Browne's particular capacity to analyze the mundane allows him to explore the memento mori from a point of defamiliarized strangeness, offering a useful (and rare) early modern analysis of this moral framework.

Browne first directs his readers to consider the frail coherence of the human body. "Men that looke no further than their outsides thinke health an appertinance unto life, and quarrel with their constitutions for being sick; but I that have examined the parts of man, and know upon what tender filaments that Fabrick hangs, doe wonder that we are not always so; and considering the thousand dores that lead to death doe thanke my God that we can die but once," Browne writes.[29] Like Amavia, Browne acknowledges that the state of living in the body is one of continual danger and perpetual suffering.³⁰ He remarks that the health of the body is tenuous at best, its material coherence hanging on by mere "tender filaments"; he recognizes that the physical body is always only one small injury or illness away from dissolution. And, like Amavia, Browne finds solace in the inevitability of death: "There is therefore but one comfort left, that though it be in the power of the weakest arme to take away life, it is not in the strongest to deprive us of death: God would not exempt himself from that; the misery of immortality in the flesh he undertooke not, that was in it immortall."³¹ As Drew Daniel points out, Browne inverts the classic Stoic logic of self-killing: Rather than bringing peace through life's eradication, "the contemplation that death is happy constitutes a means from within life through which to bear the pain that material, mortal life inevitably brings with it. We can be certain that the present form of our sufferings has a decisive end point."³² No matter what, Browne writes, we all can be comforted by the knowledge that we will die and finally leave behind the suffering of embodied existence.

However, Browne continues, physical death pales in comparison with the more truly terrifying threat of spiritual death. Through the internal logic of the memento mori, Browne uses the contemplation of decay as a devotional springboard, launching a recognition of the true spiritual nature of humanity. Without the promise of eternal life through Christ, Browne argues, a person cannot truly be alive. "I count him but an apparition" who has not received salvation, Browne writes, "though he weare about him the sensible affections of flesh."³³ However, while the spiritual self seems, at least for Browne, the more essential core of identity, the body is not abandoned entirely. Instead, embodiment remains an important pathway to understanding one's own mortality. Recognizing death means starting with the body but not ending there, Browne observes; if we want to truly understand ourselves as embodied beings, we must contemplate the relationship between body and soul, recognizing the inevitability of our end. "The way to be immortall is to die daily; nor can I thinke I have the true Theory of death, when I contemplate a skull, or behold a Skeleton with those vulgar imaginations it casts upon us; I have therefore enlarged that common *Memento mori*, into a more Christian memorandum, *Memento quator novissima*, those foure inevitable points of us all, Death, Judgement, Heaven, and Hell."³⁴

Browne's description confirms the central function of the memento mori: By contemplating the body's decay, one might "die daily" and thus become immortal. This is the same logic that underpins the spiritual work of the *ars moriendi* texts. These works provide spiritual instruction by foregrounding death, reminding readers of its inescapability. Becon, in *Sick Man's Salve*, observes that nothing is a better teacher in temperance than the threat of death. "There is not a stronger bit to bridle our carnal affects, nor a better schoolmaster to keep us in an order, then the remembrance of our latter end, then to remember that we shall not always here remain," Becon writes; "but these things seek we not to remember, but rather to forget, and therefore fall we into all kind of ungodliness, and dissolution of life."[35] Because we "forget" (repress) our decay, Becon writes, we tend to slide perpetually into sin. But by keeping death in the forefront of our minds, he argues, we can restrain our "carnal affects" and live temperately.

Browne's analysis of the memento mori's moral function highlights two key features of the form—features that Spenser draws on extensively in canto 1. First, the memento mori instrumentalizes the body's death to instructive, moral ends. Henry E. Jacobs notes that by foregrounding images of dying bodies, the memento mori form "thus creates a specific ideological matrix" that "should remind us of death, bring us to the contemplation of our own sins, detach us from the world, and move us beyond death to thoughts of God and redemption. Thus the memento mori should re-present social and religious ideology that directs the contemplative individual into normative and codified patterns of meditation which spell out a logical and authorized progression from death to salvation."[36] Decay is useful, that is, in that it can teach us a lesson about priorities: By remembering that the body is temporary, the viewer or reader is drawn away from the physical and their attention redirected toward the spiritual. Secondly, just as with the *tu fui* examples discussed in the introduction, memento mori create a relationship with time that resists sequential temporality. My claim that the memento mori is a fundamentally nonnarrative form is, admittedly, a departure from previous critical accounts. Both Neill and Rose Marie San Juan, for instance, explicitly refer to memento mori as narrative in both structure and effect. San Juan observes the ways anatomical illustrations "counter the familiar narrative of the memento mori . . . [and] ultimately questions the narrative of life's fragility and death's inevitability," thus offering a counternarrative of their own.[37] Similarly, Neill refers frequently to the memento mori as a narrative about mortality. But even more, he argues, narrative is itself a kind of memento mori: "Narrative's insistence upon ending answers the fear of mere shapeless chronicity by gratifying the desire for significant form; on the other, it acts as a kind of structural memento mori, a figure of apocalypse, and a reminder of the imminence (and immanence) of our own end."[38] For both Neill and San Juan, the memento mori provides a common template, a story of the inevitably linear and sequential experience of human life, reminding the viewer that they can travel only forward in time, toward their death.

However, I want to suggest instead that memento mori foster a nonnarrative experience of embodiment and time that more closely resembles forms like lyric. Some scholars have described the work of lyric as dilatory or meditative. Dubrow, for instance, has noted that lyric can serve "as a kind of heightening of emotion and sensation leading to its release," a mode of reflection and contemplation that can precede action.[39] This meditative structure is the same temporal process at the heart of the memento mori. The viewer or reader is directed to contemplate their own mortality, internalizing the knowledge that they too will die. It is only then, through that recognition, that the form's invited action—virtuous living—is incited. This initial phase, the act of meditation, requires the viewer to step outside narrative time. The memento mori invites the viewer to remember that they *will* die. To do so involves both a casting forward and a remaining still, recalling the inevitability of a future not yet realized and treating the imagination of one's ending as something to be remembered, something already in existence. This is underscored by the fact that the majority of memento mori iconography emphasizes not an absent or obliterated body but a decaying one. In these figures, the body is always imagined somewhere between wholeness and nothingness: a bare skeleton, not yet eroded to dust, or the fleshly fabric hanging by its tender filaments. Such images represent the gradual erosion of the individual and gesture forward toward the danger of complete annihilation in spiritual death, a threat looming but not yet realized. Within the framework of the memento mori, these images of the body's decline, death, and decomposition serve as the call to action Dubrow describes as part of the lyric function. They remind the reader or viewer that the physical pleasures of life are fleeting and temporary, urging them to turn instead to their spiritual health and true, everlasting life. Decay becomes an instructive symbol, reminding the viewer that death is a movement toward their true (disembodied) self.

The memento mori's nonnarrative relationship with time, I argue, guides Spenser's depiction of decay throughout these early scenes of book 2. First, the poem approaches death not as an event (Amavia's time of death, in particular, is notoriously ill-defined) but as a state of transitoriness and mutability, both in time and space. Having heard Amavia's cries, Guyon rushes through the trees to discover the horrors within.

> Which when that warriour heard, dismounting straict
> From his tall steed, he rusht into the thick,
> And soone arriued, where that sad pourtraict
> Of death and dolour lay, halfe dead, halfe quick,

> In whose white alabaster brest did stick
> A cruell knife, that made a griesly wownd,
> From which forth gusht a stream of goreblood thick,
> That all her goodly garments staind arownd,
> And into a deepe sanguine dide the grassy grownd.
>
> Pitifull spectacle of deadly smart,
>   Beside a bubling fountaine low she lay,
>   Which shee increased with her bleeding hart,
>   And the cleane waues with purple gore did ray;
>   Als in her lap a louely babe did play
>   His cruell sport, in stead of sorrow dew;
>   For in her streaming blood he did embay
>   His litle hands, and tender ioints embrew;
> Pitifull spectacle, as euer eie did vew.
>
> Besides them both, vpon the soiled gras
>   The dead corse of an armed knight was spred,
>   Whose armour all with blood besprincled was;
>   His ruddy lips did smyle, and rosy red
>   Did paint his chearefull cheekes, yett being ded,
>   Seemd to haue beene a goodly personage,
>   Now in his freshest flowre of lusty hed,
>   Fitt to inflame faire Lady with loues rage,
> But that fiers fate did crop the blossome of his age. (2.1.39–41)

In these stanzas, Spenser stresses that the bodies of Amavia, Mortdant, and even Ruddymane are all somewhere between life and death, "halfe dead, halfe quick."[40] This liminal status is underscored by Amavia's fluidity. Blood pours from her body, "a stream of goreblood thick," mingling with the waters of the fountain, soaking into the ground, and flowing through and out of the woods. Any sense of firm individual coherence is gone. Amavia's is now a fluid body whose borders bleed into the world and onto the bodies of those around her. She is neither entirely whole nor fully dispersed. Mortdant, too, seems to resist easy classification as dead or alive. His face is flushed and smiling, his armor smeared with blood, and he appears to be in "his freshest flower of lusty hed"—all signs that should point to life, until we realize the source of that blood is not a vanquished enemy but the dying Amavia. Spenser even goes so far as to describe him as a "dead corse," a phrase that both underscores his inanimacy and questions it. *Corse* could suggest both "a living body" and "a dead body," making the phrase a semantic echo of Amavia's "halfe dead, halfe quick."[41] Even the young Ruddymane, who, by all accounts, should be the most associated with life and vitality, is already colored by decay; Amavia's bleeding body has marked him, both literally and figuratively, for death. The bodies Spenser foregrounds here are, like the bodies of memento mori, representative not of total annihilation but of decay, the quality of instability itself.

Spenser borrows from the memento mori not only its thematic focus on active decay but also its formal response—the shift from a narrative to a contemplative mode of instruction. Spenser's debt to the memento mori tradition is underscored, particularly in this scene, by *The Faerie Queene*'s reliance on visual iconography: allegorical visual representation that conveys moral instruction through observation and meditation. By creating a detailed image of decay and then inviting the reader to dwell in their consideration of it—by literally withholding the forward motion of the quest itself until we have spent enough time looking—Spenser invites the reader into a meditative relationship with Amavia shaped through the lens of the memento mori, reminding us that we, like her, are already half dead. As Jane Grogan has argued, Spenser is concerned throughout *The Faerie Queene* with the relationship between seeing and knowing. "One of the most innovative features of Spenser's didactic poetics," she writes, "is his attempt to foreground and test the underlying visual metaphors for knowledge, learning, and moral discrimination of his culture."[42] This imagistic quality, Grogan argues, is a means to Spenser's ultimate end: the moral improvement of his readers. The poem "replicates as poetic images the same epistemological processes it demands and expects of its readers, making those acts subject to the reader's judgment and demanding increasingly sophisticated forms of readerly self-awareness."[43] Nowhere is this keen sense of self-awareness more apt than here, in dealing with the memento mori. As Browne's description reminds us, the memento mori is centrally an iconographic form; it requires an act of regarding, of simultaneous seeing and contemplation. San Juan notes that, particularly in the specific tradition of skull iconography, the memento mori functions as a mirror for self-examination. She writes that the form's "effects are only visited upon the beholder. In the exchange with the face of the skull, it is not the skull that is affected but the beholder whose very look becomes infected with fear."[44] The viewer is asked to look at the skull and, in doing so, recognize their own face within it. While the image remains static, it becomes an object by which the viewer considers their own subjectivity. Not unlike the allegorical form Spenser uses throughout the epic, the memento mori's instructive moral potential derives from the contemplation and interpretation of iconographic imagery. See this skull, this hourglass; in seeing, understand that you too will eventually die.

Spenser's visual, contemplative hermeneutic is almost impossible to miss here in canto 1. After crashing through the trees, Guyon encounters a "sad pourtraict / of death and dolour" (2.1.39). The pattern continues—in the following stanza, Amavia is twice described as a "pitifull spectacle" (2.1.40) and several stanzas later is "the ymage / of ruefull pity" (2.1.44). Once Amavia has (finally) died, Guyon and the Palmer are left with two corpses, a baby, and a choice about what to do, both literally and interpretively, with the bodies. Not only are Amavia and Mortdant an image, they are an image requiring consideration and interpretation. Guyon, the Palmer, and the reader must not only see them but also recognize the moral presented and apply it. However, as Guyon and the Palmer quickly reveal, the lesson to be taken from this scene is far from clear. Guyon delivers a brief sermon on the nature of the body, joining together the canto's iconographic vocabulary with its argument about the frailty of the flesh.

> Then turning to his Palmer said, Old syre
>   Behold the ymage of mortalitie,
>   And feeble nature cloth'd with fleshly tyre
>   When raging passion with fierce tyranny
>   Robs reason of her dew regalitie,
>   And makes it seruaunt to her basest part:
>   The strong it weakens with infirmitie,
>   And with bold furie armes the weakest hart;
> The strong through pleasure soonest falls, the weake through smart.
> (2.1.57)

The jumble of bodies, Spenser emphasizes, is "the ymage of mortalitie." By this, Guyon seems to imply that this scene—the pair of corpses actively decaying—represents the fundamental truth of the human condition. This truth is conveyed iconographically, allowing both Guyon and the Palmer to see in real time the frail coherence of the pair's "fleshly tyre." As Dolven has pointed out, this scene is one of Spenser's characteristic moments of instruction. "Amavia has become a lesson," he writes; "she has been cut out of the world of experience, with its ambiguous and continual moral claims, and repositioned in an ad hoc schoolroom that Guyon has built hastily in the little clearing."[45] The spectacle of Amavia, Mortdant, and Ruddymane has fulfilled its instructional potential as memento mori, with

Guyon drawing from these images the first of the book's lessons on temperance. Through their image, he recognizes the nature of embodiment. Bodies decay; the pleasures of the flesh are not only fleeting but dangerous temptations.

But the Palmer, seizing on this logic, tries to take things one step further. He first reinforces the scene's role as memento mori by rearticulating the moral logic of the form.

> But temperaunce (said he) with golden squire
>   Betwixt them both can measure out a meane,
>   Nether to melt in pleasures whott desyre
>   Nor frye in hartlesse griefe and dolefull tene.
>   Thrise happy man, who fares them both atweene. (2.1.58.1–5)

Like Guyon, the Palmer echoes the need for temperance to moderate between the body's appetites and the soul's capacity for reason. But unlike Guyon, the Palmer advocates for further action. That is, it is not enough that the corpses convey the message that bodies will inevitably decay; that image must also inspire any who might see it to take action. The Palmer therefore suggests that he and Guyon leave Mortdant's corpse unburied, so that anyone who might pass by could see it and, in seeing, be warned against the dangers of intemperance. In other words, he suggests doubling down, transforming Mortdant's corpse into a memento mori. Mortdant's actions were spectacularly intemperate—he embraced the pleasures of the body through the temptations of Acrasia and the Bower—and so, fittingly, he is to become a spectacle of intemperance. Through the iconographic logic of the memento mori, his body, left visible to others, can become an instructive, didactic tool.

But while the actions the Palmer proposes are in line with the moral logic of the memento mori, suggesting that an image of decay might serve as an effective way of inspiring temperance in the observer, Guyon refuses this suggestion. Instead, he argues, the virtuous thing to do is not to enshrine this corpse as a monument to temperance but to instead offer Mortdant the rites of burial.

> Palmer, quoth he, death is an equall doome
>   To good and bad, the commen In of rest;
>   But after death the tryall is to come,
>   When best shall bee to them, that liued best:
>   But both alike, when death hath both supprest,
>   Religious reuerence doth buriall teene,

> Which who so wants, wants so much of his rest:
> For all so greet shame after death I weene,
> As selfe to dyen bad, vnburied bad to beene. (2.1.59)

Guyon refuses to leave Mortdant unburied, rejecting the suggestion that the sight of his body will be helpful to others. Guyon's insistence on burial can be explained, at least in part, by Spenser's debt to previous classical epics, which often feature unburied bodies as ill omens for the fate of the quest.[46] But the refusal goes beyond that when Guyon offers a distinctly Christian explanation for his decision. Guyon's rationale for burying Mortdant is that decay is an amoral space, an equal fate for both the "good and bad, the commen In of rest." By divorcing the fate of the body from the fate of the soul—it is only "after death" that "the tryall is to come"—Guyon begins to unpick the logic of the memento mori's framework. Like Browne, Guyon here insists that the figure of the decaying body is not enough to convey the full truth of mortality; knowledge of decay is essential but insufficient on its own. But unlike Browne, Guyon goes on to suggest that seeing decay is not only insufficient but also pedagogically ineffective, failing to inspire virtuous action. Browne insists that contemplating images of decay is essential to spark the syllogistic logic of the memento mori form: If the body decays, then the pleasures of the body decay, therefore the pleasures of the body must be renounced. Guyon, however, seems here to refuse the logic of the memento mori altogether. He and the Palmer, ultimately, "both agree their bodies to engraue," and bury Amavia and Mortdant in a single grave.[47] By doing this, Guyon ensures that neither corpse is left visible; the "ymage of mortalitie" that had consumed the canto is now hidden, invisible to any who might pass by. Rather than embracing the idea initially offered up by this canto—that the sight of the pile of bodies at its center might spark temperance in the viewer—Guyon rejects this possibility. Guyon and the Palmer's quest begins, figuratively and literally, by burying the memento mori with which it began.

This initial scene in Guyon's quest for temperance ends, then, with a negation. Opening with the question of how to die temperately, Spenser first presents and then subsequently rejects the moral framework of the memento mori form. By being invited to stare at the image of mortality through the tableau of Amavia and Mortdant's bodies, the readers encounter decay through the specific hermeneutic of the memento mori. This framework for virtuous instruction dictates that by contemplating an external image of decay, the reader or viewer would recognize the decay inherent in their own bodies and the inevitability of their own deaths. The memento mori's didactic framework reinforces the desirability of death, reminding the viewer that decay is the pathway to virtue. But in these final moments, as Guyon insists on the burial of these dying bodies, the memento mori proves insufficient. As a response to the Palmer's suggestion that the bodies should be seen by others, Guyon's insistence that they should be buried should be read as a rejection of the instructive logic of the memento mori form, suggesting that viewing and contemplating an image of decay like Amavia's and Mortdant's corpses would be an inefficient way of developing one's temperance. The memento mori form, canto 1 seems to suggest, errs too close to the danger of caring too little for the needs of the body, positioning death as a desirable release from the burden of embodiment. With this, Spenser offers up the temptation to the extremes of asceticism—of the eager rejection of the body and its appetites as totally corruptive—only to subsequently reject that as well. Death comes to good and bad alike, Guyon reminds the Palmer; or, rather, the decay of the body *is* good and bad alike, and one must be careful not to too eagerly embrace death before its time.

Spenser's use of the memento mori—its presentation, followed by its subsequent rejection—also clearly illustrates Spenser's use of form, writ large, as an instructional tool for the development of virtue. Through the recognizable image of a memento mori, readers are invited into a well-known framework for understanding temperance and decay. Spenser allows for the possibility of the memento mori's logic—that decay should be embraced, even pursued, as a pathway to virtue—before then staging Guyon's denial and rejection of this moral framework. Grogan has noted that Spenser often employs this kind of readerly orientation in his poetics, providing the poem's readers with temptations that parallel those faced by the text's heroes. "Rather than seeking to inflame readers by short-circuiting their will," Grogan writes, "Spenser seeks to demonstrate both vice and virtue and to encourage readers to choose virtue, and to know what they choose. . . . The characteristic movement of the reading experience of *The Faerie Queene*, therefore, is involvement and critical distance, the pull in two directions simultaneously."[48] Not only does Spenser invite his readers to consider what to choose, but, I argue, he provides options for *how* to choose. By presenting a familiar form such as the memento mori, Spenser offers the readers an option for how to interpret decay. Here at the journey's outset, just as readers are beginning to wrestle with the difficulty of temperance, they are offered the familiar option of idealizing it—of holding up the dying body as an end to be pursued. Guyon's rejection then serves as a rejection not just of those particular values but of the framework itself, a reminder that it is just as important—if not more so—to find the right form for decay. In the quest to discover temperance, Spenser begins with the revelation that the affordances of the memento mori inevitably fall short, failing to provide an appropriate form for *The Faerie Queene*'s vision for embodied virtue.

The Bower and Carpe Diem Lyric

If the opening encounter with Amavia's death echoes the first of the *artes moriendi*'s lessons in virtue—do not care too little for the body—then it is only fitting that book 2's closing scene, Guyon's time in the Bower of Bliss, echoes the second lesson: Do not care too much for it, either. Spenser underscores the relationship between these dual dangers by carefully framing the two narrative antipodes as literal mirror images of one another, inviting readers to draw connections between the moral lessons of each.[49] Like Amavia in canto 1, Acrasia is heard before she is seen; "a most melodious sound" (2.12.70) of "soft trembling voyces" (2.12.71) draws Guyon and the Palmer closer, tempting them to peer through the "couert groves, and thickets close" (2.12.75). And like the thicket where Amavia is discovered, the Bower is cut through by a flowing fountain, the "base murmure of the waters fall" heard throughout (2.12.71). Acrasia's body itself, like Amavia's, emerges as an integrated part of this fluid landscape, flowing into the Bower and through the rest of its inhabitants.

> Her snowy brest was bare to ready spoyle
>   Of hungry eies, which n'ote therewith be fild,
>   And yet through languor of her late sweet toyle,
>   Few drops, more cleare then Nectar, forth distild,
>   That like pure Orient perles adowne it trild,
>   And her faire eyes sweet smyling in delight,
>   Moystened their fierie beames, with which she thrild
>   Fraile harts, yet quenched not; like starry light
> Which sparckling on the silent waues, does seeme more bright.
> (2.12.78)

Where Amavia's breast pours forth blood, Acrasia's body yields sweat and tears. As Schoenfeldt notes, these fluids are very similar within a humoral framework. "The blood oozing from Amavia, the tears welling from the nymph, and the sweat produced by Belphoebe's moral exertions" are all forms of "bodily excrements," not unlike the waste expelled from Alma's castle—and, I would add, not unlike the physical matter of corpses, often figured as a physical excrement from the true self of the soul.[50] Even Acrasia's vision, described in the language of extramission, extends far beyond the borders of her body, piercing those around her. Spenser again centers the scene around a body marked by its fluidity, its permeability—in short, its decay.[51]

Once Guyon and the Palmer have entered the Bower, the tableau they discover mimics even the physical posturing of canto 1's scene of destruction.

> There, whence that Musick seemed heard to bee,
>   Was the faire Witch her selfe now solacing,
>   With a new Louer, whom through sorceree
>   And witchcraft, she from farre did thether bring:
>   There she had him now laid a slombering,
>   In secret shade, after long wanton ioyes;
>   Whilst round about them plesauntly did sing
>   Many faire Ladies, and lasciuious boyes,
> That euer mixt their song with light licentious toyes.
>
> And all that while, right ouer him she hong,
>   With her false eyes fast fixed in his sight,
>   As seeking medicine, whence she was stong,
>   Or greedily depasturing delight:
>   And oft inclining downe with kisses light,
>   For feare of waking him, his lips bedewd,
>   And through his humid eyes did sucke his spright,
>   Quite molten into lust and pleasure lewd;
> Wherewith she sighed soft, as if his case she rewd. (2.12.72–73)

At first glance, Acrasia looks very much like Amavia. When Amavia is discovered, she too is found in a pietà-like position, "in her lap a louely babe" (2.1.40.5) and "beside them both, vpon the soiled gras / the dead corse" (2.1.41.1). Here, Mortdant and Ruddymane are replaced by the incapacitated Verdant. Like Mortdant, Verdant is somewhere between life and death. He lays "slombering," incapacitated and inactive.[52] Acrasia, leaning over him, devours his spirit, explicitly moving the body closer and closer to death. Unconscious, inactive, and fading fast, Verdant is indistinguishable from a corpse. Linda Gregerson, noting this, describes Acrasia's actions here as "a kind of anticipatory necrophilia," an amorous devouring predicated on (even driven by) Verdant's proximity to death.[53] Verdant is, like Mortdant, a figure of half-life, of decay and decadence embodied.

The visual and thematic parallels between this and the first canto are cemented when Spenser once again returns to the moral instructions of the *artes moriendi*'s advice on dying temperately through the use of a nonnarrative form. In response to the scene of entwined bodies, one of the Bower's "lasciuious boyes" delivers a textbook example of carpe diem poetry, a form James Nohrnberg calls "the theme song of intemperance."[54]

> The whiles some one did chaunt this louely lay;
>   Ah see, who so fayre thing doest faine to see,
>   In springing flowre the image of thy day;
>   Ah see the Virgin Rose, how sweetly shee
>   Doth first peepe foorth with bashfull modestee,
>   That fairer seemes, the lesse ye see her may;
>   Lo see soone after, how more bold and free
>   Her bared bosome she doth broad display;
> Lo see soone after, how she fades, and falls away.
>
> So passeth, in the passing of a day,
>   Of mortall life the leafe, the bud, the flower,
>   Ne more doth florish after first decay,
>   That earst was sought to deck both bed and bowre,
>   Of many a Lady, and many a Paramowre:
>   Gather therefore the Rose, whilest yet is prime,
>   For soone comes age, that will her pride deflowre:
>   Gather the Rose of loue, whilest yet is time,
> Whilest louing thou mayest loued be with equall crime. (2.12.74–75)

This song, the song of the rose, includes all the conventional markings of a carpe diem lyric—recognition of time's flight and the body's decay, used as the justification to indulge the fleeting pleasures of the body while they are still available. While this form has had a major place in the history of English lyric, the carpe diem tradition, like that of the memento mori, has suffered from overfamiliarization and, consequently, undertheorization. Wendy Beth Hyman describes it as "forever anthologized but rarely scrutinized," "a victim of its own canonicity and rhetorical blatancy."[55] She continues, "Does anyone need a literary critic to translate injunctions like 'let us sport us while we may'?"[56] Ramie Targoff concurs, arguing that "literary scholars tend to treat Renaissance carpe diem poetry as a lighthearted genre of love lyrics indifferent to the pains of tomorrow."[57] And yet, I would argue, as is the case for the memento mori, the carpe diem's strength lies in its very predictability. Such conventionality helps readers immediately recall a tradition of thinking about gender, sexuality, and decay, creating a predictable framework of interpretation—and, here in the Bower, leading toward another lesson about the possibility of virtuous decay.

Like the memento mori form, carpe diem lyrics regard decay as an instrumental force in the world that should drive the reader to action. First, just as the memento mori, carpe diem lyrics insist on death's inescapability. William H. Race, in his history of the form, observes that the form makes four distinct claims about mortality: Death is "irrevocable"; death is "inevitable"; "the immediate future is beyond our control"; and "life is transient."[58] Hyman concurs, arguing that the form's "claim to urgency can only be predicated upon the postulate that we do not have 'world enough and time.'"[59] Insisting that we all must die, carpe diem lyrics then invite the reader to use their limited time wisely. Because life is short, the form suggests, our possibilities for action are limited and therefore must be considered strategically. In the Roman period, the tradition splits into two main branches—the Horatian and the Catullan—organized around divergent responses to this question of action. Race notes that the Horatian approach, which shares a similar logic with the memento mori, "counsels the wise use of the present in the tradition of manly consolation": We are all inevitably dying, therefore let us live the most virtuous lives we can.[60] Like the memento mori, the Horatian carpe diem uses the threat of decay to throw the transience of worldly pleasures into sharp relief, directing its readers to choose permanent virtue over temporary pleasure. The Catullan strain, however, reaches antithetical conclusions, offering up an argument we more readily associate with early modern seduction lyric. The prototype of this tradition is Catullus's *carmina 5*, where the poet reflects on his and his lover's inevitable deaths—and, more importantly, the pleasure they might seize in what little time left they have left.

> Let's live, Lesbia mine, and love—and as for
> scandal, all the gossip, old men's strictures,
> value the lot at no more than a farthing!
> Suns can rise and set *ad infinitum*—
> for us, though, once our brief life's quenched, there's only
> one unending night that's left to sleep through.
> Give me a thousand kisses, then a hundred,
> then a thousand more, a second hundred,
> then yet another thousand then a hundred—
> then when we've notched up all these many thousands,
> shuffle the figures, lose count of the total,
> so no maleficent enemy can hex us
> knowing the final sum of all our kisses.[61]

Here, the threat of death spurs the poet to embrace sensual pleasure; the body dies, and so with it its pleasures. Unlike for Horace, for Catullus, that knowledge makes those temporary rewards more, not less, valuable. "Once our brief life's quenched," he writes, there is nothing left to enjoy. In a mirror image of the Horatian approach, the Catullan model uses the body's mortality as an incentive not to virtue but to pleasure. The lurking shadow of death drives the poem's forceful opening *vivamus*: We are going to die, so we should *live*.

This Catullan attitude toward decay permeates the Bower's own carpe diem lyric. The "Virgin Rose" emerges in her fairness and already is a marker of the value of fleeting pleasures; "that fairer seems," the singer reminds us, "the lesse ye see her." The song reminds the listeners that beauty—the material worth of the body—is, like all pleasures, made valuable in its scarcity. No sooner does the rose emerge than "she fades, and falls away." Recognizing the inevitability of decay, the lyric's second stanza fulfills the logic of the carpe diem form: "If we had endless time at our disposal, then this coyness would be appropriate; but we do not. *Ergo*."[62] In Spenser's poem, the second stanza's imperative—"Gather therefore"—signals the argument's logical end.[63] Because beauty is fleeting and because the body must decay, it must be seized, its pleasures consumed, before it is too late. Like the memento mori, the Catullan carpe diem lyric creates a framework in which decay is given instructive power. Because the body decays, both forms note, we must actively respond. But it is here, in the specifics of the urged action, that the forms diverge. Hyman notes that "the specter of decay that ostensibly serves as a homiletic exhortation" in the memento mori tradition becomes, in its reframing in the carpe diem, "not a reminder to contemplate the immortal soul, but its reverse: a demand to act urgently on worldly pleasures."[64] The memento mori form urges its audience to eschew the pleasures of the body, to act temperately, perhaps even ascetically. The carpe diem form, at the other end of the spectrum, nudges us away from asceticism toward epicureanism, away from the rejection of the body's pleasures and toward their embrace.

Through these two carefully paralleled scenes, Spenser underscores the inverse relationship between the carpe diem lyric and its twin, the memento mori. While the latter argues that the body's inherent decay is a reason to reject its pleasures, the former argues just the opposite: We should embrace the pleasures of the body *precisely because* they are temporary and fleeting. But just as he rejects the Palmer's nudges toward a memento mori in canto 1, in canto 12, Guyon and his actions make it clear that the carpe diem's moral message comes no closer to providing a framework for temperance that adequately accounts for decay. In what is arguably the most critically contested moment of *The Faerie Queene*, Guyon responds to the lyric's suggestion with the swift and catastrophic destruction of the Bower.

> But all those pleasaunt bowres and Pallace braue,
>   *Guyon* broke downe, with rigour pitilesse;
>   Ne ought their goodly workmanship might saue
>   Them from the tempest of his wrathfulnesse,
>   But that their blisse he turn'd to balefulnesse;
>   Their groues he feld, their gardins did deface,
>   Their arbers spoyle, their Cabinets suppresse,
>   Their banket houses burne, their buildings race,
> And of the fairest late, now made the fowlest place. (2.12.83)

The sudden shock of this passage has long troubled critics, who have debated how (or if) Guyon's actions demonstrate the fulfillment of temperance. Some have read the destruction as a victory for temperance, allegorizing the defeat of the Bower's sensual temptations. Responding to Stephen Greenblatt's reading of the razing of the Bower, which equates temperance with the exercise of power, Schoenfeldt notes that "Spenser frames his narrative in terms of an opposition between two kinds of pleasure: illicit, immoderate pleasure, which is to be resisted, even eradicated, and the salutary pleasure made possible by control, which is to be enjoyed, even relished. . . . Temperance involves a defense of the body, not a denial of it."[65] More recently, Angela Bullard has argued that destroying the Bower represents an act of humoral, ecological tempering of Acrasia's garden, with Guyon reshaping a landscape that had grown feral and "thereby remedying the Bower's imbalance and restoring 'crasis' or balance."[66]

Others, however, have insisted that Guyon's actions reveal his failure to finally achieve temperance. Paul Alpers, for instance, describes Guyon's actions as "notably intemperate" and argues that while there has been a long-standing "tendency to view [them] as morally, psychologically, or spiritually justified," the intensity of the destruction resists such readings.[67] Likewise, Joseph Campana argues for shifting the terms of our analysis, noting that "Spenser's true interest in temperance is in championing the capacity to be vulnerable to experience."[68] By this metric, Guyon and the Palmer's actions "dramatize the disastrous consequences of the attempt to moderate pleasure and deploy bodily energy as violence in the service of heroic, moral agendas."[69] Hyman, likewise, has argued that Guyon's response is less a sign of his virtuous character and more an indication of his failure as a reader. The carpe diem song "highlights the strain between the quest-like impulse of 'seize the day' on the one hand, and the demands for dilation, deliberation, and suppleness on the other. . . . [Guyon] attempts to conquer lyric profusion with unilateral epic action. But the reader's ambivalent response to the voluptuousness of the Bower is more consistent with the poetics of *The Faerie Queene* than is Guyon's single-minded obliteration."[70]

Like Hyman, I find Guyon most useful not as an object to be read but as a reader himself—a figure whose actions are less a performance to be interpreted than the performance of interpretation themselves. And in thinking about the parallels between book 2's opening scene and Guyon's actions here in canto 12, I argue that Guyon's destruction of the Bower serves as a final parallel to canto 1, specifically his rejection there of the Palmer's suggestion to leave the bodies unburied. In that early scene, Spenser presents a familiar form—the memento mori—and, along with it, the model of temperance it affords. Guyon, having given the readers ample time to succumb to the temptations of that form, rejects it, signaling its insufficiency as a form for temperate embodiment. This same pattern structures the conclusion of canto 12. Having arrived in the Bower, readers are once again offered a familiar form, the carpe diem lyric—and, here, too, Guyon rejects that form and its morality. The razing of the Bower offers a violent refutation of its lyric anthem and a suggestion that this form, like the memento mori, is an insufficient moral framework for decay. Just as the body cannot be totally abandoned, neither can it be totally indulged; the bodies of Verdant and Mortdant should not make us run toward death or away from it. Guyon's destruction of the Bower and all of its beauty is, at its core, a destruction of the morality it suggests for decay, a rejection of the notion that the ephemerality of the body's pleasures is an argument in their favor.

The Failure of Narrative in *The Faerie Queene*

These twin scenes—Amavia's death in canto 1 and the Bower's destruction in canto 12—offer *The Faerie Queene*'s readers an allegorical echo of the paired dangers of decay outlined in early modern *artes moriendi*. As Sutton, Perkins, and others caution, we cannot care too little for the health of the body, however destined for death it might be; despite the Palmer's insistence, even the most sinful body demands care, respect, even reverence. Mortdant's corpse is not waste to be left rotting above the ground, and Amavia's decay invites mercy, not condemnation. But the answer to caring too little is not, Spenser warns, to care too much. The Bower and its hermeneutic for decay are equally flawed. The body's pleasures are not an end in and of themselves. But while these moments offer clear negative definitions of temperate mortality—how *not* to care for a dying body—they offer much less in the way of positive instruction. For that, Spenser directs us not to the Bower but rather to the allegorical center of book 2: Alma's castle. In the beginning of canto 9, Alma leads Guyon and Arthur, who have just held back Maleger and his forces, around the house, surveying the castle's construction.

> First she them led vp to the Castle wall,
>   That was so high, as foe might not it clime,
>   And all so faire, and fensible withal,
>   Not built of bricke, ne yet of stone and lime,
>   But of thing like to that *Ægyptian* slime,
>   Whereof king *Nine* whilome built *Babell* towre,
>   But O great pitty, that no lenger time
>   So goodly workemanship should not endure:
> Soone it must turn to earth; no earthly thing is sure. (2.9.21)

Here, the house's most notable feature is its peculiar materiality. Made of flesh, it is "like to that *Ægyptian* slime," a substance notable for its mythical fecundity.[71] This building material—this fleshly slime—emphasizes the ephemerality of the building, a kind of planned obsolescence. Like all things, "Soone it must turn to earth," Spenser writes; "no earthly thing is sure." The allegory offered here—human body as house—would have been a familiar one for early modern readers, common both in scripture and in other early modern instructive texts.[72] Spenser's interest in reimagining it seems, in part, to stem from the way that the image of a home conveys the need for constant maintenance. Schoenfeldt has observed this in the poem's interest in the domestic labor of cooking and cleaning, which allows Spenser to reflect on the humoral and digestive temperance of the human body. But notably, this maintenance also extends to the very material of the castle. It is not just the work in the house but on the house as an object that conveys its need for constant attention. That the house is made of slime and flesh calls our attention not only to its role as allegorical body but specifically to the inevitability of that body's collapse.

Sutton, in *Disce Mori*, uses the same metaphor to describe the experience of living with decay. "We are but tenants at will in this clay farm," he writes. "The foundation of all the building is a small substance, always kept cold by an intercourse of air; the pillar whereupon the whole frame stays, is only the passage of a little breath; the strength, some few bones tied together with dry strings or sinews. Howsoever we piece and patch this poor cottage, it will at last fall *in manes Domini*, into the Lords hands, and we must give surrender when death shall say, *This or this man's time is come.*"[73] Living in a body means engaging in the work, in Sutton's words, of piecing and patching—not truly repairing. The dissolution of the structure is inevitable, and yet, as a shelter, it must be maintained nonetheless.

These metaphors of the body as clay dwelling emphasize the central paradox of temperance and decay. Temperance, as a virtue, is centrally concerned with balance and stability, with holding firm to a central mean. Alma's house, with all its activity, is a key example of this: It is the idealization of a system in which, through constant effort and activity, nothing actually changes. Notably, as Schoenfeldt has argued, the actions of temperance are those of perpetual regulation, a porous system maintaining balance through never-ending "Sisyphean effort."[74] But the reality of decay reveals that to be an impossible goal. The body is not a house; built not of bricks but slime (a generative but not a particularly stable material), the body is always already decaying, its fecund materiality also its undoing. However thorough our repairs, Sutton writes, the walls eventually fall. Caring for the well-being of the body is, this account suggests, a project doomed to fail—but it is a project we must undertake nonetheless. True temperance is the attempt not to resist decay but to moderate it, to work with it. It is the act of threading an impossibly small needle, the continual maintenance of a house that must inevitably crumble. Temperate dying aspires to the balance and homeostasis of temperate living, all the while acknowledging the inescapability of decay and the inevitability that that balance will ultimately erode.

This tension—the conflict between the body's decay, on one hand, and the desire for temperate stability, on the other—is not only a moral tension. This contrast is also, at its core, a formal tension, a collision of temporalities. Representing temperate mortality necessitates resisting the end-driven structure of narrative and the desire, as Siebers frames it, to view the body as a garment that must eventually be thrown off. Finding a version of temperance that can acknowledge that the body decays with time but that also does not attempt to speed up or slow down that movement means seeking out representational forms that can capture that tension. Many critics have noted that this interest in the strengths and limitations of narrative is a defining feature of *The Faerie Queene*.[75] Throughout his epic, Spenser demonstrates an interest in complicating (at least) and even destroying (at most) a sense of narrative wholeness. Daniel Vitkus, for example, has noted that Spenser embraces the poem's status as fragmentary text, resisting completion. As a response to Queen Elizabeth I's refusal to marry and the nation's subsequent uncertain future, Spenser offers a text that is likewise without a clear conclusion, Vitkus argues. "The shift in form and purpose restructured the poem as an intentionally 'endlesse' text," he writes, "exhibiting the sense of crisis and resembling the partial and tentative modality of signification that we have come to associate with postmodernity, rather than the finished balance and wholeness of a neoclassical structure modelled on Virgilian epic."⁷⁶ Alpers, likewise, sees in *The Faerie Queene* a keen interest in moving beyond the traditional narrative coherence of the epic tradition. Spenser disrupts the traditional Virgilian career trajectory by turning to lyric at the end of his career, Alpers observes. "Though it may seem paradoxical to say so," he argues, "Spenser's turning to major forms of the Renaissance lyric confirms the importance we have given to narration in *The Faerie Queene*, because it shows that the strains he felt in his heroic poem made him seek out other modes of rhetoric."⁷⁷ Spenser's literary career, Alpers observes, demonstrates a kind of critical awareness of the constraints and limitations of narrative approaches, an awareness also visible within the epic itself.

Recognizing this strained relationship with narrative, Dolven has argued that Spenser's poem invites readers to participate in the work of formal disruption. "Always in some sense reading itself, the poem also develops ways of figuring doubts about that interminable project," he writes.⁷⁸ Rather than offer a sense of narrative stability, *The Faerie Queene* regularly "stage[s] failures of that intelligibility not as a universal and inevitable condition but as particular events," particular scenes and moments in which the cohesion of the epic's formal logic breaks down.⁷⁹ But while Dolven suggests that such failures are indicative of Spenser's more pessimistic attitude toward the instructive potential of literature, I want to consider these failures as themselves instructional moments—formal failures that, in their shortcomings, are themselves lessons in what not to do. Guyon's quest for temperance is one such failure: the failure of narrative to represent a temperate attitude toward decay. If we view Guyon's quest as a teleological movement—admittedly errant but nonetheless linear—that progresses from his encounter with Amavia in canto 1 to the destruction of the Bower in canto 12, then it becomes clear that that structure fails to achieve the model of temperance described in *ars moriendi* texts. Guyon literally goes too far; he begins at one extreme of temperate mortality (the memento mori episode), only to arrive at another (the carpe diem lyric of the Bower). If we look to Guyon's quest as narrative to bring us to an ideal model of temperate dying, then we are left unsatisfied; if we are enmeshed in narrative time—in a narrative experience of mortality—then holding the center is impossible. As David Mitchell and Sharon Snyder have pointed out, narrative forms tend to afford a model of embodiment driven toward wholeness, one that often works against the body's imperfections and mutability. All narratives, they argue, "operate out of a desire to compensate for a limitation or to rein in excess. . . . The very need for a story is called into being when something has gone amiss with the known world, and, thus, the language of a tale seeks to comprehend that which has stepped out of line."⁸⁰ And the most unruly of narrative objects is, as Mitchell and

Snyder argue, the disabled body. "The body's weighty materiality functions as a textual and cultural other—an object with its own undisciplined language that exceeds the text's ability to control it."[81] Viewed through Mitchell and Snyder's account of narrative, Guyon's quest can be understood as an attempt to wrangle the unruly body—the decaying body—into submission.

But running counter to Mitchell and Snyder's argument that narrative seeks to eliminate excess or deficiency, the structure of Spenser's quest narrative of book 2 seems to suggest that it is *only* capable of excess or deficiency. Driven in a singular direction, ever forward, the form of the quest is at odds with the temperate desire to remain still, to be in balance. Narrative teleology is revealed to be incompatible with the temperate desire to hold the center. However, if we move outside narrative, reading book 2 against the grain, temperate mortality becomes possible. As Sutton, Perkins, and others in the *ars moriendi* tradition argued, temperance required steering between the Scylla and Charybdis of too much or too little care for the body and its pleasures. Spenser has offered readers the formal equivalent of that journey here in book 2: Canto 1 stages the rejection of the memento mori, steering the reader away from asceticism and the rejection of the body, and canto 12 offers the rejection of the carpe diem lyric, cautioning us against indulgence. Rather than reading it as a quest narrative beginning at canto 1 and ending at 12, we might instead think of book 2 as a causeway that calls us to navigate between these twin dangers without straying too far in either direction. If we can find ourselves neither in the grove with Amavia nor in the Bower with Acrasia but in the castle with Alma, we can realize the ideals of temperance. There, the reader finds a model of temperance that neither calls for the body's death nor runs from it but simply acknowledges it—a recognition of embodiment and the decay it entails. Book 2, in attempting to locate an ideal temperate death, ends by revealing the failure of narrative to achieve that goal.

By demonstrating the incompatibility of narrative and temperate decay, Spenser also hints at the potential of nonnarrative forms like memento mori or the carpe diem lyric to offer something new. *The Faerie Queene* instrumentalizes these forms to guide the reader toward a new formal solution: an embrace of nonnarrative modes that, rather than working to eliminate the body's deficiencies, offer up the possibility of dwelling indefinitely in the spaces between life and death. Guyon's journey is buffeted on all sides by these lyric and iconographic intrusions, moments that push back against a linear account of mortality. But, to use Dolven's framework, these moments are also themselves strategically staged failures. The nonnarrative forms Spenser uses in book 2 do the important work of disrupting narrative, revealing that form's insufficiency for capturing temperance. But memento mori and the carpe diem lyric also fail, in their own ways. Guyon's rejection of both forms suggests that, while the affordances of these forms offer a closer parallel to the ideals of temperate dying, the moralities they represent do not. These are the dangers to avoid, not the ideals to embrace; and so, while both forms offer the possibility of stepping outside narrative time, they also both fall short of offering an effective moral framework for decay. This absence leaves the reader of book 2 with a final question: What might an alternative form for decay look like? If narrative falls short, if the moralities of the carpe diem lyric and memento mori iconography fail to capture it—what might? These questions, I argue in the next chapter, become central to one of the period's most popular and influential literary forms, one that must negotiate an even more complicated relationship between narrative and lyric: the early modern sonnet sequence.

Chapter 2

Lyric Prosthesis

> Not marble, nor the gilded monuments
> of princes shall outlive this pow'rful rhyme,
> but you shall shine more bright in these contents
> than unswept stone besmeared with sluttish time.
>
> —Shakespeare, sonnet 55

In Shakespeare's 1609 *Sonnets*, decay appears in the first lines of the first poem.

> From fairest creatures we desire increase,
> that thereby beauty's rose might never die,
> but as the riper should by time decease,
> his tender heir might bear his memory. (1–4)

The problem, the poet insists, is that decay affects all living creatures (and especially the fair ones). What "we" want, he notes, enfolding the readers' desires into his own, is not just increase but immortality, a beauty that might, through its perpetual reproduction, never die. This first quatrain offers some tantalizing hope: The beloved's tender heir *might* bear his memory, and the fair youth's beauty *might* be memorialized through procreation. But this hope is belied by Shakespeare's opening rhyme. The quatrain sets up the expectation that *increase* will be followed by *decrease*, its perfect rhyme and total opposite. But Shakespeare instead substitutes *decease* in its place, reminding the readers that death is coming, whether we expect it or not. That sense of surprise slows the reader down and leaves us to linger in line 3, turning our backs on the solution offered in the following line. Procreation, reproduction, memorialization, immortality—these are offered by this opening quatrain as hopes only, uncertain and unstable. But buried in its center lies the truth to which the *Sonnets* continually return: All things, by time, decease. In Shakespeare's sequence, the poet addresses a young man who has refused to father a child and who will, unless other action is taken, die without any heir or memorial. But the fair youth refuses, and the poet is forced to look for alternate solutions. The explanations scholars have offered for this refusal are numerous, ranging from the biographical to the sexual to the biological to the aesthetic.[1] But while this refusal and the *Sonnets*' treatment of reproduction offer numerous inroads for thinking about embodiment, in this chapter, I turn from the young man's refusal to look instead at the solution the poet offers in its wake. Accepting that the fair youth will not reproduce (and that reproduction fails to provide the individual immortality the poet really desires), the sequence must find another option—and, as with the increase/decease rhyme, the solution we expect from the *Sonnets* is not quite the solution we receive.

What early modern (and, often, present-day) readers of the *Sonnets* likely expect is what I refer to in this chapter as the *memorial model* or *memorial solution*: the promise that while all living creatures eventually die, their memory or essence can be preserved forever in the words of the poets who loved them. In this model, literary preservation is the antithesis of biological reproduction, avoiding all the pitfalls—aging, illness, dying—that are inevitably linked to the materiality of the body. The memorial model instead promises a seemingly permanent record of the beloved's beauty across time. This strategy for poetic immortality relies on two major formal strategies, one lyric and one narrative. First, the memorial model insists on lyric's ability to stand outside time and the material world. As the carpe diem lyrics discussed in previous chapters confirm, early modern poets, whether genuinely or strategically, often imagined the world inside the lyric as a space where one might step outside time and thus escape decay. The memorial model proposes that lyric might serve as a kind of snapshot—a moment held in suspense, the lovers of the well-wrought urn forever warm and still to be enjoyed. Alongside this lyric solution, the memorial model also relies on a familiar narrative response to decay: the Neoplatonic structure of many of the period's sonnet sequences. In this narrative framework, decay is counterbalanced by the beloved's apotheosis into spiritual abstraction. The body slowly dissolves, making room for the true self: a disembodied and spiritual being unencumbered by the weight of earthly existence. Then and only then can the beloved reach the form best suited to perpetual memorialization. But, as I argue in this chapter, while Shakespeare frequently offers up this familiar model for lyric immortality in poems like sonnet 55, quoted in this chapter's epigraph, he does so only in the interest of rejecting it. With their publication in 1609, the *Sonnets* are a notably belated entry into the Elizabethan sonnet sequence tradition, and Shakespeare indicates across other works that he is keenly aware of the form's waning popularity. Orlando and Romeo, for instance, both arrive on stage as caricatures of Petrarchan obsession, only to be transformed by newer models of desire and courtship.[2] In much the same way, the *Sonnets* offer up the memorial model of poetic immortality, only to acknowledge the need for something new.

The *Sonnets*, I argue, replace the memorial model with what I refer to as the *prosthetic model*, or *lyric prosthesis*. Instead of trying to draw the beloved out of time (and thus out of their body), the prosthetic model insists on the centrality of the embodied self. It refuses the Neoplatonic desire to move beyond the material and temporal, instead choosing to acknowledge and even embrace the ephemerality of the body. Most importantly, the prosthetic model works to replace the memorial model's strategy for replication with one of relation. Rather than trying to save a snapshot of the beloved, out of time and thus immune from decay, the lyric prosthesis establishes a connection with the dying body, extending the self through writing. Like the memorial model, Shakespeare's prosthetic model offers strategies for connection both at the level of the individual poem and in the narrative shape of the sequence as a whole. First, the prosthetic model questions lyric's ability to stand outside of time, instead recognizing that lyric, like the body, is a material creation and thus subject to decay. Rather than attempting to turn away, the lyric prosthesis turns toward the physical and the temporal, highlighting its connection with the bodies of its beloved and its readers. This model of lyric, in turn, informs the narrative framework structuring the sequence as a whole. Instead of looking to move in a single direction in pursuit of the body's elimination, the lyric prosthesis imagines narrative structures for the sonnet sequence that allow for disconnection, interruption, and multiplicity. The lyric prosthesis highlights lyric's ability to establish tenuous but productive connections between body and lyric, natural and artificial, in ways that work with, rather than against, decay.

The prosthetic model provides a more detailed and accurate account of the *Sonnets'* thematic response to the young man's decay and can offer critics a new theoretical framework for imagining the relationship between lyric and embodied subject. This prosthetic model also helps to reframe two of the *Sonnets* most notable formal features, elements of the sequence that have often been framed as faults or failures. First, the lyric prosthesis can help contextualize the tenuous relationship between the quatrains and couplet in Shakespeare's sonnets, a connection that has often been described as disjointed or fractured. Read through the lens of the prosthesis, the tension present in these moments becomes a model through which we might imagine lyric's relationship with the body of the beloved—separate but connected, at once continuous and discontinuous. Likewise, the lyric prosthesis provides a better vocabulary for locating the *Sonnets* in the tradition of the sonnet sequence. There has been a long-standing disagreement among Shakespeare scholars as to whether the *Sonnets* are, in fact, a sequence at all. The sequence includes at least two beloveds in a narrative structure that falls somewhere between unclear and entirely absent. After 126 poems to the fair youth, the sequence seems to shift suddenly in a new direction, turning to the dark lady and new modes and styles of praise. Criticism of the *Sonnets* has often concentrated on the tension between the lyric and narrative dimensions of Shakespeare's work, arguing, variously, that others have paid too much or too little mind to one or the other. Those who attempt to clarify the shift from fair youth to dark lady are accused of overemphasizing the narrative mode, while those who reject the idea of a discernible superstructure are dismissed as only attending to the poems' lyric dimensions.

However, I argue, the sonnet sequence must be read as a site of collision between both forms. Built of both a narrative frame and lyric parts, the sonnet sequence requires critical models that address the two forms and their (often fraught) relationship with one another. Our reading of Shakespeare's sequence must allow for the influence of lyric on elements that have traditionally been read only through the lens of narrative. The lyric prosthesis offers just such a model for thinking about the *Sonnets*' place in the sonnet sequence tradition. Shakespeare's sequence foregrounds the moment of tenuous connection at sonnet 126, another site of prosthetic joining, as an opportunity to theorize the relationship between lyric and narrative in the sequence form. Here, the *Sonnets* refuse the traditional Neoplatonic structure, a narrative form closely associated with the memorial model, and instead substitute a prosthetic connection between parts. Like the relationship between body and lyric, the shift from fair youth to dark lady is lateral rather than ascendent; the story is not one of a single, culminating apotheosis but instead of the deepening mutual entanglement between parts. Sonnet 126 and the *Sonnets*' overall structure thus offer a model for the sequence form more overtly driven by both lyric *and* narrative, foregrounding the active collision between both forms. While I make this argument most explicitly in the final section of this chapter, this conclusion is also visible throughout in my methodology, which works to balance lyric and narrative reading modes. Aaron Kunin, in his work on the procreation sonnets, argues that Shakespeare's thinking in the *Sonnets* is "recursive, rather than progressive," and so, correspondingly, he chooses "to move freely between sonnets" when developing his analysis.[3] Though Kunin does not explicitly describe his work this way, his is an example of a fundamentally lyric-forward methodology, highlighting the nonlinear and associative rather than the developmental or sequential. I move in a similar fashion through this chapter, arguing that the *Sonnets* can and should be read not only in their printed order but also through the nonsequential exploration of linked groups or clusters of poems. This approach to reading works with, rather than against, the sequence, allowing for a more capricious readerly movement—a practice that is informed by both the lyric and narrative dimensions of the text.

Beyond the Memorial Model

The *Sonnets* seem to regularly promise their reader what I refer to as the *memorial model*: a theory of lyric that touts its ability to save its subjects from decay. The memorial model appears in the sequence as the poet moves away from the possibility of procreation, recognizing that the young man's failure and/or unwillingness to father a child demands an alternative plan of action. Across a number of these memorial model sonnets, time and the poet seem to work in opposition, respectively destroying and preserving the young man.[4] I begin here by exploring four examples of the memorial model in the sequence. These poems, which share strikingly similar themes and structures, offer a template of this model's key formal and thematic features. The first example, sonnet 19, sets up the division between the work of lyric and the effects of time. Here, the poet's description of time highlights its erosive effects—the various ways it manages to wear down the material of the world.

> Devouring Time, blunt thou the lion's paws,
> and make the earth devour her own sweet brood,
> pluck the keen teeth from the fierce tiger's jaws,
> and burn the long-lived phoenix in her blood,
> make glad and sorry seasons as thou fleet'st,
> and do whate'er thou wilt, swift-footed Time,
> to the wide world and all her fading sweets:
> but I forbid thee one most heinous crime,
> O carve not with thy hours my love's fair brow,
> nor draw no lines there with thine antique pen.
> Him in thy course untainted do allow
> for beauty's pattern to succeeding men.

> Yet do thy worst, old Time: despite thy wrong,
> my love shall in my verse ever live young.

The verbs of the opening quatrain—*blunt, devour, pluck, burn*—are all deeply physical, highlighting that time is not simply an abstraction but a real, material force. This damage however, is not unmet: Recognizing time's effects on the rest of the world, the poet forbids the destruction of his beloved's body. "Draw no lines," he warns, forbidding time from leaving wrinkles on the young man's otherwise smooth and youthful face. This challenge culminates in the couplet, where the poet declares war. "Do your worst," he defies, maintaining that despite the destructive forces of time, the man will remain young forever in the poet's verse. As Colin Burrow observes, the unexpected trochee of *ever* in line 14 places the emphasis of the poet's work squarely on its perpetuity—the young man will not just live but will live for*ever*, staying here in the timeless space of the lyric.

These same themes reappear in sonnet 60, which describes time in similarly physical and destructive terms. Here, the poet offers the familiar Petrarchan image of waves beating ceaselessly against the shore.

> Like as the waves make towards the pebbled shore,
> so do our minutes hasten to their end,
> each changing place with that which goes before,
> in sequent toil all forwards do contend.
> Nativity, once in the main of light,
> crawls to maturity, wherewith being crowned
> crookèd eclipses 'gainst his glory fight,
> and Time that gave doth now his gift confound.
> Time doth transfix the flourish set on youth,
> and delves the parallels in beauty's brow,
> feeds on the rarities of nature's truth,
> and nothing stands but for his scythe to mow.
> > And yet to times in hope my verse shall stand,
> > praising thy worth, despite his cruel hand.

While sonnet 19 offered metaphors of erosion, this sonnet develops the conceit of replacement. Each wave comes "in sequent toil" to replace the previous, leaving nothing able to resist time's inevitable forward motion. What time gives, time subsequently takes away.[5] Yet again, the young man's body is threatened with the marks of age; time "delves the parallels in beauty's brow," carving up the young face just as the mower plows the furrows of the field. And, yet again, the poet intervenes, standing against time in the poem's final couplet. His lyric can resist this destruction, he declares, remaining standing even as everything around it falls.

These first two examples explore the speaker's horror at the decay of the fair youth's body, but he is also not immune to these same effects. In sonnet 63, the opening quatrains offer an even more explicit image of the speaker's aging body, ravaged by time.

> Against my love shall be as I am now,
> with Time's injurious hand crushed and o'er-worn,
> when hours have drained his blood and filled his brow
> with lines and wrinkles, when his youthful morn
> hath travelled on to age's steepy night,
> and all those beauties whereof now he's king
> are vanishing, or vanished out of sight,
> stealing away the treasure of his spring:
> for such a time do I now fortify
> against confounding age's cruel knife,
> that he shall never cut from memory
> my sweet love's beauty, though my lover's life.
> > His beauty shall in these black lines be seen,
> > and they shall live, and he in them still green.

The sonnet's first two quatrains detail the body's decay, tracing the physical transition from youth and beauty into age and infirmity. Line 5 characterizes this transformation with an adjectival bait and switch not unlike sonnet 1's opening rhyme. The poet imagines having traveled on to "age's steepy night." A reader might reasonably expect *sleepy* here instead, a much more obvious adjective to pair with *night*. But a sleepy night would suggest a peaceful transformation, the passive and comfortable transition from youth into senescence. The shift the poet imagines is not *sleepy* but *steepy*—precipitous, cliff-like, and fraught with danger. Aging is not a comfortable transformation but a fatal falling-off.[6] Like the speaker, the young man is also vulnerable to "Time's injurious hand," which waits to push him over the very same cliff. As in the previous examples, the poet's lyric moves to the foreground in the sonnet's final lines, working against the threat of decay to ensure perpetual youth. The task here is fortification, protecting the fair youth so that he might remain both fair and youthful. That language of reinforcement spills over into sonnet 65, where time appears as a besieging force battering against the walls of the youthful body.

> Since brass, nor stone, nor earth, nor boundless sea,
> but sad mortality o'ersways their power,
> how with this rage shall beauty hold a plea,
> whose action is no stronger than a flower?
> O how shall summer's honey breath hold out
> against the wrackful siege of batt'ring days,
> when rocks impregnable are not so stout,
> nor gates of steel so strong, but time decays?
> O fearful meditation; where, alack,
> shall Time's best jewel from Time's chest lie hid?
> Or what strong hand can hold his swift foot back,
> or who his spoil of beauty can forbid?
>> O none, unless this miracle have might,
>> that in black ink my love may still shine bright.

Here, the poet's gaze broadens, focusing not only on his or the young man's body but on beauty writ large. Once again, time levels everything in its path; brass, stone, rocks, and steel are all subject to decay. If these must fall, the poet asks both the readers and himself, what can the delicate objects of beauty offer? Flowers, "summer's honey breath," objects of ephemeral and insubstantial beauty—these, too, are doomed. The only escape, the poet notes, is through the miracle of verse. Once more, in its couplet, the sonnet turns to promise lyric as a haven free of decay. Like the couplet of 63, sonnet 65's last lines promise the paradoxical preservation of color in black and white. It is only in his verse, the poet argues, that beauty's brightness can remain unchanged.

Taken together, these four sonnets illustrate the central features of the memorial model of lyric preservation. Like other poets discussed throughout this book, Shakespeare represents decay as the legible effects of time on the material world, particularly on the body. As these examples suggest, time, on its own, appears neutral. Many of the images Shakespeare chooses for time—waves, tides, seasons, days—are cyclical, underscoring a sense of constant and unending change that underlies the sequence and its concerns. But paradoxically, these changes, on their own, are not changes at all; summer eventually returns, just as it did last year, and the sun rises again in the morning, just as it will tomorrow. These immaterial cycles of time inflict no decay, no destruction. Decay only occurs when time encounters the material world, the rocks and steel and, in particular, bodies that fill these poems. One of the recurring images Shakespeare uses to underscore this effect is of the wrinkles that will eventually fill the fair youth's face—the carving of the young man's face in sonnet 19, the "parallels in beauty's brow" in 60, the "lines and wrinkles" of 63. Time's cruel knife is visible only in the incisions it leaves behind.

Lyric, on the other hand, emerges in the memorial model as a disembodied, immaterial alternative space, immune to decay, a preservation technology akin to memory. In sonnet 63, while "confounding age's cruel knife" threatens to mar the young man, the poet can keep him from being "cut from memory" through writing—line 9's deictic declaration that "I now [in the act of inscription] fortify." The claim that lyric is like memory, a comparison the poet will return to several times over the course of the sequence, suggests two very important preservative advantages. First, it frames lyric as an immaterial medium, the stuff only of imagination; lyric is the antithesis of the material objects that fills the quatrains of these poems, intangible and weightless. Because of this, lyric is then outside the reach of decay. If, as these poems seem to suggest, decay only occurs when time encounters matter, then lyric's immateriality places it beyond time's reach. Lyric's comparison with memory underscores this: To remember and to be remembered is, fundamentally, to transcend time. Remembering makes the past present again, bringing back to life what was lost. In sonnet 3, for instance, the poet notes how the young man's beauty "calls back the lovely April" of his mother's prime. His mother's youthful beauty, long absent, cannot be made present again in her own body. But by evoking the memory of it, the speaker is able to effectively turn time back, defying decay. Lyric's power, under the memorial model, is thus twofold: The poet's writing is able to step outside the material world and, in doing so, escape time's destruction. Lyric promises a timeless, unchanging world, free from decay.

These four poems are by no means the only poems in the sequence to offer a version of the memorial model; sonnets 55, 71, 74, 81, to name only a handful, offer a similar framework for literary immortality. In fact, the frequency with which the *Sonnets* appeal to their memorializing capacity has become one of their defining characteristics. Kunin writes that the *Sonnets* "repeatedly and almost obsessively" pursue the question of how and why the poems might achieve this kind of preservation, making them "the most familiar and influential statement of the value of preservation in English literature."[7] Anne Ferry likewise argues that "Shakespeare, most of all poets, was obsessed with the eternizing conceit," the idea that lyric could preserve its subjects indefinitely.[8] But while Shakespeare is perhaps the most overtly interested in lyric's memorial function, the *Sonnets* are not the first works of literature—nor even the first sonnet sequence—to try to keep their beloved alive for posterity. Rather, as both Kunin and Ferry point out, Shakespeare's role in the history of the memorial model is one of intensification, rather than invention. Kunin notes that the kernels of this trope appear earlier, in Horace and in Spenser, and argues that, "in fact, the earlier poems [in the sequence] have no original ideas at all" but are "distinguished by the explicitness by which" they pursue this concern.[9] Similarly, Ferry contends that "the boast that his art 'gives life' that 'shall not fade' recalls the promises of Petrarch and Ronsard, whose verses had proven themselves to be 'eternall lines' in which the poets, even more triumphantly than their mortal loves, could escape universal decay."[10] Shakespeare's critique of the memorial model invites readers to look back over this tradition. By repeating this familiar argument, the *Sonnets* explore not only its speaker's ability to save the fair youth but the ability of lyric as a form to engage in the work of preservation.

While the speaker of the *Sonnets* repeatedly seems to insist on the memorial model's viability, I want to suggest that these moments, rather than reinforcing his position, reveal the limitations of this theory of lyric preservation. Shakespeare foregrounds the memorial model not to endorse this solution to decay but to highlight its flaws. The apparent guarantee these sonnets offer—the promise that poetry will transcend time and thus decay—is undermined by several of the sequence's formal strategies. First, the very fact of the memorial model's repetition erodes its reliability, making the sentiment more diluted and ironic with each subsequent appearance. Readers might be tempted to see this use of repetition as evidence of Shakespeare's rhetorical prowess, the ability to present this familiar sentiment in more numerous and beautiful ways than his predecessors and rivals. But, particularly in a sequence that so forcefully thematizes the impossibility of perfect replication (see, for instance, the language around copying in sonnet 11), any repetition inevitably becomes an alteration.[11] For the poet to promise once or twice to save the young man might read as hopeful or optimistic; for the poet to declare so more than a dozen times shifts that optimism toward desperation. Joel Fineman notes this same strategy of repetition and erosion in what he terms the sequence's paradoxical praise—the poet's repeated insistence on the young man's beauty revealing, through its many reiterations, that the goal is in fact to praise the poet himself:

> In the rhetorically self-conscious tradition of sonneteering praise, this [*ostentatio*] will be reflected in the enthusiasm for Petrarchist artifice, the striking oxymorons, the catachretic imagery, the ornamental diction, the formal and the complicated syntax with which radical conceits are developed through and to their bold conclusions. . . . Even

when it is elaborately artificial, the rhetoricity of the poetry of praise is understood authentically to express poetic intention, to do so in a straightforward way, for, finally, its laudation is understood to define its poet's purpose. In contrast, the paradox of praise deliberately distances itself from the rhetoricity to which it draws attention, belying itself by means of a hyperrhetoricity whose ironic intention is most fully realized when understood to mean something other than what it seems to say. This is the oddity of paradoxical praise.[12]

The distancing work of praise paradox occurs, Fineman argues, via reoccurrence: "Both the novelty and the effect of Shakespeare's sonnets derive in good measure from the way they call attention to the fact that they repeat, with a difference, the epideictic tradition they succeed."[13] The same holds true for Shakespeare's treatment of lyric as a tool for preservation. With each instance of the poet's claim that poetry can save the young man, the stability of the memorial model erodes further and further, with lyric's victory over decay becoming increasingly less and less sure.

In addition to exploiting this process of transformation by repetition, Shakespeare uses the inherent ambivalence of the English sonnet's couplet to further undermine the memorial model. In each of the four examples cited here—sonnets 19, 60, 63, and 65—the poet's claim to lyric's permanence reaches its height in the couplet, following the *volta*. In earlier Italian sonnets, the similar length of the octave and sestet allowed for a general sense of parity in perspective; whatever problem the sonnet opened with, the poet might devote as much detail to its reimagination after the turn. In the English form, however, the unevenly weighted structure complicates the possibilities for thematic relationships between the two sections, often resulting in a sense of rhetorical imbalance. Some critics contend that this results in a kind of semantic compression, with a couplet that serves as an aphoristic encapsulation of the previous poem's argument. Stephen Guy-Bray argues that "English sonneteers are markedly more likely to write a final couplet that is in some way a comment on the previous twelve lines, typically either as a summary . . . or as a contradiction."[14] Jessica Rosenberg notes that Shakespeare's couplets, both in tone and in typesetting, mirror the couplets found in typical early modern husbandry manuals like Thomas Tusser's *A Hundreth Good Pointes of Husbandrie*. In husbandry manuals, Rosenberg observes, the couplet compressed advice for household management into aphorism, creating memorable and widely applicable linguistic tools for readers' later use. Both Tusser's and Shakespeare's couplets, she writes, "bring with them expectations of a future of iteration and detachment—a hermeneutic and material practice that links the provision of husbandry with the form of the sonnet."[15] Like the mnemonically convenient couplets of these manuals, Rosenberg argues, Shakespeare's couplets offer compressed and portable summations of the poems that precede them, inviting readers to think of these sentiments as practical, axiomatic truths.

Others, however, insist that the couplets should be read not as summaries or encapsulations but as a gesture of refusal or distancing at the poem's close. Rosalie Colie argues that the often-reactive tone of the couplets is reflective of Shakespeare's engagement with the epigrammatic tradition. "Even when they are syntactically hooked to the quatrains preceding them," she writes, Shakespeare's couplets can often be read "as if they were intense, dramatic epigrams," detachable and emotionally removed from the quatrains.[16] Helen Vendler maintains that readers should approach Shakespeare's couplets "not as resolution (which is the function of [the 3rd quatrain,]) but as coda," standing in a "number of relations (summarizing, ironic, expansive) to the preceding argument."[17] Dubrow argues that while readers have been "conditioned to expect [Shakespeare's] couplets (like those of many other sonneteers) to be reasoned statements of objective truths . . . expect[ing] them to function rather like the chorus's commentary in a play or the narrator's judgments in a novel," it is more accurate to say that Shakespeare's couplets "reflect the chaos in the speaker's mind, a purpose to which a couplet that merely summarized the preceding twelve lines would prove inadequate."[18] Colie, Vendler, and Dubrow share a common suspicion of the couplet's stability and tone. Rather than simply intensifying or distilling (a preservation method Shakespeare's sequence also approaches with some suspicion) the meaning of the preceding quatrains, the couplets frequently destabilize whatever certitude the speaker has managed to achieve. In place of a conclusion—because of x, therefore y—Shakespeare's couplets offer more of a gesture toward the futility of action or the impossibility of resolution. Instead of resolving neatly into the satisfaction of a major chord, the poem turns, with its last note, to dissonance and complication.

It is in this more ambivalent tone that we must read Shakespeare's couplets and, consequently, the memorial model's promise that lyric might easily save the beloved from decay. The promise that, in the poet's verse, the fair youth will be forever green, forever young, forever bright, and forever unmarred by time appears in each of these sonnets in lines 13 and 14, following a trio of quatrains detailing just how destructive time can be. Take, for instance, sonnet 65's couplet:

> O, none, unless this miracle have might,
> that in black ink my love may still shine bright.

If we read this couplet as a confirmation of the previous lines, then the memorial model is a reliable preservation technology. Despite the decay that threatens him, the young man can remain beautiful and untouched here in the black ink of the poem; the work of lyric is unironically miraculous. However, if we read it as a self-conscious commentary on the possibility of preservation, we see the tone shift dramatically. The invocation of a miracle underscores not the possibility but the *im*possibility of the task; the couplet's continued conditional language (the pun on *might*, terms like *unless* or *may*) shifts the reader's gaze away from the certainty of the promise toward the unlikelihood that it might ever work. The overt contradiction between the black ink and the brightness of the beloved widens the space between what the poet wants and what is possible in the medium available to him.

If we read these couplets with the expectation that the sonnet's quatrains and couplet are rhetorically related as problem and solution—because you are dying, I will save you with my poetry—then these moments are confirmations of the memorial model's promise. Lyric offers a straightforward replacement for the dying beloved, a solution to the problem of decay. However, if instead we read them as contradictions or complications, the *Sonnets* begin to look less like a promise that lyric can preserve the fair youth and more like a critique of its ability to do so. This is not to suggest that the couplet is wholly cynical—far from it. Rather, as this and the other examples discussed seem to confirm, Shakespeare's couplets reveal the paradoxical position the speaker and writer of these poems finds himself in. What emerges is a genuine, deeply felt desire for poetry to somehow intervene in the fight against decay and, simultaneously, an implicit acknowledgment that it is ill-suited to do so. The critique the *Sonnets* offer in these moments is not necessarily of the desire at the heart of the memorial model—to save that which it loves—but of the way it might do just that.

Alongside these formal strategies for undermining the memorial model, the *Sonnets* also levy a thematic critique of the relationship with the body that such a model imagines. As previously discussed, the memorial model imagines the poet's creation as the total antithesis of decay. Under this framework, lyric is imagined to be immaterial and therefore not subject to the same destruction that will inevitably befall the young man's beauty. The poet envisions his work allowing him and his subject to overcome the limitations associated with embodiment. But the opposite of this is also true: Because the memorial model of lyric refuses materiality, it shares no common ground with the body of its beloved, for better or for worse. And for a sequence that so insistently praises the fair youth's physical beauty, any distance between lyric and the body quickly becomes a problem. The *Sonnets* underscore this disconnect by repeatedly describing the poet's creation as barren or sterile. In sonnet 83, for instance, the speaker calls his writing "the barren tender of a poet's debt" (4). Later, in sonnet 76, the poet opens with the same fear, that lyric offers a fundamentally sterile medium. The poet calls his verse "barren of new pride" (1) and bemoans its inability to grow with the times. The issue of poetry's sterility is of particular concern near the end of the procreation sonnets, where the choice between biological and literary reproduction is foregrounded. In sonnet 16, the poet asks the young man once again why he refuses to father a child.

> But wherefore do not you a mightier way
> make war upon this bloody tyrant Time,
> and fortify yourself in your decay
> with means more blessèd than my barren rhyme?
> Now stand you on the top of happy hours,
> and many maiden gardens, yet unset,
> with virtuous wish would bear your living flowers,
> much liker than your painted counterfeit:
> so should the lines of life that life repair,
> which this time's pencil or my pupil pen
> neither in inward worth nor outward fair
> can make you live yourself in eyes of men:
> > to give away yourself keeps yourself still,
> > and you must live drawn by your own sweet skill.

Reproduction, the poet insists, is the mightier way to defeat time, a biological response to a biological problem. The young man is urged to husbandry, reminded of the "many maiden gardens" that would happily bear his flowers. Alongside this image of fertile soil are reminders that verse, in contrast, is a "barren" medium. The poet notes that artificial means of reproduction—verse, painting—must necessarily fail to capture the fullness of the young man's beauty. Nothing, he writes, can "make you live yourself"—nothing except reproduction.

This anxiety about the distance between lyric preservation and biological reproduction intensifies in sonnet 17, which offers what seems at first glance like flattery typical of patronage lyric: The young man is *so* beautiful, so exceptional, that no art form could ever capture his true worth. But behind that flattery lies a fear that lyric's rejection of the body will be its undoing.

> Who will believe my verse in time to come
> if it were filled with your most high deserts?
> Though yet, heaven knows, it is but as a tomb
> which hides your life, and shows not half your parts.
> If I could write the beauty of your eyes,
> and in fresh numbers number all your graces,
> the age to come would say 'This poet lies:
> such heavenly touches ne'er touched earthly faces.'
> So should my papers (yellowed with their age)
> be scorned, like old men of less truth than tongue,
> and your true rights be termed a poet's rage,
> and stretchèd meter of an antique song.
>   But were some child of yours alive that time,
>   you should live twice: in it, and in my rhyme.[19]

Once again, following a set of quatrains detailing the destructive effects of time on the material world, the poet turns to the memorial model. In one of the sequence's last appeals to reproduction, the poet, while still promising to save the fair youth in verse, suggests that a child would double the odds. The couplet promises the fantasy not just of immortality but of double life—twice kept alive, in a child and in rhyme. But a poem is not a child, and the promise of easily exchangeable afterlives in yet another couplet raises questions about the degree to which these are really alternatives at all.[20] This promise, like those promises of lyric immortality previously discussed, is first undermined by the form in which it appears. By placing it in the couplet, Shakespeare frames the parity of these options with suspicion, suggesting these two are not as evenly matched as they appear. This ambivalence is underscored by the parallel the poem invites readers to draw between this final binary, poem and child, and the imagery of the first quatrain. There, the poet calls his verse a tomb for the young man, one that, while it "were filled with your most high deserts," ultimately "hides your life, and shows not half your parts." Here, the poet divides the young man's afterlife in two: what remains in the poem and what remains in the grave. What remains in the poem is the disembodied memory allowed by the memorial model: the epitaphic inscription on the outside of the tomb, the beloved's name and description only.[21] What remains on the inside is the body, in all its decay—the life and the parts that cannot be translated into writing, the reality of embodied existence offered by reproduction. The immortality offered by verse and by a child, when read against this image, are two very different futures. Verse can preserve the individual identity of the young man, something that generational immortality cannot; as sonnet 16 notes, there is nothing that "can make you live yourself." But while a child cannot preserve the individual identity of the young man, it offers something the poem cannot: a body. The poet's verse is deemed fantastical by its readers because the body it imagines is necessarily absent. A child would be a living, material reminder of the beloved and the beauty the poet so desires.

These two sonnets, which appear at the end of the sequence's initial procreation subsequence, confirm the issue at the heart of the memorial model and reveal one of the major reasons for its failure. The problem to which the *Sonnets* respond from their outset is decay: The young man's beauty is fading, his body is aging, and his death is inevitable. And while the procreation sonnets urge reproduction as an initial solution, sonnet 16's "mightier way," that avenue is foreclosed before the sequence has even begun. Not only does the young man refuse, but, as these sonnets remind the readers, reproduction does not preserve anything of the young man's individual identity. The only option that remains, seemingly, is the memorial model. The poet can preserve the name and memory of the fair youth in an immaterial form that appears timeless and thus safe from decay. But, as the countless lines of praise for the fair youth's beauty confirm, the beloved *is* his body. As sonnet 1 declares, the desire is that beauty's rose—not just beauty, but the body in which it is realized—might never die. A memorial lyric that can, as sonnet 17 suggests, offer at most a name for a gravestone strips the fair youth of an essential part of his being. This is, of course, an essential part of the memorial model's plan—by rejecting the body, this mode of preservation can avoid decay entirely. But in avoiding decay, the memorial model necessarily loses part of what it loves. This model of lyric erects a monument around the dying body, pushing the beloved's inevitable rot deep underground while offering a bodiless and thus necessarily incomplete immortality. The very strengths that the memorial model can claim for lyric—immateriality and immunity to decay—are also its central weaknesses. A lyric that stands outside time and the material world is a barren one, one that cannot yield the embodied beauty the poet so desires. But while the *Sonnets* reject the memorial model's desire for immateriality and timelessness, they do not abandon lyric entirely. That is, Shakespeare's sequence does not reject lyric's preservative potential as such, only the narrow vision for lyric found in the memorial model. Returning to sonnet 76, a poem that seems to repeat several of the memorial model's central claims, we can see how the *Sonnets* concurrently question whether these fundamental assumptions about lyric really are true. Here, the poet repeats the claim that lyric offers a sterile medium but then suggests that biological reproduction might not be the only way to grow.

> Why is my verse so barren of new pride,
> so far from variation or quick change?
> Why with the time do I not glance aside
> to new-found methods, and to compounds strange?
> Why write I still all one, ever the same,
> and keep invention in a noted weed,
> that every word doth almost tell my name,
> showing their birth, and where they did proceed?
> O know, sweet love, I always write of you,
> and you and love are still my argument;
> so all my best is dressing old words new,
> spending again what is already spent:
> > for as the sun is daily new and old,
> > so is my love, still telling what is told.

This poem offers a new perspective on the idea that lyric might exist outside time's reach. Under the memorial model, lyric's resistance to time and decay is one of its primary advantages. But here, that same immutability becomes a flaw, rather than a strength. Poetry offers a barren salvation at best, the poet seems to suggest. It is not the lines of writing but the genealogical "lines of life," the poet notes (the pronunciation of which would have echoed *loins*, as David and Ben Crystal argue), that can create embodied life.[22] The poet reminds both the fair youth and the reader that lyric's disembodied qualities, while guarding it from time, also strip from it any sense of vitality. If, as sonnet 1 reminds us, all things that grow eventually die, then the reverse is also true: Things that cannot die also cannot grow.

But while this sonnet makes clear that a timeless lyric is a barren one, it also questions the assumption that lyric resides outside of time. In sonnet 17, the poet describes a future in which his poetry has been aged not just by shifting styles and tastes but by actual decay: The pages, like the poet, are "yellowed with their age," reminding the reader of the lyric's material form.[23] Here, in sonnet 76, the poet's references to the "noted weed" of his verse and the "old words" of his subject matter suggest an awareness that the Petrarchan love lyric he offers the young man—and, more specifically, the memorial model at its heart—belong to an era long gone. The poet has gotten too much of what he desires: By confidently declaring his writing free from decay, capable of total and complete timelessness, his poetry has gotten stuck in time. The poet's writing fails to move forward or keep up with evolving trends; his lyric decays anyway, not as the result of time's effect on the body but as the direct consequence of refusing time itself. The poet's work becomes a memorial not just to the young man but to itself, a reminder of the past rather than a bastion for the future. Lyric might not be able to grow as a body does, but it can grow stylistically and formally. There are, as the poet reminds us, newfound methods and variations available to him; there are new kinds of poems he might write. A lyric that looks to remain outside time is doomed to achieve what it desires: an existence perpetually out of sync with the times. But by leaning *into* time, the poet seems to suggest, his creation might cease to be quite so barren.

Throughout the sonnets discussed in this section, Shakespeare uses the uneasy formal connection between quatrains and couplet to foreground the tension inherent in lyric's relationship with decay. The memorial model offers readers the hope that an immaterial lyric, immune from the movement and change of time, can preserve a version of the young man that is completely safe from decay. But the *Sonnets* offer this traditional sentiment only to undermine it; by concentrating such promises in the couplets, Shakespeare reimagines the memorial model not as a solution but as itself an additional problem. The memorial model's central promise—that lyric can escape decay because it leaves the material world behind—becomes its key failing. An immaterial version of lyric ensures only that the beloved's body and beauty, both of which are central to his being, would necessarily be abandoned. This kind of lyric "shows not half your parts," the poet mourns; the body he loves, that he desires, must be left behind. These couplets offer the solution of lyric only to immediately question its efficacy. And likewise, while the memorial model of lyric seems to promise stability, what it delivers is only stagnancy. For Shakespeare, writing in a Petrarchan mode already well on its way out of favor, the question of a tradition's lifespan was an urgent one: Even if the *Sonnets* could keep a version of the fair youth alive, how much longer would readers be interested in it? The *Sonnets* explore the limitations of this memorial model of lyric, recognizing that it cannot fulfill its promise to circumvent decay. The only option, the poet seems to recognize in sonnet 76, is to turn to "compounds strange," the joining of unlike elements. Shakespeare's pun here joins the verbal with the bodily: *Compound* could suggest both a compound word and a medicine made by combining two or more elements (or "simples") into a single whole, both a textual and a material act of joining.[24] For Shakespeare's *Sonnets*, the solution to the stark binaries of the memorial model lies here, in the act of compounding the disparate—life and death, body and text—into a new, unified being.

The Lyric Prosthesis

Shakespeare responds to the flaws of the memorial model—its failure to preserve anything of the beloved's body and the dangerous stagnation that can result from rejecting time—by offering the *prosthetic model*, or *lyric prosthesis*, in its place. This model reframes lyric's response to decay as connective rather than preservative, imagining how the poet's creation might become an extension of the beloved's living (and decaying) body. While the brief reference to "compounds strange" offers a glimpse into this model, one of the most discussed articulations of the *Sonnets'* lyric prosthesis appears in sonnet 15, a poem that at first glance looks very much like another example of the memorial model.

> When I consider everything that grows
> holds in perfection but a little moment;
> that this huge stage presenteth naught but shows,
> whereon the stars in secret influence comment;
> when I perceive that men as plants increase,
> cheerèd and checked even by the selfsame sky,
> vaunt in their youthful sap, at height decrease,
> and wear their brave state out of memory;
> then the conceit of this inconstant stay
> sets you most rich in youth before my sight,
> where wasteful time debateth with decay
> to change your day of youth to sullied night,
> > and, all in war with time for love of you,
> > as he takes from you, I engraft you new.

Many critics argue that the grafting metaphor of these final lines, and the historical discourse it represents, is essential to understanding the sequence's vision for poetry's relationship with its subject. Grafting, a relatively new horticultural technology in England at the time of the *Sonnets*, represented the ability to shape plant husbandry to the desires of gardeners in ways previously unthinkable.[25] Some have asserted that Shakespeare's reference to this reproductive technology affirms the queerness that lies at the heart of the *Sonnets*. Vin Nardizzi argues that Shakespeare uses grafting to embrace a model of "seedless generation, a genealogy unmoored from an act of conjugal procreation."[26] In Nardizzi's reading, sonnet 15 brings together queer and heterosexual models of reproduction, uniting biological and literary preservation. Both Nardizzi and Claire Duncan note that cultural anxieties about grafting also ran parallel to antipoetic sentiments in early modern English culture, with both discourses critiquing art's dangerous capacity to displace nature. Even the husbandry manuals dedicated to teaching grafting techniques cautioned readers against taking these technologies too far, Duncan writes. "These manuals exhibit an anxiety about the limits of this intervention," she argues, "suggesting that gardeners must not be allowed to pervert the natural boundaries of kind.... These gardening manuals suggest that humans can and should interfere with nature, but to make it better, not perverted."[27] Grafting, like poetry, offered the dangerous ability to intervene in nature. As Nardizzi points out, the speaker in sonnet 15 seems to try to literalize Sir Philip Sidney's vision that literature might "grow, in effect, into another nature."[28]

However, while cultural debates around early modern grafting provide a useful context for this moment, I want to suggest that, for some of the same reasons discussed earlier, sonnet 15's promise to engraft is deeply ambivalent about that mode of preservation and that, while illuminating, the graft is still an incomplete model for the relationship the poet desires between his work and his beloved. The promise that poetry might intervene against decay appears, yet again, here in the couplet. Just as in sonnet 17, this placement destabilizes the poet's claim of equal exchange. This couplet also offers the false promise of a balanced equation: *As* time takes from you, *so in turn* I engraft you anew. Like the gardener, the poet augments the natural order with their own creation; but unlike the gardener, the poet offers a supplement that is materially incompatible with the stock onto which it has been grafted. Throughout these memorial model sonnets, the poet continually insists that bodies and lyrics are made of fundamentally different stuff. Nardizzi argues that the metaphor of grafting in sonnet 15 underscores the poet's desire for "continuity" between biological reproduction and poetic generation.[29] Within the narrow context of this single sonnet, the turn to grafting seems an attempt to erase the differences between lyric and beloved: While horticultural grafting might link different varieties or qualities together in unnatural ways, the plant bodies it joins together are fundamentally the same and thus able to be seamlessly continuous with one another. Indeed, many of the anti-grafting responses focused on the how dangerously invisible this interference might be; the predominant anxiety was that outside observers might not be able to tell "natural" from "cultivated." But the tension in poetry's relationship with the beloved in the memorial model sonnets throughout this sequence emerges from the reality that here, the relationship between graft and stock is precisely the opposite: These two objects are discontinuous and materially dissimilar. There is no risk, the sequence assures us, of ever mistaking lyric for body.

While Shakespeare offers the metaphor of the poet's creation as a grafted limb, it is its inorganic twin, the prosthesis, that fully captures the lyric ethos of the *Sonnets* and that answers the shortcomings of the memorial model.[30] First, the prosthetic model rejects the claim that lyric can exist outside the material world. The memorial model of lyric preservation insists on language's fundamental immateriality; it promises a space outside the temporal and physical limitations of a body, a space outside decay. However, as the *Sonnets* repeatedly confirm, the poet's creation is, in fact, a physical object: The recurring invocations of yellowed pages and black ink keep the materiality of the text in the foreground, reminding readers that the lyric resides not just in their mind but in their hands. And while that materiality means that the poet's creation is not as immune from decay as one might imagine, it also means that body and text have much more in common than the memorial model allows. Shakespeare's prosthetic model aspires to what Elaine Scarry describes as a "materialist conception of language," the insistence that "language is capable of registering in its own contours the contours and weight of the material world" and that "language itself may enter, act on, and alter the material world."[31] Scarry continues, "When language and the body are placed side by side, the weightlessness of any language that has lost its referential aspirations becomes especially noticeable."[32] The *Sonnets'* rejection of the memorial model is, in part, the process of noticing that weightlessness, of seeing the shortfalls of an immaterial model of lyric preservation. To imagine lyric not as a memorial but as a prosthesis means insisting on the physicality of language, on poetry's ability to find a site of connection with the body, despite the distinctions between the two.

This is not to suggest, however, that the prosthetic model insists that poem and beloved are totally identical. Rather, while maintaining that the poet's creation does in fact exist in the world, the prosthetic model also recognizes the distance between poem and body. This is borne out, most immediately, in the repeated descriptions of lyric's sterility discussed earlier. In part, these critiques reinforce the sequence's procreation argument: If the primary goal of the *Sonnets* is to convince the young man to father a child, then it is to the poet's advantage to stress the difference between that and all other modes of preservation. As I have suggested, these critiques also underscore the danger of a lyric that tries to live outside time. Unlike a child, a memorial lyric is incapable of growth or development in the world, making it particularly susceptible to becoming outmoded, as the speaker of the

Sonnets fears his work may already be. But the other major effect of these comparisons is to underscore the material difference between a poem and a child. The first, the poet's creation, is associated with inorganic, artificial matter; it is a thing made of ink and paper, not unlike the statues and monuments from which it tries to distinguish itself. The second, a child, belongs to the realm of the organic; it is linked with the days, seasons, plants, and creatures that fill the *Sonnets*, the living beings that manage (with the exception of the young man) to be able to remake themselves. These comparisons concentrate one of the primary thematic tensions of the *Sonnets*, the division of art and nature. While this distinction often manifests as a difference in qualities of action—whether something is the result of natural forces or of artistic intervention—the sequence also thematizes this difference at the level of material. The distinction between manner and matter is one that the grafting metaphor obscures—intentionally and strategically, I argue, in a way similar to the child and rhyme comparison in the couplet of sonnet 17. While the graft is artisanal in its method, it is natural in its matter, and indeed in its afterlife; the graft, once joined, goes on to grow and reproduce like any other living limb. But the poet's creation, unlike a branch, is never natural; it remains squarely in the realm of the artificial, making it, instead, prosthetic.

But while a prosthetic model of lyric recognizes the distinct material qualities of poem and body, it also insists that this difference does not prevent the two from joining. Unlike the memorial model, which views lyric and biological reproduction as entirely antithetical, the prosthetic model insists on lyric's materiality, which creates the opportunity for a meeting place where text and body might, despite their differences, join together—and, in joining, might create a new kind of life. In sonnet 16's discussion of reproduction and lyric, the third quatrain tries to tease out the qualities each kind of afterlife might preserve and the qualities each might miss.

> So should the lines of life that life repair
> which this time's pencil or my pupil pen
> neither in inward worth nor outward fair
> can make you live yourself in eyes of men.

The explicit claim here is that memorialization in poetry is not the same as remaining alive and thus cannot actually prevent the body's decay; neither the "inward worth" of the fair youth's character nor the "outward fair" of his beauty are safe, despite the work of the poet's pen. However, while acknowledging that lyric does not live in exactly the same sense that the beloved lives, the poet imagines another model of animacy for his creation, fostered not through memorialization but through prostheticization. While his poem cannot live on its own, it can nonetheless be alive—not just metaphorically but in a very real sense. Despite its artificial nature, David Wills argues, a prosthetic is nonetheless imbued with animacy. This vitality emerges not from the material of the prosthetic itself—the plastic or carbon fiber of a bionic limb is not alive, per se—but through the relationship with the body with which it joins. "The natural body [is supplemented] *by*, but also *in*, its artificial appendage," Wills writes, "the body recognizing its own artificiality even as it enlivens its new inorganic member."[33] As Wills suggests, the extent to which a prosthesis feels or is perceived to be alive is defined less by its material composition and more by its activity. The prosthesis is alive not because it is made of living material but because it is an integral part of a body engaged in the work of living. As these lines underscore, none of the reproductive technologies available—not writing, not painting—can create something that is on its own alive. But yet, the poet suggests that the "lines of life" might succeed—the loins, yes, but also lines as a connectional practice. The poet shifts the readers' gaze from the tools to the act of connection, of lineation, of extension.

The enabling animacy of prosthetic connection drives sonnet 18, in which the poet returns to the trope of life-giving lineation. Promising his beloved will grow "in eternal lines" (12), the poet then confidently declares that

> So long as men can breathe or eyes can see,
> so long lives this, and this gives life to thee.

This couplet joins the others already cited in making a bold promise for immortality in verse. The speaker here makes a clear reference to the poem itself; *this*, the poet's creation, lives and gives life in turn to the beloved. However, immediately following sonnet 17's complaint about the barrenness of verse, this promise seems already demonstrably false. This, like the many other memorial model couplets, seems to guarantee something it knows it cannot deliver. However, the conditional—"so long as men can breathe or eyes can see"—signals the promise of the prosthetic model in its place. Instead of focusing on *this*, the poet's creation, the poem nudges us back to the *so* of line 13, allowing us to focus on the conditions that might enable such an outcome. The poem only lives through its relationship with the living bodies of others; only through their eyes or in their mouths does the work come to life. The prosthetic model inverts the poet's claim in the final line: It is not the case that lyric gives life to the beloved, but rather that bodies like the beloved's—living but also decaying bodies—share their lives with the poem. Shakespeare revisits the connection between articulation and animation in sonnet 81, where, in the third quatrain and couplet, the poet again compares his verse to a memorial for the beloved.

> Your monument shall be my gentle verse,
> which eyes not yet created shall o'er-read,
> and tongues-to-be your being shall rehearse,
> when all the breathers of this world are dead.
>   You still shall live (such virtue hath my pen)
>   where breath most breathes, even in the mouths of men.

The poet again seems to reveal the limitations of his own argument, demonstrating the shift from memorial model to prosthetic in the process. The speaker claims, brashly, that his verse will be the monument to the young man, that his pen holds the power of immortality. But in the same lines, Shakespeare assigns the act of animation to the body parts of the text: eyes, tongues, and mouth. It is through the poem's connection with the bodies of its readers that both poem and subject, lyric and beloved, share in mutual animacy. Neither on their own but only in connection with one another—this is the only way that both might, in any sense, live.

This site of connection underscores the final crucial element of the prosthetic model. For a relationship between lyric and beloved to be truly prosthetic, the boundaries between subject and poem, self and other, must become blurred in both directions. Many prosthesis users describe that while others might see their prosthesis as an object separate from their "real" body, they do not experience that same sense of differentiation. Instead, the prosthesis becomes an integral part of their bodily map—part of themselves. The Cyborg Jillian Weise, for instance, rejects the notion that her bionic leg is not a part of her body. Recalling those who describe her bionic limb as "not her leg," Weise responds, "I always have to be wearing 'not my leg,'" noting that her prosthesis is "as essential to [my] personhood as any biological limb."[34] Vivian Sobchack writes that distinctions between self and other or real and artificial are not useful binaries for describing her relationship with her prosthesis. Sobchack writes, "My 'real' leg and my 'prosthetic' leg are not usually lived as two absolutely different and separate things since they function as an ensemble and are each a part of my body participating in the whole movement that gets me from here to there. Thus, they are *organically related in practice (if not in material)*."[35] She continues, "those who successfully *incorporate and subjectively live* the prosthetic . . . sense themselves neither as lacking something nor as walking around with some 'thing' that is added onto their bodies. Rather, in most situations, the prosthetic as lived in use is usually transparent . . . as is the rest of our body when we're focused outward to the world."[36]

While the prosthesis and body remain distinct from one another, the site of connection becomes less clear the more closely we examine it; the elements remain themselves, but the space between them is imperceptible. Despite any material difference between prosthesis and body, the relationship between the two results in a shared sense of being—of mutual animacy, of a united and embodied self. It is this model of the lyric prosthesis, ultimately, that the *Sonnets* offer as a replacement for the memorial model of lyric preservation. The many references to the yellowing pages, the black ink, and the physicality of the printing process reveal that the poet recognizes that his work lives in the same physical world as the young man. But, as the repeated insistence on poetry's barrenness confirms, the poet's creation is not part of the same organic world as the fair youth. The inorganic matter of the prosthesis is necessarily different from the organic (decaying) matter of the body with which it joins.[37] On its own, divorced from the body, lyric cannot grow, cannot reproduce, cannot create life in the same way that a child might—yet it is only by joining with this living and decaying world that lyric has any possibility for life itself.

The *Sonnets* and Prosthetic Form

The *Sonnets*' prosthetic model of lyric immortality shapes the thematic claims within individual sonnets about the work poetry might accomplish and the effect it might have on the fair youth's future. Unlike the stark dissimilarity imagined by the memorial model—a decaying, ephemeral beloved and a timeless, immaterial lyric—Shakespeare's sequence instead seems to imagine that lyric and body might, despite or even because of their differences, find themselves joined together. But while thematically significant, Shakespeare's lyric prosthesis exerts its most profound influence on the formal relationships that shape the sequence. Wills argues that, at its core, a prosthetic relationship relies on the coexistence of difference and contiguity. A prosthesis joins "two putatively distinct orders," he writes, two nonidentical entities "whose difference is the whole matter at stake, and yet whose rigorous differentiation would entail the collapse of this entire critical edifice."[38] In a prosthetic relationship, the point of connection is both identifiable and indistinguishable; one might recognize the presence of two nonidentical elements within a single whole that are nonetheless inextricable from one another. This differentiated structure provides an alternative to traditional formalist concerns about a text's wholeness, the Brooksian well-wrought urn of total coherence. This previous ideal of the whole overlaps significantly with the memorial model of lyric preservation and its vision for lyric. Both idealize consistency and timelessness, embracing figures like the monument as a template for the kind of stability and uniformity to which they aspire. A prosthetic model for formal unity, on the other hand, argues that wholeness is entirely compatible with bifurcation, difference, and discontinuity—that these sites of difference can be, simultaneously, sites of connection.

One area in the *Sonnets* on which this concern around wholeness has concentrated is, as I have already suggested, the relationship within individual sonnets between the couplet and the quatrains. As the previous critical histories confirm, scholars have long regarded the relationship between these two elements as tenuous and struggled to establish critical models that acknowledge this disconnect while still allowing for a sense of formal unity. The very descriptions of the couplet's connection to the poem in these accounts underscores the need for a new prosthetic model of wholeness. Take, for instance, Rosenberg's description of the critical history surrounding the couplets, which frequently appeals to ecological metaphors for unity. "To many of his mid-century critics," she writes, "Shakespeare's couplets seem abrupt, pat, or flat-footed, ill-suited to the lines preceding them and *a threat to the organic form of the sonnet*."[39] A few lines later, she describes how the couplets often stand in "syntactical independence" to the rest of the poem, "which makes them seem superfluous and easily detached, a part that does not belong to *the organic poem*."[40] Later, she writes, "The disunity threatened by the couplet seemed to pose *a danger to the organic lyric identity of the sonnet*."[41] She notes, "In *its inorganic relationship* to the rest of the poem, a couplet threatens to forget *the organic life* the sonnet had seemed to possess."[42] Rosenberg's appeal to the poem as an organic being is not entirely unexpected, given her focus on early modern husbandry manuals. And yet, these metaphors reveal an underlying dichotomy that echoes through many of these accounts. To be whole is to be organic: The body of the poem is a living body, and its coherence is the expression of material unity across that body. Most importantly, this coherence is a fundamental expectation; it is natural, organic, to be without break or difference. On the other hand, the couplet feels inorganic; against the natural matter of the quatrains, it feels artificial and created. The connection of these two elements is, in this description, unnatural. The inclusion of the artificial element of the couplet threatens the unity of the otherwise organic whole.

To be clear, Rosenberg does not make these particular claims as part of her own argument. But the language of these comparisons underscores the need for a prosthetic model of form, particularly for the *Sonnets*. Seen through the lens of the lyric prosthesis, the visible seams between organic and inorganic, whole and part, are not formal failures but in fact a model of unity consistent with the thematic relationship the sequence imagines between lyric and body. Under such a model, the couplet can be inorganic *and also* not a threat to the whole; the poem can join the natural with the artificial, sustaining both while not eliminating either. This prosthetic model provides a better critical framework for discussing the relationship between couplet and quatrains. But in addition, the lyric prosthesis offers a more effective vocabulary for discussing the *Sonnets*' generic classification, another long-standing critical debate about the sequence's formal identity. The *Sonnets* have long been described as an outlier in the sonnet sequence genre, with some critics insisting that the work is not, in fact, a sequence at all because of the unclear narrative structure of the work. These readers argue that there is not a clear cast of characters, plotline, or resolution. These disagreements are, in part, about the acceptable or appropriate balance of lyric and narrative within the sequence form. From their Petrarchan origins, sonnet sequences have always included some degree of narrative, a discernible if limited story that readers might use as a framework to orient their readings of individual poems. But simultaneously, the form of the sequence has also always resisted narrative coherence. Petrarch, famously, opens by telling his readers

> *Voi ch'ascoltate in rime sparse il suono*
> *di quei sospiri ond'io nudriva 'l core*
> *in sul mio primo giovenile errore,*
> *quand'era in parte altr'uom da quel ch'i'sono*

> [You who hear in scattered rhymes the sound of those sighs with which I nourished my heart during my first youthful error, when I was in part another man from what I am now.][43]

While Petrarch acknowledges his narrative framework (the transition from the man he was then to the man he is now), that framework is already fragmentary, the rhymes scattered from the outset. Much like the form of the romance epic, discussed in the previous chapter, the narrative element of the *Rime sparse* is rooted in error, in winding paths rather than direct routes. This is also true of the sequence form more broadly: Whatever narrative does exist comes to life in and through the lyric forms of individual poems, songs, and sonnets. Because of this, readers and scholars who look solely to the narrative elements of a sonnet sequence for meaning are bound to be disappointed. Guy-Bray notes that modern readers are often incorrectly predisposed "to see sonnet sequences as narratives in which nothing happens," arguing that such an approach obscures the many things that lyric does achieve.[44] Dubrow goes so far as to suggest that critics should reject the category of sonnet sequence altogether. She argues instead that "the presence of narrativity varies so much from one collection to another and often within a given collection that we should discard the term 'sonnet sequence' in favor of 'sonnet cycle' when generalizing about the English tradition," as that description better captures the predominantly lyric nature of such works.[45]

As these accounts suggest, finding a model to accurately capture the interplay between lyric and narrative in the sonnet sequence (not to mention the variety with which such relationships are realized) has proven difficult, with many critics turning to metaphor as a way of capturing the dynamic balance of the form. C. S. Lewis offers a geographic analogy for navigating a sequence's shifting waters: "The first thing to grasp about the sonnet sequence is that it is not a way of telling a story. It is a form which exists for the sake of prolonged lyrical meditation. . . . External events—a quarrel, a parting, an illness, a stolen kiss—are every now and then mentioned to provide themes for the meditation. Thus you get an island, or (if the event gives the matter for more than one piece) an archipelago, of narrative in the lyrical sea."[46] Michael Spiller suggests the metaphor of a photo album, with individual snapshots organized into a collection. "Each photograph is a formal discrete item," he writes, that "has its own meaning and justification, and may also be framed and viewed on its own. . . . However, their separateness challenges the album compiler to become aware of [their] principles of aggregation."[47] Like the photo album, Spiller suggests, a sonnet sequence might be organized via a range of principles that highlight different dimensions of its construction; one might put more emphasis on narrative (akin to sorting photos chronologically, for instance) or instead choose to emphasize lyric elements (choosing aesthetic or thematic groupings, for example). Regardless of the structure, the form derives its imaginative energy from the collision of these two elements, the negotiations between part and whole, frame and object. This relationship, as I suggest in the introduction, entails a constantly shifting dynamic—like an optical illusion, with elements moving, transforming, emerging, or receding according to the viewer's focus. Lewis's and Spiller's metaphors suggest the difficulty and perhaps even the impossibility of pinning down the relationship between lyric and narrative in these works. Sea and island, photograph and album—these metaphors work to capture the mutually constitutive relationship at the heart of the sonnet sequence, to determine how we might best read and interpret these texts.

Even within the context of this generic difficulty, Shakespeare's *Sonnets* have proven to be an exceptionally difficult example to classify. Critics have long debated whether Shakespeare's sequence is, in fact, a sequence at all, with some suggesting that the text is purely lyric. Walter Cohen, editor of the *Sonnets* for *The Norton Shakespeare*, asserts that it is "easy to overstate the internal organization of the sonnets as we have them." He continues, "The division of the sequence into two main groups is arguably unwarranted. Most of the poems are not explicitly about either the youth or the mistress, not even designating the sex of the person discussed. Only their relative position in the collection has produced the standard simplification adopted here. Furthermore, the sequence as a whole is relatively uninterested in plot."[48] Dubrow concurs, arguing that the *Sonnets* are marked by "a resistance to narrativity that characterizes a number of [other] sonnet sequences" and that Shakespeare "did not arrange these sonnets in a way that tells a clear story and unmistakably signals the direction of address of each lyric."[49] This rejection of sequential structure is exemplified by Paul Edmonson and Stanley Wells's edition of Shakespeare's poetry, which organizes the sonnets by probable date of composition rather than the print order in the 1609 edition. Edmonson and Wells argue that the poems of the *Sonnets*, while likely intentionally arranged in the order in which they are first published, do not "hang together in the manner of the published sonnet cycles of other writers."[50] They characterize the *Sonnets* as "a collection of often highly personally inflected poems written over at least twenty-seven years, rather than a sequence aimed at catching the mood and developing the taste for a literary fashion."[51] For Edmonson, Wells, and others, the *Sonnets* lack the narrative scaffolding necessary to support even a loose sequential reading, rendering the text an object closer to an early modern miscellany than a sonnet sequence.[52]

Other editors, however, including Katherine Duncan-Jones and Burrow, argue in favor of approaching the *Sonnets* as an intentionally structured sequence that clearly participates in the generic tradition. Both Burrow and Duncan-Jones assert that the 1609 printing order is authorized by Shakespeare, the product of careful consideration and revision. Burrow concludes, "the sequence as it is printed in Q does have some fixed points which indicate that the order in which the poems appear had been carefully considered, at least in the part of the sequence up to 126."[53] Burrow is careful to note, however, that sequentiality does not necessarily equal narrativity. "Readers of the poems in their sequence in Q are not invited to weld them into an immutable numerologically determined structure, but to make sequences, of time, of sound, of sense, of narrative, and of argument," he writes. "The satisfaction offered by each of these differing systems is left so artfully partial that some poems seem to call to others from which they are separated by long intervals, and to invite rearrangement."[54] Unlike the more strictly organized sequences that predate him, Burrow argues, Shakespeare's *Sonnets* offer a more capricious (and much less narratively oriented) framework for readers; still, he notes, capricious does not necessary mean free of narrative. Other influential studies of the *Sonnets*, including those by Imtiaz Habib and Margreta de Grazia, likewise insist that the sequence contains a recognizable and influential narrative element.[55] The sequence is ordered sequentially and intentionally, these critics maintain, and its meaning is at least partially constructed by this narrative dimension.

At the heart of this disagreement about whether the *Sonnets* contain any narrative dimension and should thus be considered a sequence is a shared observation: Shakespeare's *Sonnets* do not replicate the particular Neoplatonic narrative structure that shaped Petrarch's sequence and its many imitators. Instead, Shakespeare's sequence offers a new model for the sonnet sequence form, a model similarly guided by the lyric prosthesis. As I discuss in the introduction, the Neoplatonic narrative structure commonly associated with Petrarchan poetics in early modern England regarded the body's decay and eventual eradication as the teleological end point toward which forms like the sonnet sequence should be oriented. Laura dies and her body dissolves, but Petrarch's sequence steps in to gradually replace that physical form with a textual one. While later sequences replace this specific narrative structure with ones of their own, the Petrarchan mode continued to move in the same general direction: up and away from the decaying body, toward the spiritual and literary apotheosis of both subject and author. This is the same lyric ethos that the *Sonnets* interrogate and reject in the memorial model, the hope that poetry might help one abandon the material world altogether. This Neoplatonic strategy is primarily narrative, relying on those specific formal affordances to replace the decaying body with an everlasting one. Mitchell and Snyder describe this act of progressively replacing the body as the prostheticizing work of narrative. They argue that narrative prostheticizes by orienting itself around the eradication (or the attempted and failed eradication) of the perceived failures of the disabled and decaying body.

> A simple schematic of narrative structure might run thus: first, a deviance or marked difference is exposed to the reader; second, a narrative

consolidates the need for its own existence by calling for an explanation of the deviation's origin and formative consequences; third, the deviance is brought forth from the periphery of concerns to the center of the story to come; and fourth, the remainder of the story rehabilitates or fixes the deviance in some manner. The fourth step of the repair of deviance may involve an obliteration of the difference through a "cure," the rescue of a despised object from social censure, the extermination of the deviant as purification of the social body, or the revaluation of an alternative mode of being.[56]

The Neoplatonic structure so often associated with the sonnet sequence and distilled in the memorial model promises to do just that. By centering the beloved's decay as the primary crisis to which the poet must respond, the sequence then engages in the work of rescue that Mitchell and Snyder describe, transforming the abject decaying body into an object worthy of spiritual elevation.

But the sonnet sequence is not purely narrative—and Shakespeare's *Sonnets* are particularly, insistently, not purely narrative. Rather than engaging in the work of narrative prosthesis, the *Sonnets* offer a model of lyric prosthesis that resonates not only at the level of the individual poem but at the level of the sequence itself. By recognizing the fact that the *Sonnets* attempt to prostheticize the fair youth through a lyric rather than a narrative strategy, we can better understand how Shakespeare's sequence foregrounds its lyric dimension while still acknowledging the presence of a narrative structure. The lyric prosthesis, that is, helps to foreground the collision between lyric and narrative at the heart of the *Sonnets* as a generic success rather than a failure. At the center of this prosthetic sequence structure is sonnet 126, after which the *Sonnets* seem to abruptly shift their gaze from the fair youth to the dark lady. This moment of apparent fracture has attracted significant discussion from readers and critics of the sequence. While some, such as de Grazia and Fineman, argue that this narrative division is supported by shifts in pronouns, tone, and theme, others, such as Dubrow and Habib, suggest that readerly expectations for narrative have overinflated the degree of difference between the pre- and post-126 poems. And yet, readers from all camps seem to agree that 126 itself, one of the most formally anomalous sonnets in the sequence, is working to signal some kind of major thematic transition in the *Sonnets*.

> O thou my lovely boy who in thy power
> dost hold Time's fickle glass his sickle hour;
> who hast by waning grown, and therein show'st

> thy lovers withering, as thy sweet self grow'st—
> if Nature (sovereign mistress over wrack)
> as thou goest onwards still will pluck thee back,
> she keeps thee to this purpose, that her skill
> may Time disgrace, and wretched minutes kill.
> Yet fear her, O thou minion of her pleasure;
> she may detain, but not still keep, her treasure!
> Her audit (though delayed) answered must be,
> and her quietus is to render thee.
> [   ]
> [   ]

While in earlier poems, the young man found himself the victim of time's destruction, here, the balance of power has been reversed. The fair youth now wields time's glass and scythe himself; he holds the weapons that once threatened him. The result of this shift of power is a kind of stalemate. The poem foregrounds patterns of oscillation and oppositional movement, suggesting that the once-irresistible destruction of time has now met its match. The youth has "by waning grown," sprouted and withered, and is simultaneously propelled onward and plucked back. Standing in the eye of time's hurricane, pulled in every direction and yet rendered immobile, the fair youth finds himself stuck—but not still. This ambivalence is echoed in the poem's exclusive use of the couplet form. All the poem's rhymes are opened and then immediately closed, offering another layer of static movement as the reader progresses through the sonnet.

Through these contrasts between stillness and motion, stability and change, the *Sonnets* reflect one final time on lyric's ability to resist decay. The speaker's lingering desire to keep the fair youth out of time's power and safe from decay are the last gasps of the memorial model's promises for literary immortality, the fantasy that the young man might shed the limitations imposed on him by his body by transforming into an object of pure lyric. But unlike in those earlier sonnets, in this case, the poet seems, at last, to have acknowledged the limitations of his ability to preserve the young man's youth and fairness. Here, instead of his own writing emerging to battle time, the poet identifies nature as the sole source of any extra life the young man might claim. Contrasting the memorial model's promise to exist indefinitely, the preservation offered by nature is merely a delay—detained, the poet writes, but not kept. While nature extends the fair youth's lifespan (to the sole purpose, the poet notes, of disgracing time), she also ends it, her inevitable audit eventually answered. This shift from complete resistance to time to temporary delay fulfills the promise of the prosthetic model. Unlike the memorial model and its attempt at indefinite preservation, the lyric prosthesis aspires to the work of nature as described in this sonnet. The prosthetic model imagines the possibility that it might expand, rather than preserve, the beloved—extending him through time, into the poem, into the minds and mouths of Shakespeare's readers—while acknowledging that decay is inevitable and that the poet and his works must exist within time. Changelessness is illusory, the *Sonnets* seem to acknowledge, and can result only in losing the readers necessary for the work's continuation and thus the young man's literary afterlife. And by aligning the poet's desires with nature, sonnet 126 reinforces the importance of the beloved's body in its response. The fair youth exists—living, growing, decaying—in the real world, not the world of the poem. Where before nature and the poet existed in opposition, the poet's work permanent and lasting and nature's work fragile and ephemeral, here they join together, collaborating to prolong the young man's life in its fullness. Rather than opposing the rhythms of nature, as he has in so many of the sonnets that lead up to this moment, the poet find himself allied with nature, both laboring to keep the young man, if only for a moment longer. This, then, is the goal of the lyric prosthesis—not to replace or remove the young man from the world but to imagine a model of lyric that might become an extension of, and not a replacement for, the body it loves.

The full realization of the prosthetic model is thematic and formal, evident in 126's unique approach to the couplet. After 125 poems in which couplets have fulfilled the function not of conclusion or narrative culmination but of increased ambivalence, their overwhelming presence here emphasizes that this sonnet is not a moment of resolution or even of clear transition. Rather, it is a moment of dynamic tension, of movement both backward and forward. As readers of the *Sonnets* have noted, the poems before 126 and after are marked primarily by their difference from one another. This is the meeting point of, variously, masculine and feminine, Platonic and erotic, rich and poor, linguistic and visual, whiteness and Blackness, queerness and heteronormativity, frustration and consummation, desire and repulsion, maturity and youthfulness. While readers have attempted to fit those binaries into narrative structures, positing one as problem and the subsequent as solution (or vice versa), the proliferation of such models suggests that in fact any narrative arc that might exist is far from clear. As the forms within 126 suggest, the *Sonnets'* overarching narrative structure is instead one of ambivalence. Rather than offering a landmark by which readers might orient themselves—one of Lewis's islands of narrative in the sea of lyric—this sonnet subverts expectations by offering a model of connection marked by contingency. The sequences changes and moves in a way not recognizable to the familiar narrative patterns associated with the sonnet sequence as genre. However, as the lyric prosthesis emphasizes, ambivalent connection is an effective, even desirable model for formal cohesion. Fineman, after discussing the distinct qualities of the two subsequences, notes that the *Sonnets* demonstrate an undeniable sense of both division and wholeness.

> Yet the sequence as a whole refuses to be thus discriminated into two distinct and isolated parts. Assuming we read them both, the two parts of the sequence cannot be kept separate from each other, for when we begin to compare them each with each the second sub-sequence retroactively undoes the first, with the latter "forswearing" the former in a definitive revisionary way. For this reason, if the young man sonnets and the dark lady sonnets together form a homiletic diptych, it is one the two sides of which fold over upon each other in a mutually refractory collation, closing over upon each other in so conflicted and displacing an articulation that it is the very opposition between the two sub-sequences that turns out to complicate their opposition.[57]

The models that scholars have developed to try to capture the relationship between the sequence's two parts—Fineman's "mutually refractory collation" and diptych of an entangled continuity that simultaneously offers two distinct identities and yet an undeniable wholeness, Nardizzi's "hinge" between heterosexual and queer models of reproduction—describe a narrative structure run through with the ethos of the lyric prosthesis. The sequence's two halves are stitched together, moving the reader not directly forward (or backward) but, in an echo of sonnet 126, everywhere and nowhere all at once. Shakespeare's return to the couplet here is an intentional formal marker signaling that the link between the sequence's two uneven halves should be read as analogous to the connection between quatrains and couplet. That is, rather than moving toward a summation or encapsulation, the *Sonnets* turn toward ambivalence, complication, and uncertainty.

The formal relationships in the *Sonnets*, particularly those that come to a head in sonnet 126, make clear the need for a prosthetic model of lyric. This moment demonstrates, for instance, that Shakespeare's sequence requires a critical vocabulary that can better capture the collision between the lyric and narrative elements of the sequence form. As previously mentioned, this sequence does not offer the kind of Neoplatonic narrative typically associated with the memorial model—and, in refusing that, it also refuses the kind of prostheticizing work that Mitchell and Snyder allocate to narrative. Instead, Shakespeare's sequence demonstrates that models of prosthesis developed in and for narrative do not translate cleanly over generic lines and that lyric requires its own theory of prosthesis that fully captures the different affordances of that form—its relationships with time, change, and subjectivity, to name only a few.

Some disability theorists have begun to take up the question of what it might mean for lyric to prosthetically relate to its subject and how that differs from narrative. Jonathan Hsy, for instance, notes that lyric's prosthetic function works primarily through formal intervention. "A concerted turn from narrative prosthesis (plot progression) to lyric prosthesis (mode of expression)" is rooted, he argues, in "close formal analysis," calling critics to attend to the relationship between specifically lyric forms and the body.[58] Julie Singer similarly offers a definition of lyric prosthesis as "the use of lyric forms to bridge gaps or compensate for lacks, be they in the body of the narrator, in relationships between characters, or in the structure of a text. . . . A lyric prosthesis allows for the free articulation of a 'hybrid' text's formally diverse components."[59] Writing of late medieval courtly romance, Singer argues that what scholars had previously identified as "lyric insertions" into an otherwise narrative text were in fact not interruptions but prosthetic extensions that, through formal experimentation, offered a sense of bodily wholeness in response to impairment. Singer notes that by offering a structured poetic form, the text establishes a logic of metonymic replacement. "The fixed form poem's ties to the rhythms and structures of the body enable an innovative healing technique whereby the textual body corrects the lover's physical body by completing it," she writes. "This therapeutic strategy consists in the replacement of a missing part with its *like*, with a related structure or device. In language we call this process of substitution metonymy; in surgery, we call it prosthesis."[60] Lyric prostheticizes not through narrative transformation but via formal echoes, through what Singer calls its reliance on "fixed forms," defined structures that offer a sense of wholeness and ordering. Shakespeare's sequence takes this approach to heart; by foregrounding forms like the English sonnet or this unconventional sequence structure that highlight moments of connection without assimilation, the *Sonnets* use lyric forms to define a new model of preservation.

Sonnet 126's silent final couplet, indicated by the printers' brackets, gestures toward the young man's eventual death. There in the empty space, nature, who has clung to the young man's body, delaying the inevitable quietus demanded of her, must turn the youth over to decay at last. After countless couplets promising literary immortality, 126 offers a clear message: If lyric's goal is to defeat death, it will inevitably lose. However, these blank brackets also send a message about what lyric *can* do. While the poet cannot eliminate decay, he can, through the form of his work, create space for it. These brackets become a final inversion of sonnet 17's opening image. There, the poet compares his work to the writing on the outside of the tomb, foregrounding the memory of the young man while burying his body deep within its walls, out of sight. Here, however, the interior of the tomb—the space for the young man's body, held open by this final bracketed couplet—is pulled into the poem itself. The text of the poem becomes the structure that surrounds and supports the young man's mortal body. If, as Singer and Hsy suggest, the work of lyric prostheticization occurs through forms, then Shakespeare's message is clear. The form of 126, like the form of the couplet and *The Sonnets* as a whole, is not of a perfect and unbroken whole but of the union of parts—of life and death, beloved and poet, lyric and decay.

Chapter 3

Time of Death

> like the revolution
> of life and death and life.
>
> —Hester Pulter, Poem 47
>
> Crip time is grief time.
>
> —Ellen Samuels, "Six Ways of Looking at Crip Time"

Death does funny things to time. Joan Didion, in *The Year of Magical Thinking*, writes that one of the most profound symptoms of grief following her husband's sudden death was her sense of being unmoored in time. Returning over and over to the night of his heart attack, Didion tries to reconstruct the events into a narrative sequence. One attempt to do this involves an examination of the bureaucratic records of the event, the sheaves of paperwork that have come to be associated with modern dying. Didion constructs various timelines "according to the hospital's Emergency Department," "according to the log kept by the doorman," or "according to the autopsy report."[1] But while such objective measures of time exist, Didion writes, they exist fully outside the subjective time of grief. This feeling of time—an experience that feels separate from linear, sequential, objective measures—appears as a feature of many grief memoirs. C. S. Lewis, in *A Grief Observed*, describes grief time as "waiting; just hanging about waiting for something to happen."[2] He continues, "It gives life a permanently provisional feeling. It doesn't seem worth starting anything. I can't settle down. I yawn, I fidget, I smoke too much. Up till this I always had too little time. Now there is nothing but time. Almost pure time, empty successiveness."[3] Roland Barthes, in the diary he kept after the death of his mother, writes, "There is a time when death is an *event*, an ad-venture, and as such mobilizes, interests, activates, tetanizes. And then one day it is no longer an event, it is another *duration*, compressed, insignificant, not narrated, grim, without recourse: true mourning not susceptible to any narrative dialectic."[4] Grief rejects linear time, rejects the teleology we might try to impose. "In the version of grief we imagine," Didion observes, "the model will be 'healing.' A certain forward movement will prevail. The worst days will be the earliest days."[5] But, in reality, "grief comes in waves, paroxysms, sudden apprehensions"—anything other than a straight line.[6] To encounter death is to be pulled out of time and to be thrust more deeply in it. Time moves slower, faster, not at all.

Perhaps the early modern poet who knew this best was Hester Pulter. Pulter was, as Elizabeth Kolkovich has described, "an expert in grief," outliving only two of her fifteen children and surviving not only several major national plague outbreaks but also the English Civil War that resulted in her family's relative isolation from London and the aristocratic social circles with which they had been previously connected.[7] So many of her poems wrestle with the deep and abiding grief she felt for her children, her nation, and herself, and this chapter explores the forms through which that struggle takes shape. Grief may at first seem tangential to embodied mortality compared with the concerns at the heart of Spenser's allegory or Shakespeare's *Sonnets*; one might be tempted to think of it as a way of feeling rather than being. But, as Pulter's lyrics make clear, the experience of grief is an integral part of the larger concept of decay at the center of this project. First, while modern Cartesian frameworks work to associate emotion solely with the intellect, rather than with embodiment, it is important to place Pulter's grief within the context of early modern affect. As Erin Sullivan notes, excessive emotion—particularly sadness—was understood in the period as an ailment or illness like any other, experienced as a state of bodily dis-ease.[8] In fact, Sullivan argues, sadness was the most potent and dangerous affect of all: London's Bill of Mortality for 1630 attributes thirty deaths that year to, simply, "griefe."[9] As I discuss in greater detail later in this chapter, grief's pathological nature means that it was and is subject to some of the same temporal expectations around cure, recovery, and eradication that shape impairment and disability. For Pulter and her contemporaries, the experience of grief was not simply a response to decay but a brush with decay itself—embodied suffering that could lead to one's own death. To dismiss it as mere emotion not only misses the affective reality of grief but contributes to the misogynist trivialization—both then and now—of feminine suffering.

And secondly, as Pulter's poems make abundantly clear, the experience of grieving for others inevitably means contemplating one's own mortality. Grief is simultaneously specific and universal; it involves not only the felt absence of a particular individual but also the impact of recognizing the ephemerality of all life. Didion writes that for her, grief at the loss of her husband was just as much a recognition of her own inevitable death. "We are imperfect mortal beings," she notes, "aware of that mortality even as we push it away, failed by our very complication, so wired that when we mourn our losses we also mourn, for better or for worse, ourselves. As we were. As we are no longer. As we will one day not be at all."[10] Barthes, likewise, notes that his grief, by disrupting his sense of time, brings his own mortality to the forefront of this mind. "To think, to know that *maman* is dead *forever, completely* ('completely,' which is inconceivable without violence and without one's being able to abide by such a thought at length), is to think, letter by letter (literally, and simultaneously), that I too will die *forever and completely*," he writes. "There is then, in mourning (in this kind of mourning, which is mine), a radical and *new* domestication of death; for previously, it was only a *borrowed* knowledge (clumsy, had from others, from philosophy, etc.), but now it is *my* knowledge."[11]

In Pulter's poetry, there is little if any distance between grief for others and grief for herself. While spurred by the specific loss of her children or the impact of the war, Pulter's lyrics quickly shift in focus to her own mortality and that of humanity in general. As I explore in this chapter, these accreting individual losses are the moments when decay becomes visible and in which she must begin to make sense of her own body's ephemerality. And as Pulter considers the decay present in her own body, her relationship with time is complicated further. For seventeenth-century English Protestants, thinking about one's death also meant reckoning with the hope of resurrection, a theological premise with its own temporal paradox. Like grief, the hope of resurrection pulls one out of the stability of sequential time. Life is both finite and infinite; death is the end of all things and beginning of all things, a moment within time and an escape from time altogether. Even as she turns from despair to hope, Pulter, through her encounters with decay, recognizes mortality as a fundamentally disruptive temporal force.

Pulter expresses this relationship with time throughout her poetry, exploring form's capacity—both the forms of lyric and metaphorical and aesthetic forms within her lyrics—to capture the disorienting temporality of decay. One of the primary metaphorical forms she foregrounds is the circle. The image of the circle seems to mirror her experience of time as a series of unceasing cycles: of day and night (of special significance to the insomniac Pulter), of years and growing seasons, of astrological revolution, of reproduction, of grief, and of resurrection. But she just as often describes the temporality of decay through the figure of the speck. As with her circles, Pulter's specks vary in their realization; they are sometimes dust, sometimes ash or calcinated bodily remains, sometimes atoms. In "View But This Tulip," a poem I return to later in this chapter, Pulter writes to God of her death that

> then, though I to atoms scattered be,
> in indivisibles I'll trust in thee. (21-22)[12]

The primary feature of the speck is this quality of indivisibility that Pulter describes here—the smallest possible material unit to which any body might be eventually reduced.[13] This materiality then translates into a model of temporality. In contrast to the never-ending motion of the circle, the speck represents for Pulter a moment of pure presence, without change and without movement.

But while she offers models of time based on both forms, what Pulter's lyrics ultimately conclude is that neither circle nor speck, on their own, can capture the temporality of decay. Rather, the two are locked in balance with one another, with neither offering a totalizing or dominant model for the effect of mortality on time. While we might expect the hope of resurrection to replace the despair of grief, Pulter resists that narrative, instead allowing both death and life, pain and joy, finitude and infinity to stand together. For Pulter, the time of death is best expressed in the collision of circle and speck, with the concurrent push and pull of both forms capturing the experience of living and grieving in a mortal body. Levine notes that when two forms collide, the encounter "produces unexpected consequences, results that cannot always be traced back to deliberate intentions or dominant ideologies."[14] Others observe that Pulter frequently explores the collision of various conceptual forms in her poetry. Elizabeth Scott-Baumann, for instance, identifies the union of revolution/dissolution as one of Pulter's "signature rhymes," in which opposing thematic forces are unified through the formal coherence of tightly rhymed couplets.[15] Just so, circle and speck are locked in balance, simultaneously complementing and contradicting one another. By yoking circle and speck, Pulter is able to explore the "unexpected consequences" of decay—time as infinite, terminal, and profoundly disorienting.

The sense of time that emerges from this collision is what disability theorists refer to as *crip time*, a temporal framework that reflects the body's ephemerality, privileging flexibility and contradiction over structure and linearity. In particular, crip time resists the teleological drive toward a cure—the desire to respond to decay by erasing it or repressing it—and instead focuses on the present moment and on alternative ways of imagining the future. Echoing Ellen Samuels's claim in this chapter's epigraph, I suggest that the grief time Pulter identifies is, in fact, crip time. This temporal model allows

Pulter to acknowledge the disparities between circle and speck, death and resurrection, without needing to choose one or the other. Pulter's embrace of crip time offers lyric scholars a richer, more nuanced model for thinking about the temporality of lyric. Lyric studies has long agreed on what lyric time is not; it is not narrative, not linear, not tied to teleology in the same way or to the same degree as narrative forms. But these existing theories of lyric time fail to account for the temporal complexity Pulter develops through these forms, as they fall short of capturing the simultaneous movement and stasis she evokes. Pulter's work offers us a template for new ways of thinking about lyric time that resist easy binaries of movement/stasis or change/stagnation in favor of more complex theorization. These poems demonstrate that, by theorizing lyric temporality in ways more akin to crip time, we can develop more effective and capacious theoretical models.

Pulter's work provides an ideal case study for the many valences of form and formalism that lie at the heart of this book for several reasons. First, her use of conceptual forms like the circle and speck signals her interest in literary form as a framework for knowledge. Pulter approaches lyric forms as something more than metaphor—as structures that shape and organize the possibilities of what might be. This ideological approach can help critics reimagine the relationship between forms and critical histories. As Marshelle Woodward argues, Pulter's work offers the possibility for alternative feminist histories of formalism that reject New Critical investment in formal wholeness in favor of models of permeable and dispersed identities.[16] But in addition to this conceptual vein of formalism, Pulter is also invested in form in the narrower sense, through specific poetic types and traditions. The Leeds manuscript is full of fixed forms and formalist lyric: highly regular poems in couplets or tercets, sonnets or sonnet-like short poems, and, above all, an overall sense of careful engagement with early modern lyric traditions. Pulter's many emblem poems, for instance, demonstrate the kind of gleeful invention only possible within such a formalist ethos; using the structural affordances of the emblem, she writes fifty-four wildly different poems on as many different subjects. Finally, Pulter brings together these two strands of formalism to engage with what we might describe as generic formalism, an interest in the forming work of lyric. Throughout her manuscript, she is clearly thinking about lyric as form, about what kinds of knowledge its structures and details make possible.

In writing about Pulter, I am also pursuing a secondary but no less important critical project. Pulter's work is clearly here to stay in early modern lyric studies, with good reason. Her poetry provides invaluable insight into early modern thinking about areas as diverse as alchemy, motherhood, ecology, grief, resurrection, Royalist politics, astronomy, and poetics, to name only a few. Joining with scholars who have already begun the monumental task of bringing Pulter out of the attic and into the classroom, I aim in this chapter, wherever possible, to help further locate these lyrics the intellectual networks of her day and ours. This means, for instance, thinking about how Pulter may fit into the metaphysical tradition of the late seventeenth century, particularly that movement's focus on embodiment and resurrection. This also involves thinking about the network of Royalist thinkers and writers who she may have read or engaged with. And, finally, this means thinking about the role Pulter's work will continue to play in early modern lyric studies and lyric theory in general and about what it adds to our understanding of lyric and the work of form.

Circle and Speck

Pulter's fascination with circles is probably best evinced by the fact that she titled four of her 120 poems simply "The Circle." Since not all Pulter's poems received titles, the fact that they are not only named but share a single title suggests that she likely conceived of these poems as linked texts; we might consider these as sequent drafts of the same poem or renewed attempts to capture this concept of circularity in verse. Pulter's many Circles are presented as an act of rewriting and returning, coming back around to reconsider something anew. In particular, the first three Circle poems each explore the experience of grief or reckoning with decay and the disorienting sense of time that accompanies it. The first, "The Circle [1]," opens with a meditation comparing the speaker's feeling of ceaseless grief with a never-ending circle.[17]

> In sighs and tears there is no end;
> my soul, on heaven alone depend.
> Sighs like the air doth clouds condense
> which tears from our sad eyes dispense.
> Trust me: in sighs there is no ease,
> no more than wind doth calm the seas
> and tears (ah me) descend in vain,
> to sighs they rarify again:
> in this sad circle I run round,
> till giddily I tumble down. (1–10)

These opening lines quickly capture the poem's preoccupation with circularity. Here, Pulter puts forward the circle as a form of cycle and ceaselessness.

To be in a circle, temporally speaking, means being in a state of perpetual motion, in constant change; such a form of time has no beginning or end, just constant and unyielding activity. This circular experience of time is provoked by the speaker's proximity to decay. Her grief embeds her in the circling pattern of despair. In the poem's opening lines, the speaker's suffering becomes an ecological cycle: Sighs, like clouds, condense into precipitating tears, raining down over the poet's face. In turn, those tears are themselves a new beginning. The water, she writes, "descend[s] in vain," because, almost immediately, "to sighs they rarify again," evaporating to begin the grieving process all over again.

It is worth noting that Pulter's circles are layered with possibilities, and critics have identified numerous circular forms operating simultaneously here and throughout the Leeds manuscript. "By using 'The Circle' as their title," Scott-Baumann writes, "these poems demand to be read with circles in mind; but . . . they leave the reader to determine what 'the circle' of the poem's title really is."[18] The circle as a form is inherently ambiguous; it may be two- or three-dimensional, sealed or open, dynamic or static. Kolkovich writes, "Sometimes Pulter's circles appear truly closed . . . and other times she describes something more akin to a spiral that circles around until it reaches an eventual end."[19] Noting Pulter's significant interest in alchemy, Jayne Archer remarks that the circle represents several distinct functions in that philosophical system. "On one level," she writes, the circle "refers to the ouroboros, the self-birthing snake (sometimes dragon) that devours its own tail. This is the ancient symbol of eternity, the perfection of art and of the completion of the alchemical opus (the *opus circulatorium*)."[20] The alchemical circle could also stand for various spheres—"the womb and the alembic (the vessel or retort, within which alchemical processes take place). Both spaces are associated with the creation of new life and both are enclosed ('hermetically sealed')."[21] Pulter's interest in the circle as a symbol of enclosure also seems to shape her choice of lyric forms. Scott-Baumann notes that Pulter continually returns to closed forms like the couplet and the sonnet, forms that offer the reader a sense of encapsulation and completion.[22] "The Circle [1]" is a prime example of this mode, written in a series of tetrameter couplets that come together to form a tightly knit whole. Wherever we look, Pulter is ready with another circle.

In these lines from "The Circle [1]," however, Pulter is specifically concerned with temporal circles. Less a noun and more a verb, the circle of "The Circle [1]" seems to be a cycle—or, to use one of Pulter's favorite terms, a *revolution*. To experience time as a circle, the poem suggests, is to be caught up in the experience both of continual change and, paradoxically, of overwhelming stasis. The cycle of grief is both endlessly changing and never evolving; it is self-sustaining, making possible its own perpetual existence. Just as the evaporation of water creates the circumstances necessary for its future precipitation, the poet's weeping—an act that should be the culmination of grief—creates the conditions for continued mourning. This causal loop, the speaker notes, makes escaping from grief impossible.

> But should poor I suspire to air,
> I know the sad fruits of despair;
> or should I into tears dissolve,
> what horror would my soul involve. (11–14)

Even if she could "suspire to air" and break out of this hydrological grief cycle, the speaker realizes, the only result would be more pain and suffering. The odd phrasing of this line underscores its internal tension. To *suspire*, according to the *Oxford English Dictionary*, means both to sigh and to yearn, typically to yearn for or after something.[23] But Pulter is not sighing for or after but to. Suspiring to air creates a sense of hyperbolic sighing so extensive that the body is transformed into pure airy matter.[24] This is compounded by the primary sense of yearning, suggesting that such a transformation would not be incidental but intentional. To "suspire to air" is to actively seek a full transformation, willingly exchanging one's body for another material altogether. And if not to air, she proposes, she might melt away into tears, exchanging the solidity of her body for the fluidity of water. Either choice imagines breaking out of the endless cycle of grief. The speaker fantasizes that, rather than endlessly changing forms, she might remain in a single material state, escaping the motions of perpetual grief.

But whether by suspiring or dissolving, escape from the cycle of grief is ultimately impossible; the circularity of time is all-consuming. In fact, the poem notes, attempts at escape result only in "the sad fruits of despair" and the involving of her soul in horror. *Involve*, one of Pulter's most frequently used verbs, implies the continuation of the circle through reabsorption. Seventeenth-century definitions for this verb included "to roll or enwrap in anything that is wound round, or surrounds as a case or covering; to enfold, to envelop," or "to wind in a spiral form, or in a series of curves, coils, or folds; to wreathe, coil, entwine."[25] Kolkovich notes that Pulter often uses *involve* as a verb of ambivalence, especially around the subject of grief. In "Upon the Death of My Dear and Lovely Daughter J. P.," she writes, "Pulter uses 'involve' to signify absorption or enwrapping, an action evoking both warmth and suffocation."[26] There, in another poem centered around the inescapability of grief, the poet is likewise caught up in a never-ending cycle. Pulter's elegiac verse "reveals a striking refusal of linearity," Kolkovich argues; "the speaker's grief [is] evolutionary, and not in a healing way. Her tears are not medicinal. Releasing them does not lessen her sorrow, yet she cannot stop crying."[27] Pulter's characterization of her grief as involving further reinforces how much proximity to death disrupts linear time. Even here, as the speaker imagines trying to escape from the continual cycles of grief, the circle reasserts itself. Any attempt to break free results only in being reabsorbed into the cycle of time, these couplets seem to suggest; there is no resistance, only further encirculation.

But while escape seems impossible, Pulter does offer another alternative: annihilation. Recalling's Donne's offer in the Holy Sonnets to be battered and broken or George Herbert's call in "Love II" to be burnt, the speaker of "The Circle [1]" seems to conclude that the only true alternative to revolution is dissolution.[28] The gaze of the poem shifts from the cyclical experience of grief to the terminal experience of death.

> Then, gracious God, in Thee I'll trust,
> although Thou crumble me to dust.
> No grief shall so emergent be
> to separate my soul from Thee;
> of nothing Thou didst me create
> and should'st Thou now annihilate,
> abrupt, or consummate my story
> Oh let it be unto Thy glory. (15–22)

Here, Pulter offers the formal counterpart to the circle: the speck. Her lyrics often describe destruction as the process of reducing something to the smallest possible unit of matter imaginable: a mote of dust, an atom, a fragment of ash. The poem turns from the cyclical and fluid state of grief to the process of erosion, a transformation that results in a single, definitive end. Turning to God, the speaker recognizes that the sole alternative to her endless grief is total destruction. "No grief shall so emergent be," she writes, that it will intervene between herself and God. In her edition, Scott-Baumann glosses *emergent* as "unexpected [or] pressing," suggesting that there is no level of grief so great that God has not already anticipated it. However, *emergent* also evokes a sense of perpetuity, describing that which "arises from or out of something prior; consequent, derivative."[29] This definition accords more closely with the way "The Circle [1]" characterizes grief: self-perpetuating, a cycle always already in motion. The speaker declares that there is no grief so continual, so cyclical, that God cannot interrupt its motion. She seems to find, finally, a way out of the circle. "Crumble me to dust," she invites, "annihilate, / abrupt, or consummate my story." The poem turns away from the inescapability of perpetual grief and toward the promise of finality in these speck-like forms.

In these final lines of "The Circle [1]," Pulter's two forms for the experience of time come face to face with one another. On one side, she imagines the circle, a form of cyclical time in which pain seems unceasing; this form evokes the sensation of perpetuity, of movement without direction, of constantly resurging grief. On the other, Pulter offers the speck, the dust to which the speaker imagines her body reduced in her own inevitable death. The speck is time in pure presence, the total absence of change or movement; it is the moment, in death, when time has arrived where it was always heading and can travel no further. But even as Pulter offers these two forms, she makes clear that neither exists independently of one another—that, in fact, both forms of time are locked in balance with one another. This is apparent, for instance, in the way the speaker describes her desire for eradication. Pulter offers three different verbs to describe being reduced to a speck: *annihilate*, *abrupt*, and *consummate*. All three evoke the sense of termination the poem so desperately longs for, and all suggest that the perpetual grief that has consumed the speaker might finally end. But each also offers a slightly different shade of transformation. *Annihilation*, for instance, suggests total material eradication, destruction to the point of nothingness. As *annihilate* provides the rhyme for *create*, Pulter seems to suggest the two are antithetical—making and unmaking. *Abruption*, in comparison, emphasizes motion rather than matter; it suggests an unexpected halt, stopping in one's tracks. Thomas Browne, in *Religio Medici*, uses *abrupt* in a very similar context—a short poem that shares not only a theme but a rhyme with "The Circle [1]"— to describe death's destruction.[30]

> There will I sit, like that industrious flye,
> buzzing thy prayses, which shall never die
> till death abrupts them, and succeeding glory
> bid me goe on in a more lasting story. (19–22)

For both Browne and Pulter, *abrupt* is appropriate because it evokes a sense of violent interruption, an ending that comes about entirely unexpectedly. *Consummate*, however, does almost the opposite. While on one level, the verb hints that death consumes the self, *consummate* also implies completion—conclusion rather than destruction or interruption. Through Pulter's rhymes, *consummate* is linked with *separate*, *create*, and *annihilate* in a constellation of terms concerned as much with creation as with separation or destruction. "Of nothing Thou didst me create," the speaker says to God, asking now to be returned to the same state. While the speaker yearns for the static temporality represented by the speck, the very act of being made into dust also marks the reemergence of circular time. At the very same moment that dissolution offers a way out of grief, it also brings the speaker back to the beginning, finishing the cycle of embodied life begun at the moment of creation—one final existential circle.

The interwoven circles and specks in these final lines express the tension produced by the collision of these two forms, creating a disrupted sense of time brought about by the speaker's grief at the loss of others as well as the act of imagining her own end. Pulter is not alone in the early modern period in her interest in the relationship between decay and time. Many of the period's philosophers, theologians, and writers were deeply invested in defining what, precisely, happened to time as the moment of death drew near. On the one hand, as the specks to which Pulter's speaker asks to be reduced suggest, dying was often thought of as a transition out of time. Unlike the time of the living, which felt more akin to the circular and never-ending movements Pulter associates with the circle, time after death was often seen as the total absence of any movement or change. D. Vance Smith points out that many late medieval scholastic philosophers argued that mortality had the unique quality of never existing in the present. Smith writes that a "profound demonstration of the exceptionality of death is in the way the word itself alters and is altered by the regular rules of Latin grammar. There is no past participial form of *moritur*, strictly speaking, because it is declined with a double u: 'mortuus est,' which gives it the form of an adjective, is declined *sine tempore*, without tense."[31] Once the moment of death had passed, the idea of distinguishing between past and future was irrelevant. In this philosophical tradition, to be dead is to enter eternity, the absolute singularity of the speck. To exit the world of humanity and enter the divine means, on one hand, to abandon circular time in favor of absolute time—the absolute time of nonexistence.

By the mid-seventeenth century, this belief had solidified into a central tenet of mainstream English Protestant theology. Jeremy Taylor, in his popular 1651 treatise *The Rule and Exercises of Holy Dying*, accuses Catholics of erroneously applying worldly standards of time to the afterlife.[32] In the dedicatory epistle to Richard Vaughan, Taylor specifically condemns the practice of distinguishing temporal and eternal punishments.[33] Under Catholic doctrine, temporal punishment referred to a finite period of penance for sin, completed either in life or in purgatory, that, once finished, was considered complete; eternal punishment, on the other hand, referred to a permanent state of damnation. While he accepts the idea of a temporal punishment in life, Taylor writes that such distinctions are ineffective, even meaningless, after the moment of death.

> In the Church of Rome they reckon otherwise concerning sick and dying Christians than I have done. For they make profession that from death to life, from sin to grace, a man may very certainly be changed, though the operation begin not before his last hour, and half this, they do upon his death-bed, and the other half when he is in his grave. And they take away the eternal punishment in an instant, by a school distinction or the hand of the Priest, and the temporal punishment shall stick longer, even then when the man is no more measured with time. . . . The distinction of temporal and eternal is a just measure of pains, when it refers to this life and another, but to dream of a punishment temporal when all his time is done, and to think of repentance when the time of grace is past, are great errors.[34]

In his discussion of doctrinal differences concerning salvation, Taylor makes an important point here about the relationships among death, time, and eternity. He describes eternity as a state in which "all . . . time is done," when man is "no more measured with time." For Taylor and most seventeenth-century Protestants, the categories of eternal and temporal were fundamentally exclusive: Time either exists, or it does not. Once an individual has transitioned into a state of eternity—either through damnation or salvation—time becomes flattened, and distinctions of now/then cease to exist.

And yet, simultaneously, time after death was also seen as part of the larger circle of existence, another phase of a single, continuous timeline. As the final lines of "The Circle [1]" show, dying—especially when described through the metaphor of dust—was characterized as a return, a circling back to some previous origin point. In part, this reflected ecological models of time that linked death with renewal and regrowth. Frances Dolan notes that Pulter and many other women poets of the period keenly observed "the transformative power of the soil" and shared a "theological investment in dung and dust as the matter from which we come, the matter to which we return, the means by which we escape embodiment."[35] The dunghill, Dolan argues—a space where the materials of dust, ash, lime, and, on occasion, dead bodies themselves were collected to decay into new matter—becomes an emblem of this transformation. "The composting that takes place in the dunghill is how death becomes life," she writes, "how matter decomposes and then re-matters."[36] Dust's ecological resonance overlapped with its theological symbolism. In Christian liturgical language, dust comes to represent death's transition as a moment of continuity rather than rupture. The final lines of "The Circle [1]" recall, for instance, the language of the Church of England's burial orders. In the seventeenth century (as today), the priest is instructed to offer the following as part of their prayer as the body of the deceased is covered with dirt: "We therefore commit this body to the ground; earth to earth, ashes to ashes, dust to dust."[37] The dust of the decomposing body—the dust that would, like that of the dunghill, return to earth—mirrors the dust of Adam's creation; to be reduced to dust was to bend the circle of time back to its beginning, arriving where it first started.

Ars moriendi authors used this association between death and cyclical time to console their readers against fears of dying. Taylor reminds his readers not to fear their own deaths, arguing that dying only extends a state of being they have already come to know. Time moves constantly, he writes, and the distinctions between living and dead are to be feared only as much as the line between past and present or sleeping and waking. "First we change our world, when we come from the womb to feel the warmth of the sun. Then we sleep and enter into the image of death, in which state we are unconcerned in all the changes of the world," Taylor writes, "and if our Mothers or our Nurses die, or a wild boar destroy our vineyards, or our King be sick, we regard it not, but during that state are as disinterested as if our eyes were closed with the clay that weeps in the bowels of the earth."[38] Life is nothing but time, Taylor argues; death is no more or less catastrophic than being delivered from the womb or waking from a nap. Birth and death are thus parallel moments, recurrent events in the same cycle of time.[39] And, Taylor suggests, it is only by dying that the faithful can perceive the fullness of divine temporality. The small events of the world fall away, and the dead are able to understand the shape of time as it really exists. Drawing on the doctrine of eternal life, these early modern Christian models embrace the idea that mortality exists within time, not outside it. Death is a transition, not an eradication.

These two concurrent understandings of time—death as the absence of time and as the revelation of continued time—collide in Pulter's poem. Even as the speaker imagines moving outside the cycle of her unending grief, transitioning from circle to speck, that movement only further reinscribes her within another, higher cycle of time. The closer Pulter gets to death, the more both forms seem to fit, and the more time seems to be both continuous and interrupted. These collisions are amplified in the subsequent circle poem, "The Circle [2]," where Pulter adds another vocabulary—that of alchemy—that highlights the tension between these two forms.[40]

> Those that the hidden chemic art profess
> and visit Nature in her morning dress,
> to mercury and sulphur philtres give
> that they, consumed with love, may live
> in their posterity and in them shine
> though they their being unto them resign (1–6)

This opening image describes the alchemists' pursuit of the philosopher's stone, a panacea offering immortality. "Pulter imagines love potions ('philtres') being used to bring together these chemicals," Scott-Baumann notes, "which were often imagined as male and female, and to generate their offspring or 'posterity.'" Alice Eardley, in her edition, notes that this union was often referred to as a "chemical wedding."[41] The two elements, yielding their individual identities to each other, are then joined by love to form the mythical philosopher's stone, which subsequently grants the holder immortality. These dense lines require Pulter's readers to navigate a confusing sequence of pronouns, particularly the six instances of *they*, *their*, and *them* in lines 4–6. Both Scott-Baumann and Eardley, in their respective editions of the poem, assign antecedents that would render these lines, roughly, as follows:

> That [the mercury and sulfur], consumed with love [for one another], may live
> In [the combined elements'] posterity, and in [the elements] shine
> Though [the element's identities] unto [the philosopher's stone] resign

The primary *they* of these lines, in this reading, is the combination of mercury and sulfur, the two elements joined together to forge the philosopher's stone. This reading confirms Pulter's nuanced understanding of alchemy, reflecting a careful attention to the philosophy's approach to chemical transformation. Archer notes that Pulter's work, both here and across the manuscript, is marked by "a sophisticated use of terms, images and conceits drawn from alchemy," indicating Pulter's deep familiarity with the practical details of natural philosophy.[42] What seems central here, in particular, is the alchemists' ability to unite disparate elements: to move from fragmentation, or speck-like existence, into a cohesive union. Resigning their individual beings, the foundational elements coalesce into a unified whole.

But the poem offers another option for the pronouns' antecedent, announced in the first line—"those that the hidden chemic art profess," the alchemists themselves. *They* may also, both grammatically and logically, refer back to the individuals introduced in the first line whose response to decay offers a second possible reading of these lines. Built into the poem's description of these transformations is a critique of those who attempt to manipulate the rhythms of nature. This critique first emerges in the pun of line 2: While Scott-Baumann glosses *morning dress* as Nature's daily, informal wear, the description also suggests that Nature appears in *mourning dress*.[43] Overlaying these dual idioms of *morning dress* (everyday wear) and *mourning dress* (clothing specially designated for grief and mourning), Pulter also invites the reader to think of nature as a space marked by decay. Especially given the close connections Pulter imagines between revolutions of time and the experience of grief in "The Circle [1]" (here echoed in the cycles of day and night), the repetition of that connection at the beginning of "The Circle [2]" ensures that readers associate nature with not only generation but also dissolution. As a result of this pun, the alchemists' encounter with Nature becomes a confrontation with death and their response an even clearer attempt to subvert it. If we read the alchemists, and not the union of elements, as the referent for the pronouns of lines 4–6, these lines then become:

> That [the alchemists,] consumed with love [for the philosopher's stone], may live
> In [the alchemists' own] posterity, and in [the elements] shine
> Though [the alchemists' identities] unto [the philosopher's stone] resign

Rebelling against the presence of death in the world, these alchemists pursue immortality by creating the philosopher's stone. In doing so, they attempt to extend their own lives into posterity; they try to outlive their own natural lifespan, instead overlapping with the next generation. This particular rebellion against death and time may have hit especially close to the heart for Pulter, who outlived most of her own children in a tragically disrupted generational narrative of her own.[44]

This second possible reading, which centers the alchemists rather than their materials, underscores the speaker's response to what she frames as an unnatural relationship with death and time. To live into one's own posterity suggests an over-continuation, a stretching beyond the natural borders of one's lifespan. This desire, Scott-Baumann notes, is echoed by Pulter's choice of form for the poem itself, a "sonnet-like fourteen-line form."[45] "Sonnets were often connected to ideas of memorialisation," Scott-Baumann writes, offering their subjects and their authors a way of living forever in verse.[46] As I argue in the previous chapter, early modern sonnets—particularly, though not only, those in the Petrarchan tradition—were especially concerned with decay, often recognizing that while poetry could provide a vehicle for the beloved's memory, there was nothing to be done to save the material self.

The early modern sonnet and its offshoots simultaneously offer and undermine the promise of disembodied immortality, the idea that one might live forever in verse. Pulter enters this debate by presenting a group of subjects—the alchemists—similarly engaged in a war with time. By the poem's close, they, too, are inevitably subject to death.

> By time and fate to dust are all calcined
> lying obliviated in their urn
> till they to their great ancestors return.
> So man, the universe's chiefest glory,
> his primitive's dust (alas) doth end his story. (10–14)

As death reasserts itself, Pulter's speaker once again finds herself at the nexus of circle and speck. The alchemists' attempts to escape the circles of time—diurnal time, biological time, generational time—have failed. They are now fated to join "their great ancestors." Linear time and the generational hierarchies of ancestry reemerge, and, as they do, circle and speck are brought together once more. The alchemists' desire for wholeness and incorporation, manifest in their attempt to combine disparate elements into a single philosopher's stone, has resulted instead in dissolution; rather than making a new element, the alchemists are reduced to their primary materiality. The dust to which they are finally dissolved is associated both with their ending and their beginning. The matter of those long past, the "primitive" dust of Adam, offers the future at which all eventually arrive. These alchemists, who have tried desperately to escape death by creating a life of infinite linearity and total cohesion, are instead reinscribed in the circles and specks of mortality. To end, the speaker seems to suggest, is to return to where you once began.

And if Pulter's criticism of those who try to escape death is subtextual in "The Circle [2]," the terse lines of "The Circle [3]" ensure that message is not missed.

> To be unwilling or afraid to die
> in the whole world's society,
> is a sign of huge impatiency.
> That many things revolve thou mayest explore
> and when thou dost dissolve it is no more,
> for so this earthly transitory mound
> in an eternal motion still runs round.[47]

The speaker meets thanatophobia with direct criticism: Humanity as a whole, she declares, suffers from an unwillingness to confront death. Pulter adapts a core trope of early modern *artes moriendi*, the idea that a fear of death derived from a flawed attitude toward time. As Pulter does here, these treatises commonly described such an attitude as "impatience." Sutton, for instance, dedicates a chapter to explaining how "the impatient may be persuaded to endure the pains of sickness." Taylor likewise spends several sections of his treatise advising readers of "the practice of patience." He argues that individuals become too attached to the pleasures of the world. "Hence it comes that men are impatient of the thoughts of death; hence comes those arts of protraction and delaying the significations of old age."[48] To accept death, Taylor writes, is to acquiesce to God's temporality—to face death neither too eagerly nor with too much resistance. These attitudes toward time are closely linked with the approach to temperance described in the first chapter; by caring just enough for the body and its health, readers were encouraged to live in sync with divine time, allowing their bodies to age and decay at the rate God intended. John Milton, Pulter's contemporary (and possible family friend), likewise uses *patience* to describe accepting the slow time of mortal existence.[49] In Book 10 of *Paradise Lost*, after Eve suggests suicide, Adam rebukes her.

> No more be mention'd then of violence
> against our selves, and wilful barrenness,
> that cuts us off from hope, and savours onely
> rancor and pride, impatience and despite,
> reluctance against God and his just yoke (10.1041–1045)

Impatience, in discussions of decay, reflects less a sense of urgency and more a discomfort within time, a "want of endurance" or "failure to bear suffering."[50] Both those who yearn for death and those who refuse to accept its inevitability find themselves at odds with divine time, struggling against the changes that, Pulter notes, are only too clearly inevitable.

After critiquing the world's impatience, the poem then offers a model for the right attitude toward time. The speaker notes that we must accept the cyclical nature of time; "many things revolve," she writes, and the earth is a "mound" that "in an eternal motion still runs round." And yet, "when thou dost dissolve it is no more." This ambivalent insertion in line 5 in the midst of these cyclical images, Scott-Baumann argues, "signals not that a person's dissolution or death is their destruction (that they are no more); rather, it suggests that death is nothing but another revolution, a mere turn of the circle." Scott-Baumann glosses "it is no more" as axiomatic, meaning "it is of no consequence." The *it* of the sentence, she argues, refers back to the individual's dissolution—that the single death is, in fact, of no consequence (and certainly no impediment) to the ceaseless revolutions of the world. But *it* remains uncomfortably ambiguous; even if the world continues, the individual (as well as their impatience) is also, literally, no more. This ambiguity is echoed in Pulter's description of the earth as "transitory." Pulter uses this adjective in several other poems to describe impermanence (that is, decay). In "A Solitary Discourse," she writes that since "Adam fell from glory" (79) humanity now lives "a life most transitory" (80). In "The Eclipse," Pulter addresses mortality itself:

> But O, Mortality, 'tis thou alone
> that dost obscure bright glory from my soul.
> 'Tis thou that fett'rest me with flesh and bone
> and mak'st me here in dust and ashes roll,
> presenting to me transitory toys
> and hidest from my soul celestial joys. (37–42)

For Pulter, the term *transitory* captures the colliding affordances of circle and speck. On the one hand, it emphasizes ephemerality. Unlike the unending movement of the spheres, life is brief, a single heartbeat. But *transitory* also suggests the transitional, a bridge between places. To be transitory is to be in transition, to be in motion from one world to the next. To be mortal, "The Circle [3]" warns, is to find oneself caught up in the circles and specks of time.

Crip Time, Lyric Time

In "Grief," Herbert writes of the tension between despair and the formal restraints of his poetry.[51]

> Verses, ye are too fine a thing, too wise
> for my rough sorrows: cease, be dumb and mute,
> give up your feet and running to mine eyes,
> and keep your measures for some lover's lute,
> whose grief allows him music and a rhyme:
> for mine excludes both measure, tune, and time. (13–18)

Not only does language fail to capture the depth of the speaker's grief, but the regularity of verse itself is at odds with the roughness of his sorrow. Like Pulter, Herbert finds his grief to be unmeasured, not just subsuming his entire affect but fundamentally out of sync with the rhythmic predictability of his verse. Meter is fine for some lover's lute, but the speaker's grief resists "measure, tune, and time." But unlike Pulter's Circle poems, "Grief" seems to conclude by explicitly denouncing the possibility of finding a form that suites despair—though, of course, Herbert offers this sentiment in alternate rhyming lines of iambic pentameter, immediately belying the claim that lyric must necessarily fall short. Pulter's vision of the relationship between decay, time, and lyric forms is more explicitly affirmative, identifying the collision of two forms—circle and speck—that can reflect the disrupted temporality brought about by decay. The form of the circle affords a sense of perpetual movement and activity, suggesting constant, endless motion, the same kind of ceaselessness Shakespeare invokes in his *Sonnets* with the turning of the seasons or the lapping of the waves on the shore. But, Pulter is careful to note, constant movement is not the same as total transformation. The circle is not linear or teleological but cyclical. Like a treadmill, the circle turns in place, moving and going nowhere. The speck, however, rejects all sense of movement; it is a form of stability and separation. If the circle is pure movement without transformation, the speck is its opposite—total transformation without movement. To become a speck is to be pulled out of the flow of time, to exist without time. And for Pulter, just as for Shakespeare and Herbert—just as for Didion and Barthes—the brush with decay reveals these colliding forms of time.

Disability theorists have long recognized this, observing that the body's inherent material instability is incompatible with traditional approaches to time. Crip time, modeled in part after Halberstam's notion of queer time, offers a framework for resisting these normative models of temporality and the compulsory able-bodiedness imposed by them.[52] In part, crip time describes the resistance to imperatives to move at the same pace as the rest of the world. "When disabled folks talk about crip time," Samuels writes, "sometimes we just mean that we're late all the time—maybe because we need more sleep than nondisabled people, maybe because the accessible gate in the train station was locked."[53] Like many other facets of disability, crip time is the product of a built environment—in this case, what Moya Bailey calls the expectation of pace—that creates the conditions of disabling. "We make disability where there was none," Bailey writes, "because of our need for speed," because of the expectations brought about by late capitalism for constant, unyielding productivity.[54] Crip time describes the exclusionary temporal environment built on the demand for more, faster. It identifies the way such environments subsequently categorize anyone not up to speed as disabled.

But while crip time may be a result of the environment, it can also be a response to it, even a protest against it. The slowness associated with crip time can also be an act of resistance to prevailing attitudes about what it means to be on time or at pace. Petra Kuppers writes, "Many spiritual traditions know these times out of time, these nondriven moments that turn their back on modernity's insistent tick. Meditation and prayer bring many people to a welling of empty time, to a fulfillment, in halting."[55] To embrace crip time is to refuse to acquiesce to "the need to move quickly simply for the sake of moving quickly."[56] However, as Samuels and Elizabeth Freeman note, crip time is also often involuntary; while an act of protest, living in crip time might also be the only option for many. Crip time is "paradoxically both liberating and confining," Samuels and Freeman write, "because it breaks open rigid socioeconomic structures of time and affords others, and because that breaking is not a choice but a necessity, an enforcement issued by the physical and mental strictures of the crip bodymind."[57] Kuppers asserts that it is essential to note that the resistance of crip time often originates in pain—in the physical pain of impairment, in the social and emotional pain of disability. But while pain blurs the question of agency, it does not erase it. Choosing crip time often means choosing to lessen one's pain, a choice that, while seemingly straightforward, is often dismissed by normative attitudes to time and productivity. And yet, Kuppers contends, even in the presence of pain, crip time can offer valuable self-knowledge. She writes, "many disabled people speak or type or gesture to the blossoming of attention in attenuation, in waiting in abeyance. To the other side of crip time."[58] One may, in choosing to live in crip time, carve out new ways of being.

At the core of these features is crip time's resistance to linearity and teleology. This is most visible in the ways crip time disrupts the medicalized teleology of recovery and cure. As Alison Kafer notes, disabled individuals are often forced into "curative time," the temporality of compulsory able-bodiedness. Under a curative ideology, the only body defined as worthy is an able one; all bodies that deviate from that ideal are then defined by their progress toward it—or their failure to achieve it. "Futurity has often been framed in curative terms, a time frame that casts disabled people (as) out of time, or as obstacles to the arc of progress," Kafer writes. "In our disabled state, we are not part of the dominant narratives of progress, but once rehabilitated, normalized, and hopefully cured, we play a starring role: the sign of progress, the proof of development, the triumph over the mind or body. Within this frame of curative time, then, the only appropriate disabled mind/body is one cured or moving toward cure."[59] The curative imaginary, Kafer observes, expects consistent, linear progress away from impairment and toward wholeness, away from disability and toward "normalcy." Anything else becomes pathologized. When someone deviates from this narrative teleology and begins to live in crip time, Samuels notes, they become a kind of time traveler. "Disability and illness have the power to extract us from linear progressive time with its normative life stages and cast us into a wormhole of backward and forward acceleration, jerky stops and starts, tedious intervals and abrupt endings," she writes. "The medical language of illness tries to reimpose the linear, speaking in terms of the chronic, the progressive, and the terminal, of relapses and stages. But we who occupy the bodies of crip time know that we are never linear, and we rage silently—or not so silently—at the calm straightforwardness of those who live in the sheltered space of normative time."[60]

These normative temporalities likewise shape our treatment of grief; we expect those suffering to move steadily in the direction of healing, pathologizing any who refuse to keep pace with what has been deemed healthy or "normal" grief. This impulse toward narrativization has led to the popular trope of the five stages of grief as a progressive narrative from denial to acceptance, a fundamental misappropriation of Elisabeth Kübler-Ross's foundational work in *On Death and Dying*.[61] Kübler-Ross's framework was meant to describe the cognitive process of accepting one's own mortality, derived from her work with hospice patients. It was only as the work gained widespread popularity that these stages were misread as a template for how to grieve for others. Kübler-Ross later clarified that these stages were not meant to be, nor were they regularly experienced as a linear progression; rather, the five stages described the distinct dimensions of the grieving experience—five shades of grief rather than five steps in a journey. Despite the overwhelming desire of readers to transform these stages into a narrative of progress—a cure narrative whereby grief can be neatly eradicated—Kübler-Ross's original concept places grief squarely in the realm of crip time. These nonnarrative, nonnormative temporalities move against the stream, below the stream, across the stream; they operates outside the directional movement of the cure narrative, of the capitalist workflow, of the linear time of the world.

Crip frameworks for time are rooted in the body's decay, taking the overlapping, nonlinear, paradoxical temporalities that emerge from encounters with mortality as their model. Samuels, writing of her own disability, recounts that "with each new symptom, each new impairment, I grieve again for the lost time, the lost years that are now not yet to come. This is not to say that I wish for a cure—not exactly. I wish to be both myself and not-myself, a state of paradoxical longing.... I wish for time to split and allow two paths for my life and that I could move back and forth between them at will."[62] This is precisely the temporal paradox invoked by decay, the same paradox Spenser and the other early modern writers attempting to define temperance tried to navigate. On the one hand, crip time acknowledges that death is the end of all things. Bodies decay; people become ill or injured or old. Rather than working to repress or delay that inevitable future, crip time calls us to face it unflinchingly, to acknowledge that we all move inevitably toward dissolution. And yet, on the other hand, crip time also calls us to resist being drawn preemptively toward the future. It refuses the teleological projection that Siebers argues drives the ideology of ability, the fantasy that death itself—and with it, all manner of disability—should be overcome. This same teleology resonates at the level of the individual body through the curative impulse. The curative imaginary can only accept a future in which the body becomes more whole, not less. Crip time, alternately, refuses to assign greater narrative value to the future than the present, instead working to keep them in balance. The paradoxical temporality of disability—the desire to erase disability and to live in it, the acceptance and fear of the end of the body—those impulses brush up against one another and even coexist.

Crip time offers an important framework for resisting, reframing, or reorienting the teleologic narrative structures that form the foundation of ableist ideologies. But while Siebers, Kafer, Samuels, and others have written extensively on how crip time can resist these narrative impulses, disability theorists have had comparatively little to say about how nonnarrative forms like lyric might offer a model for new temporal systems. As I note in the introduction, lyric theorists have long argued that that form's relationship with time is fundamentally different from that of narrative. Some suggest that lyric affords only a continual presence, a thin vertical slice of time in which everything is compressed into a single eternal now. Northrop Frye, for instance, argues that in lyric, "we turn away from our ordinary continuous experience in space and time."[63] Instead, he writes, lyric creates a space out of time: "The private poem often takes off from something that blocks normal activity, something a poet has to write poetry about instead of carrying on with ordinary experience."[64] Lyric, for Frye, affords inaction and blockage, an inability or refusal to move through time. Others suggest that while lyric is not outside time entirely, it occupies only the present moment, a similar refusal of progressive or sequential temporality. Jonathan Culler contends that lyric occupies only the "now" of articulation. "Apostrophes give us a ritualistic, hortatory act," he writes, "a special sort of event in a lyric present."[65] The "fundamental characteristic of lyric," Culler argues, "is not the description and interpretation of a past event but the iterative and iterable performance of an event in the lyric present, in the special 'now' of lyric articulation."[66] Likewise, Sharon Cameron asserts that lyric "rises momentarily from the enthusiasms of temporal advance to the flow of time that ultimately rushes over and drowns it."[67] Lyric "casts off its knowledge of remembered life," she writes, "driving past and future apart and away with the wedge of the eternal now."[68] She continues, "Concerned neither with ends nor with beginnings, concerned with etiologies only on occasion and sometimes, then, by chance, the context of the experience narrated in a lyric will need to be reconstructed from the particularities of the moment. It is the speaker's words that matter, not her past or future."[69] For Frye, Culler, Cameron, and many others, lyric offers a way out of time, the ability to exempt oneself from the motions of change; lyric allows the reader to immerse themselves fully in a single, atemporal moment, not unlike the specks Pulter imagines.

However, as others have pointed out, these theories fail to capture the full range of lyric's temporal affordances. Dubrow, for instance, argues that treating lyric as wholly antithetical to narrative obscures the complex possibilities of lyric time. "Lyric meditation can propel narrative action," Dubrow writes; it can intensify emotion, reframe a perspective in anticipation of action, or "may more directly generate narrative action by releasing whatever is blocking it."[70] Dubrow suggests a new critical category, what she calls the "anticipatory amalgam." These are lyrics that imagine future action, willing those events to become reality. "If narrative generally, though of course not always, involves a story that is set in the past (which differs of course from the time of discourse) . . . and lyric is generally the mode that focuses on the lyric present or overlapping time schemes," Dubrow explains, then the anticipatory amalgam represents the collusion, rather than competition, of both narrative and lyric to access the future.[71] A similar relationship is visible in the carpe diem lyrics discussed in the introduction and first chapter. These poems explicitly rely on the lyric's ability to both stand outside time—to work in opposition to the decay that threatens the lovers' pleasure—and to move time forward toward the goal of consummation. Marvell reminds his reader that

> Thus, though we cannot make our sun
> Stand still, yet we will make him run. (45–46)

While these examples of the anticipatory amalgam and carpe diem poems describe only a limited number of lyrics, they speak volumes about the need for new, more expansive models of lyric temporality. Lyric studies continues to struggle to find a suitable vocabulary that rejects an exclusive binary of stasis or movement in favor of something that better captures the complex potential of lyric time.

Pulter's poetry, however, provides a useful example of other ways we might approach time in the lyric—ways that are inextricably linked to how she embraces crip time. The overlapping temporalities of circle and speck evoke the sensation of being thrust out of normative linear time, calling the speaker and reader to recognize the inadequacy of those narrative models to capture the decay central to these poems. The body's refusal to adhere to a narrative—the ebb and flow of suffering, the disordered genealogical lines through child loss—and the speaker's desire to both flee from and embrace the decay within her own body make any singular temporal framework, whether purely linear or purely static, inadequate. And so, through her poetry, Pulter turns to create something else: a lyric temporality that can sustain these paradoxes without trying to resolve them. By rooting her poetics in crip time, Pulter imagines a lyric temporality that rejects the binary models of action/inaction or temporary/timeless in favor of a dynamic collision like that of the circle and speck. Drawing on crip time's insistence that one might embrace stasis and change simultaneously, Pulter looks to lyric as a form that can be, to use Samuels and Freeman's description of crip time, both liberating and confining. Rather than defining lyric's temporality in singular terms, Pulter's poems imagine lyric time as a cacophony of possibilities.

The End of Time

Pulter's Circle poems illustrate a speaker wrestling with the reality of her grief against the normalizing pressure of the curative imaginary Kafer describes. As Didion, Barthes, and others make clear, there is often a strong impulse to fit grief into a teleological framework, imagining suffering moving constantly in the direction of its own eradication, hope slowly replacing pain, bit by bit, until the loss has evaporated. For early modern authors, this narrative ideology included a specific theological conclusion. In Pulter's poems, and in much mainstream Protestant theology of the seventeenth century, the ultimate culmination of grief and all decay was not only the absence of pain but the moment of resurrection. In the Church's burial orders, the priest is first instructed to remind those gathered at the graveside that life is "full of misery." But, as the body is lowered into the ground, the mourners are then told to remember that this is done "in sure and certain hope of the resurrection to eternal life."[72] Their grief and, subsequently, their attitudes about their own mortality are then molded into this narrative, reminding the faithful that their present suffering can and should move steadily toward eternal reward.

However, as her lyrics on resurrection make clear, Pulter is somewhat resistant to this teleology. Making similar use of the collision of circle and speck from her poems on grief, Pulter imagines resurrection not through the form of narrative but as another temporal paradox. For her, resurrection and the hope it entails are not the antithesis of grief but its complement a recognition that decay's paradoxical temporality is true both at the level of individual suffering and of universal mortality. This revisionist theology is made possible by Pulter's embrace of crip time as an alternate social framework. The turn from grief to resurrection indicates her concern not simply with the individual experience of time but also with the systems that create that experience—not only with the suffering of one but with the ideology in which that one suffers. Like the many contemporary scholars who reject the clear distinction between disability as an individual impairment (like the medical model) or as a purely systemic construction (like the social model), Pulter places decay in both contexts. Kafer notes that "drawing a hard line" between the social and the individual "makes it difficult to explore the ways in which notions of disability and able-bodiedness affect everyone," the ways that all bodies are "affected by cultural ideals of normalcy and ideal form and function."[73] The vision for resurrection that emerges in Pulter's lyrics considers the decay of not only her own body but of all bodies and of the systems of belief that shape the body's relationship with time.

One of the central early modern scriptural touchstones for resurrection theology, particularly bodily resurrection, was the metaphor of the seed Paul offers in his letter to the church at Corinth. There, he assures the young church of the promise of eternal life. Paul imagines his recipients' disbelief, writing, "But some man will say, How are the dead raised up? And with what body do they come?" Pressed to explain the specifics, Paul offers an explanation that has, historically, raised more questions than answers.[74]

> Thou fool, that which thou sowest is not quickened, except it die. And that which thou sowest, thou sowest not that body that shall be, but bare grain, it may chance of wheat, or some other grain: But God giveth it a body as it hath pleased him, and to every seed his own body. All flesh is not the same flesh: but there is one kind of flesh of men, another flesh of beasts, another of fishes, and another of birds. . . . So also is the resurrection of the dead. It is sown in corruption; it is raised in incorruption: It is sown in dishonor; it is raised in glory: It is sown in weakness; it is raised in power: It is sown a natural body; it is raised a spiritual body. There is a natural body, and there is a spiritual body.[75]

As Caroline Walker Bynum points out, Paul's seed metaphor is "the oldest Christian metaphor for the resurrection of the body."[76] Much like the memento mori forms discussed in the introduction and first chapter, this description simultaneously insists on total dissimilarity and complete similitude. On one hand, "all flesh is not the same flesh." Because the body that arises after the resurrection is and must be totally different from the body of the living, the material body is therefore incompatible with immortality. Our physical selves are mortal and so must die; the body that lives forever, therefore, cannot be that same body. And yet, Paul explains, the difference is like that between seed and grain—which is no difference at all. The seed planted has within it already the wheat that will emerge in the spring. In the same way, the body that rises again at the resurrection was immanent within the living body, guaranteeing that the resurrected self was continuous with the previous self—that it was the same subject, and not some other being entirely, that would enjoy eternal life.

Pulter offers her own version of Paul's seed metaphor in "View But This Tulip," one of her many emblem poems. Pulter opens with a detailed description of palingenesis, an alchemical ritual that aimed to regrow a plant from its own ashes. This process provides an obvious metaphor for thinking about the possibilities of bodily resurrection. But against this alchemical method for immortality (a method not unlike the experimentation she critiques in "The Circle [2]") Pulter offers an alternative, an adaptation of Paul's seed metaphor:

> As wheat in new plowed furrows rotting lies,
> Incapable of quickening 'til it dies,
> So into dust this flesh of mine must turn,
> And lie a while forgotten in my urn.
> Yet when the sea, and earth, and hell, shall give
> Their treasures up, my body too shall live—
> Not like the resurrection at Grand Caire,
> Where men revive then straight of life despair—
> But with my soul my flesh shall reunite,
> And ne'er involved be with death and night,
> But live in endless pleasure, love, and light.
> Then hallelujahs will I sing to thee,
> My gracious God to all eternity.
> Then at thy dissolution patient be.
> If man can raise a flower, God can thee. (31–45)

Echoing Paul, Pulter compares the body to wheat. Like the "rotting" seeds of sown grain, the speaker's own body is reduced to dust and left to molder in its urn. She is clear to underscore that there is an unbroken material connection between the body that dies and is interred and the one that rises again. It is not just any body, but *her* body—"this flesh of mine" in "my urn." Like Paul, the speaker insists that her resurrected self must be continuous with her living, fleshly body.

Pulter also describes a resurrection body that will be fundamentally distinct from the living body. As Dolan points out, "And ne'er involved be with death and night" looks to be a later addition to the manuscript, inserted between lines 39 and 41 to create the only triplet in a poem otherwise made entirely of couplets. Without this line, the couplet would read:

> But with my soul my flesh shall reunite,
> But live in endless pleasure, love, and light.

The *but* at the start of both lines suggests that these were likely never intended be a standalone couplet. But even so, the later insertion also suggests a close semantic relationship between these two lines that is, in some sense, more intuitive than the whole tercet. If we consider them as a couplet, these lines offer a more canonical account of resurrection: body and soul reunited for an infinite future of pleasure, love, and light. However, with the inserted line, Pulter muddies the waters:

> But with my soul my flesh shall reunite,
> And ne'er involved be with death and night
> But live in endless pleasure, love, and light.

There is an implied *again* in the middle line that throws the poem off its axis. The grammatical subject of the lines is "my flesh," subjugating "my soul" to the status of object, the thing with which the flesh will be reunited but not, at least, the thing that shall "never be involved with death and night." The speaker has, in the lines just before this, described the future of her earthly body (a future that includes rotting and dissolution). Those nearby images contradict this claim and remind both reader and speaker that her body will intimately be involved with death, with all the physicality that implies. We might rightly assume that Pulter means to suggest that her flesh will never *again*, after death, be involved with death. But that absent term leads this line and tercet to feel uncertain. The body's dissolution is guaranteed, but as the subject of its resurrection approaches, Pulter's form and syntax become irregular, unsure.

Without the absent *again*, Pulter's description of resurrection relies on a temporal paradox: *never* (line 40) and *endless* (41). In one respect, these are complementary; to never be linked with death—to be forever alive—means, literally, to be without end. Exchanging a previously mortal state of embodiment for this new immortal existence allows the speaker to imagine entering into a state in which all time is absolute, without beginning or end. And yet, these two terms also describe completely opposing relationships with time. *Never* is "at no time," outside of time, while *endless* is in all times, always.[77] That this new body might be both never and endless suggests that the resurrection body will be both without time and within it, always and never alive. In this moment resurrection becomes, for Pulter, the point at which these forms of cyclical and fragmentary time most clearly collide.[78] For Paul, particularly in the seed metaphor, the central paradox of resurrection is material: The body must die in order to live, must be dissolved and destroyed in order to grow and rise again. Pulter adapts this, using the collision of circle and speck, into a metaphor that is both material and temporal. The body must be within time, capable of existing within the cyclical ecological rhythms of germination, growth, and decay. The body must also be outside time; it must never decay and be endlessly alive.

This tension between ending and endlessness appears again in "The Hope," written in 1665 and thus one of the last additions to the Leeds manuscript. As Scott-Baumann points out in the headnote to her edition, this is another example of Pulter's use of sonnet-like or sonnet-adjacent forms. The poem, which like "View But This Tulip" is almost entirely in couplets, stretches out to fifteen lines with its final tercet. And, like many of Pulter's other near-sonnets, "The Hope" imagines a speaker attempting to reconcile the inevitability of death and the possibility of eternal life.

> Dear Death dissolve these mortal charms
> And then I'll throw my self into thy arms
> Then thou mayest use my carcass as thou lust
> Until my bones (and little luz) be dust
> Nay when that handful is blown all about
> Yet still the vital salt will be found out
> And when the vapor is breathed out in thunder
> Unto poor mortals loss, or pain, or wonder
> And all that is in thee to atoms turned
> And even those atoms in this orb is burned
> Yet still that God that can annihilate
> This all, and it of nothing recreate
> Even He that hath supported me till now

To whom my soul doth pray and humbly bow
Will raise me unto life. I know not how[79]

As the *Pulter Project* editors point out, the manuscript text of this poem has only one full stop, the period in the middle of the final line. Liza Blake notes that "the relative scarcity of punctuation in this poem may be authorial. While the majority of the manuscript is written in a neat (and likely professional/scribal) roundhand, this poem, and a few others, are written in a spiky italic hand that also has made frequent corrections to other poems in the manuscript. Though we don't know for sure to whom any of the hands belong, most editors assume that the spiky hand . . . is Pulter's."[80] The absence of punctuation on its own does not seem to substantially differentiate "The Hope" from Pulter's other works. "The Circle [1]," for instance, a poem of twenty-two lines, also only includes a single, final full stop; "The Weeping Wish," also in Pulter's hand, includes only a single full stop at the end of the final line. Others, like "Universal Dissolution" (another poem with evidence of Pulter's own editorial intervention), are punctuated irregularly, with some sections full of punctuation while others include few or none.

But while the limited punctuation is stylistically consistent with Pulter's other poems, it also serves an important semantic purpose here, amplifying the poem's sense of wandering as the speaker attempts to pin a narrative terminus on her physical existence. Asking Death to "dissolve" her physical body, she then imagines that her presence with death will continue on "until my bones (and little luz) be dust." As in the Circle poems, the speck—the mote of dust to which her corpse is reduced—emerges as a form symbolizing the end of time, the cessation of all change. But here, that finality is called into question. The next line—"nay when that handful is blown all about"—undermines the previous speck, pushing the new end point of dissolution forward in time, when those dusty remains are scattered to the ends of the earth. The next line compounds these doubts further still: "Yet still the vital salt will be found out." Even at this new assumed ending, there is yet another level to which the body can be reduced—specks all the way down. The dust of the desiccated body is replaced with the vital salt of alchemical remains, which is in turn replaced by atomic dissolution. As line builds on line, Pulter's open syntax enacts the very doubts it captures; each point that seems like it might be a conclusion reveals itself as yet another false ending. The speaker's train of thought never really ends but instead flows on into the next line, and the next, and the next. The poem becomes a catalog of temporal continuation—"and then," "then," "until," "nay when," "yet still," "yet still." Here, circle and speck collide with full force. Everything is an ending; nothing ever ends.

This catalog of dissolution comes to a head with the implied pause of line 10, underscoring the influence of the sonnet form here with a *volta*-like shift in perspective. Having extended the depth of disintegration as far as atoms, the speaker doubts even this represents an end: "Even those atoms in this orb is burned." As Scott-Baumann notes, the orb represents not only the earth but also the alembic, the alchemic vessel in which reduction occurs. Pulter's declaration that "even those atoms" are burned suggests that they themselves possess a future state, that they can be reduced further and made even more speck-like. No matter the level of material reduction the speaker can imagine, it seems, there is another layer beneath it, waiting to be revealed. And "yet still," she writes, there's more. With the poem's building desire for finality—to find what is eventually, somewhere, at the bottom of all these many specks—the reader's anticipation builds that the turn will, finally, reveal the end of everything. Line 11 teases this; the readers' expectations may be that the line will read "Yet still that [material] God can annihilate," suggesting that God's intervention signals the ultimate, final end. But Pulter pulls the rug out from under us once more. The active verb in the final section of the poem is not *annihilate* but *raise*. Even God, who has the capacity to achieve total eradication—the total end that these speck-like images aspire to—does not provide it. Instead, God both continues and reverses the experience of time in the poem. Rather than stopping time, God extends it, drawing the speaker into eternal life. This shift represents a complete change of direction; rather than continuing this pattern of infinite fragmentation, God begins the process of reassembly.

This process, however, pulls up short in the poem's final, fragmentary line. The half phrase—"I know not how"—breaks off without conclusion, leaving the reader (and speaker) in a state of uncertainty. This is compounded by the fact that this fifteenth line makes up the only tercet of the poem, underscoring the sensation of unfulfillment. This moment echoes the ambivalence of the final line of "View But This Tulip": "If man can raise a flower, God can thee." Can man raise a flower?[81] Pulter's long and detailed descriptions of decay are answered with a fragmentary and ambivalent description of the resurrection. This imbalance is, in part, a feature of the sonnet form. As discussed in the previous chapter, the English sonnet is often marked by a pronounced tension between its quatrains and couplet. With so much space dedicated to the "problem" of the poem, if we can call it that, any solution offered in the concluding two lines must consequently feel insufficient. Pulter intensifies even that existing structural imbalance; so much of this poem explores the dissolution of her body in great detail, making the single final line—God "will raise me unto life. I know not how"—feel impossibly small in comparison.

The two tercets discussed in these resurrection poems—lines 39–41 in "View But This Tulip" and lines 13–15 in "The Hope"—capture the collision of temporalities that Pulter locates in decay. In these moments, the poems' speakers recognize the inherent paradoxes of resurrection: The body ends, and in fact must end, but the body must also live forever. The material self is necessarily temporal and temporary (one must die to be raised again) and eternal and lasting. Time begets death; death begets more time. These tensions are then made manifest in the very form of the lines themselves. With the inserted center line in "View But This Tulip" and the fragmentary fifteenth line of "The Hope," Pulter grounds these discussions of resurrection temporality into self-consciously anomalous couplets-turned-triplets. The couplet form is, by definition, a closed form; comprised solely of beginning and end, it performs its own limitation. And yet, as the idea of resurrection approaches, Pulter's poetry stretches out beyond its own boundaries. Inserting these extended tercets into her lyric, Pulter creates moments of suspended time in which the couplet, if only briefly, suddenly feels as if it might go on forever. Such moments are, in general, indicative of how both Scott-Baumann and Woodward describe Pulter's formalist ethos. Both note that Pulter reimagines traditionally enclosed forms to push back on that sense of enclosure, replacing containment with a sense of permeability. These resurrection lyrics, with their overflowing tercets, demonstrate Pulter's ability to draw on the language of lyric forms to capture the collision of times found in the body's decay. The poems enact these two contradictory temporalities at the level of the line: time as both limited and infinite, closed and open.

Pulter is not alone in using the subject of resurrection to explore the limits of what the lyric form can do. Daniel Juan Gil argues that the metaphysical poets of the seventeenth century were particularly interested in the question of what happened to the body after its earthly death. While the rise of dualist philosophy in the period meant that mainstream Protestantism was beginning to move away from the doctrine of corporeal resurrection, poets like Donne, Vaughan, and Herbert embraced this earlier theological tradition, demonstrating a shared interest in the resurrection's immanence in the living body—Paul's germinative glorious body, already within the seed husk of the living body. But, Gil notes, these poets were not only interested in bodily resurrection for its own sake. Rather, for these writers, bodily resurrection provided the opportunity to explore lyric's ability to reflect the complexity of embodiment. Gil argues that these poets viewed the body's paradoxical resurrection materiality as the perfect subject through which to explore the avant-garde critical potential of poetry. He contends that their work demonstrates an approach to lyric that "does not present itself as a representation of the world or as a monumental aesthetic object but as a transpersonal practice that is valued primarily for the effects it creates in readers. . . . [It] is designed to provoke readers into a new way of life built on a new way of understanding themselves in their bodily life and in their relationship to their historical world."[82] Through "radical formal experimentation," these poets explored how their work could make the body felt and known in new ways.[83] Notably, Gil does not include Pulter in his analysis or in the cohort of poets he identifies at the center of this theoretical movement. And yet, Pulter is nonetheless clearly at the heart of these intellectual and poetic conversations and must be considered another essential voice in this movement. These resurrection lyrics offer readers a glimpse of Pulter's relationship with form—not only forms as organizing principles, as with the circles and specks of time, nor only just as technical structures, as with the couplet experimentations described earlier, but with the generic form of Pulter's work, with the work of lyric as a whole. Like Herbert, Donne, Vaughan, and others, Pulter sees in the material of the body, the temporal paradoxes of decay, and the concurrent in/finitude of time that gathers around mortality the opportunity to explore the possibilities of lyric form. Through formal experimentation of all kinds, Pulter's lyrics make legible the body's tenuous place in time.

Pulter's forms—the circle and speck, the couplet and tercet, the sonnet and emblem—all work to advance what I argue we must recognize as an early critical theory of lyric temporality. In Pulter's poetry, lyric time is pushed beyond binary distinctions such as action or inaction, stasis or movement, teleologic or recursive, present or past. Unlike past theories offered by Frye, Culler, and others, Pulter's is not an account of lyric time that insists on a single, unified temporality; hers is not an atemporal model of lyric that steps entirely outside the flow of linear time. Instead, these poems seem to suggest that lyric's temporality is in fact closer to the kinds of collisions Pulter identifies in grief, resurrection, and the body's decay, moments in which time runs in all directions at once. For Pulter, lyric can capture the friction between subjective and objective time, moments when one feels out of sync with time but in time nevertheless. This is clear, for instance, in the Circle poems, where the speaker, in her grief, is thrust deeper within and further outside time simultaneously. Lyric can convey both stasis and motion; it can capture the collision of the two, the disrupted time of grief. And, as these resurrection poems suggest, lyric can sit at the nexus of never and always, the vehicle for all time and no time. If past theories of lyric time have insisted on a lyric present, then Pulter imagines lyric presents, a gallery full of clocks ticking at different rates: diverging, syncing, overlapping, but always ticking.

Lyric time, in these texts, is accretive rather than reductive—always capable of more than one time.

This vision for a more dynamic model of time is made possible by a lyric ethos grounded in the body's decay—of an intimate understanding of crip time. Kafer notes that, at its core, crip time challenges "normative and normalizing expectations" by placing embodiment at the center of our temporal calculus.[84] "Rather than bend disabled bodies and minds to meet the clock," she writes, "crip time bends the clock to meet disabled bodies and minds."[85] Pulter confronts the reality of decay head-on in these lyrics: She is surrounded by the death of the body, of others and, inevitably, of her own. But faced with the realities of embodiment, Pulter does not attempt to remold that decay to fit a normative model of time. She does not shape her grief or her hope for resurrection into a fixed narrative form, imagining only cure or eradication. Rather, she chooses forms of time that reflect back the realities of impairment and decay. Instead of a normalizing model of lyric time, Pulter offers an adaptable model, one that makes space for the many temporalities of the body. Through these many forms of time, Pulter's work captures the contradictory, overlapping, and paradoxical temporalities of the decaying body, offering not resolution but (to use Pulter's favorite term) revolution.

Chapter 4

Intimacies of Decay

> Poetry leads to the same place as all forms of eroticism—to the blending and fusion of separate objects. It leads up to eternity, it leads us to death, and through death to continuity.
>
> —Georges Bataille, *Eroticism*

The last place we might expect images of decay to appear is in the celebratory scenes of a marriage poem. And yet, Donne, true to style, manages to surprise us. Donne's "Epithalamion Made at Lincolns Inne" has established its place as an outlier in the catalog of early modern marriage poems, displaying a subtle antagonism toward the genre's standards of tone and decorum.[1] Amid the customarily happy subject matter of the wedding procession, Donne includes imagery that evokes a looming sense of death. At the poem's opening, as the bride departs her chamber, the speaker describes the bed she has left behind as an open grave.[2]

> Leaue, leaue, fayr bride your solitary bed.
> No more shall you returne to it alone.
> It nourseth sadnes and your bodyes print
> Like to a graue the yielding Downe doth dint. (2–5)

The prenuptial bedroom is transformed into a gravesite, the bride's body likened to a corpse sinking into the burial plot. Readers might be tempted to hear this moment as a hyperbolic extension of the carpe diem genre—the virginal body's decay the result of her chastity—but that disappears as the language of decay extends past the marriage and into the scene of consummation. Returning to bed after the marriage rite, the bride is described as "an appointed Lambe" (89) who regards her bridegroom as "the priest [come] on his knees to'embowell her" (90). Elsewhere in the poem, Donne describes the "faire Temple" (37) of the church as the "leane and hunger sterved wombe" (40) that, at the lovers' death, may "expect their bodyes and ther tombe" (41). Decay is not linked exclusively to the virgin body, as might be expected, but to the spaces where the marriage is performed and consummated. Unification and connection are, in Donne's epithalamion, paradoxically described in the language of decay and decomposition.

But while these images may have startled some early modern readers (or even modern ones), they also provide a textbook example of Donne's signature metaphysical conceit. Samuel Johnson famously described this technique as "heterogeneous ideas . . . yoked by violence together," a description that is, in this particular example, technically accurate.[3] Using metaphors of decomposition, Donne links the body's decay with the intimacy of the marriage bed—two individual bodies yoked through the violence of destruction into a single, blissful whole. And while the union between decay and intimacy (an intimacy that, in Donne's epithalamion, is both sensual and sacred) might provoke an initial flash of repulsion, that visceral reaction may be the point. As Richard Rambuss observes, the conceits of poets like Donne and Richard Crashaw created "such palpable effect that we are jolted into experiencing anew (or perhaps even for the first time) the expressive strangeness" of existence. "Such an effect," Rambuss argues, "is nothing short of the very aim of metaphysical wit."[4] While Donne's works offer no shortage of invention when it comes to conceits, he repeatedly returns to this union of decay and intimacy.[5] Using vivid metaphors of decomposition to anchor scenes of intimacy, Donne creates a persistent metaphysical conceit that links the reproductivity of consummation with the destruction of decay across his lyrics. Lovers are frequently described as dying or decaying, their bodies characterized as fluid, ephemeral, and—most importantly for Donne—penetrable.

For Donne, this conceit and its many iterations serve two immediate purposes. First, these moments help confirm Donne's investment in an embodied poetics. Like Shakespeare, Donne uses the affordances of lyric, particularly its capacity for this kind of complex extended metaphor, to reject the narrativizing impulses of Neoplatonism. These poems suggest that the body and its pleasures, even its decay, are not barriers to be overcome or moved past but are an end in and of themselves. The connections made possible by decay are not secondary to the emotional and spiritual bonds forged between lovers; rather, bodily intimacy is the highest degree of connection these poems can imagine. Because of this, decay also serves as a conceit for lyric itself. In these moments, when the physical boundaries of bodies dissolve through decomposition, Donne sees radical potential. The decaying body becomes a fantasy of permeability, the site of (impossible) total physical intimacy between lovers and between humanity and the divine. And it is the form of lyric that allows such a fantasy to come to life. Donne treats these poems as an imaginary space unbounded by the limits of rationality and everyday language. Lyric, like decay, becomes a tool by which the poet might make real their most impossible desires. Like the decaying body itself, lyric offers the potential for connection and invention beyond the limits of reality. This lyricizing influence is so significant that its effects transcend Donne's poetic works, crossing over to shape his later sermons and prose. In Donne's theological writing, decay persists as an instrumental part of the intimacy between God and humanity realized through bodily resurrection. It is because of our decay that we can see God face-to-face, Donne argues; it is not despite but because of these bodies that we can be raised again.

This continuity between Donne's lyrics and his theology confirms what generations of scholars have since observed—that, rather than any abrupt discontinuity between poet and pastor, Donne's career overwhelmingly suggests a stable and coherent set of beliefs. As Blaine Greteman notes, "Donne's engagement with bodies forms a consistent creative thread from his earliest paradoxes and witty poetic performances to his final, brooding meditations and sermons."[6] The persistence of the conceit of decay bears that out: Even in these final, theological works, Donne centers and celebrates the dying body. This theological argument relies, in large part, on the work of the metaphysical conceit, of the lyric form itself. In this, Donne's later writing illustrates the usefulness of the collision model when thinking about formal relationships. As discussed in the introduction, my interest in collision as a model for formal interaction is grounded in the wide range of possibilities such a model allows. While previous chapters focus on examples where lyric and narrative affordances run counter to one another—the forward drive of epic and the meditative inclination of the carpe diem poem, for instance—here, collision takes the form not of contradiction but of intensification. Lyric overflows its banks to spill into Donne's sermons, meditations, and other theological writing, bringing its unifying capacity along with it. Donne's theology is ultimately a lyric theology, borrowing from the metaphysical conceit the idea that language might bring radically disconnected things into communion with one another. And so, Donne's use of this conceit in his sermons and theological writing offers a final example for this book of the shaping work of form. By attending to Donne's work with the metaphysical conceit, we can see how lyric enables new ways of thinking about decay—not as destruction, but as creation.

In these moments of decay, Donne dwells in the bodily, resisting the impulse to move beyond it. His theology, particularly his theology of resurrection, offers an early instance of disability theology that centers, rather than alters, the decay inherent in the body. At the end of the chapter, I identify several core features of Donne's theology of embodiment that provide the foundation for disability theology, both in the early modern period and in contemporary theological studies. First, as I argue throughout, Donne rejects a Neoplatonic model of being, finding the body's value not in some future state of perfection but in its present decay. Donne likewise privileges interdependence over independence, finding connection to be of a higher spiritual worth than individualism. Donne sees the contingency and dependency of the body as its inherent potential for intimacy and pleasure rather than as a source of individual weakness. And, finally, as I have already suggested, Donne recognizes the instrumental work of metaphor in transforming belief. In a way that anticipates the work of contemporary theological scholars, Donne's work demonstrates the necessity of metaphor—particularly metaphors that center and celebrate decay—in building systems of belief. In outlining these features, I offer a framework of how we might identify other early modern disability theologies. Disability studies, particularly premodern disability studies, has long recognized the influence of Christianity on cultural attitudes around embodiment and ability. Reading the many stories of "monstrous births" in the period, Julie Crawford argues that, despite attempts toward secularization and rationalism, Protestants continued to interpret stories of bodily deformity through the lens of providence, assigning disability (whether real or fictitious) religious significance.[7] However, while scholars have allowed for the influence of belief on disability, the opposite has not been true. By suggesting we begin to read Donne's theology as disability theology (rather than as a theology of disability), I want to explore what it might look like to allow disability to speak back to the period's systems of belief. Decay, I argue, exerts a surprising and significant influence on early modern Christianity that we have only begun to map.

Much has already been said, of course, about Donne and death. Critical accounts of Donne's apparent fascination with death have varied widely, from claims that the poet barely contained his own suicidal ideations to assertions that he suffered from a crippling fear of mortality. Donald Ramsey Roberts, for instance, argues that Donne was exceptional in his fascination with death, particularly his own. He notes, "Contemporary ritual demanded no such presumptive measures as preaching one's own funeral sermon, arranging one's body for the coffin, and preparing a posthumous monument."[8] In contrast, Targoff contends that Donne's continual return to death and decay suggests an overwhelming dread of the separation between body and soul made manifest in the secular lyrics' repeated scenes of lovers taking leave of one another.[9] Others take up more intermediary positions, noting that Donne straddles the line between desire and horror when describing the body's eventual demise. Guibbory suggests that Donne "both fears and is fascinated by such changes. . . . In a universe where all decays, the only things that grow are disease and corruption."[10] John Carey describes Donne's "unmistakable relish" in listing the anatomical details of human decomposition as the expression of pure "imaginative energy," a rush of "exhilaration" at the poetic mastery of the body rather than actual joy at its loss.[11] My aim is not to discern the motivation behind death's prominence in Donne's work but instead to suggest that these images are better understood in terms of their poetic function. That is, rather than asking what has caused Donne to focus on decay, I concentrate on the work of form, on how the conceit itself shapes the possibilities of meaning. Since Donne's descriptions of decomposition are arresting in their level of detail, critics tend to pathologize their presence. But rather than symptomatic, Donne's use of decay is a strategic, carefully constructed conceit that through its unexpected unions transforms the seemingly grotesque materiality of the decomposing body into an opportunity to explore the most extreme potential of intimacy.

Made of One Another

Decay and intimacy first find one another in Donne's secular poems and their sustained interest in embodied love. Some of the clearest examples of this conceit appear in the linked poems "The Funeral," "The Relique," and "The Dissolution," keystones in a short sequence on the process of death in Donne's 1633 *Poems*.[12] The first two of these lyrics share a distinctive central image: a memorial token described by the speaker in "The Funeral" as a "subtile wreath of haire, which crowns my arme" (3) and becomes, by the beginning of "The Relique," "a bracelet of bright haire about the bone" (6) of his now-cadaverous limb. Immediately, the specific material of this object focuses readers' attention on the interconnection of decay and intimacy. Donne and seventeenth-century contemporaries would have regarded hair as a liminal substance, not part of the body proper but an outgrowth. Megan Kathleen Smith notes that it was an "excrement" in the most fundamental sense of the term, a quality shared by other bodily waste including, importantly, the corpse itself.[13] Not only was hair categorized in the same material class as the dead body, but—importantly for Donne's purposes—it also served as a common synecdoche for decay. This substitution was, in part, based on first-hand observations; as those who tended the graveyards of early modern churches would have been well aware, hair was one of the last traces of the living body on skeletal remains. Browne, in his detailed description of decomposition in *Hydriotaphia*, notes that while the soft tissues of the body quickly dissolve in the grave, "teeth, bones, and hair, give the most lasting defiance to corruption."[14] Hair was one of the last traces that gestured backward at the body that used to be, a visible reminder of the changes endured in the grave. Closely associated with advanced decomposition, hair and bone enter Donne's lyrics as emblems of extreme decay through which he can explore the furthest reaches of corporeality.

The hair bracelet appears early in "The Funerall," where the speaker considers the effect of his mistress's remains on his own living body. The bracelet

> 'tis my outward Soule,
> viceroy to that, which then to heaven being gone,
>   will leave this to controule
> and keepe these limbes, her Provinces, from dissolution. (5–8)

The speaker seems first to imply that the bracelet will guard his own body from decay, resisting decomposition and maintaining a state of permanent wholeness. This, however, is manifestly fruitless; the request is made by the speaker's reanimated corpse, confirming that his own decay is inevitable. The hair of the bracelet does not keep the speaker in a state of fleshly fullness but instead creates a different kind of wholeness, one reliant on the union between speaker and mistress. In the second stanza, the two individual bodies are joined in a single, erotic union. There, the speaker begins with a conditional: "If the sinewie thread my braine lets fall" (9) can effectively work to "tye those parts, and make mee one of all" (11), then his body may remain whole. But, as the previous stanza has already shown, the body's own internal thread is insufficient. On its own, the individual body might make "one of all" both by unifying its many parts into a single system and by distinguishing that individual system from those around it. But both these acts of differentiation are completely undone in death. The internal thread of the sinew is then replaced by the external thread of hair—a decaying strand replaced by a more resistant and long-lasting thread. The bracelet, made of "those haires which upward grew" (12) from his mistress's head, is more effective and "can better" (14) unite the poet's own body. The true act of making "one of all" is the process not of unifying disparate body parts into a closed system, the speaker realizes, but of uniting separate individuals into a single, unified whole. This action is decidedly erotic. The upward growth of the mistress's hair suggests an erection, and the poem's central image is one of penetration—the speaker's arm encircled by the remnants of the mistress's body. Modeled after the intimacy of sex in life, the joining of the two lovers through their bodily remains creates a new union, achieving "one of all" and, in the process, creating a connection more enduring than either of their individual bodies.

Donne's language here focuses on the primacy of the body's materiality, even—and especially—in death. The posthumous union described is not the consequence of previous emotional connections but instead the very act producing the intimacy in question. The joining of bodies is the cause, not the effect.[15] The speaker notes that the bracelet was not intended as a token of mutual love; instead, it was given as a cruel reminder of his own unrequited affection.

> she meant that I
> by this should know my pain,
> as prisoners then are manacled, when they'are condem'd to die. (14–16)

But the intent behind the bracelet is overshadowed by its effect. Because the speaker possesses the mistress's remains, he can manufacture the intimacy denied to him while she was alive, enacting posthumous revenge. "What ere shee meant by'it, bury it with me" (17), he proclaims, taunting her memory; "since you would save none of mee, I bury some of you" (24). Even in the face of contrary desires, the physical location of the body or its parts—not the actions or emotions of the subject—ultimately determines its fate. This moment, like so many in Donne's lyrics, affirms the body's ability to create, and not just simply reflect, intimacy. Much like "The Flea," where the lovers' mingled blood serves as the starting point from which the poet develops his seduction argument, "The Funerall" grants the body a controlling influence over the spiritual or intellectual self; the poems' speakers, in the absence of romantic connection, manipulate their lovers' corpses in order to create the intimacy they desire.

The speaker of "The Relique," now seemingly aware of the potential for his remains to be manipulated, spends much of that poem offering instructions for how to correctly interpret decay's effects. Echoing the misuse of his mistress's body in "The Funerall," the speaker's own remains in "The Relique" are now transformed against his will. Unearthed along with the hair bracelet and dragged from the privacy of the grave-bed into the public eye, his and his lover's bodies become the objects of "mis-devotion" (13). While many have noted an implied critique of Catholicism here, the poem's place in this group of lyrics on death requires its treatment of devotion to also be considered in the context of materiality more broadly.[16] The speaker does not reject relic veneration outright, in fact, and finds no inherent error in identifying the corpses as divine objects. Rather, he protests the reason behind their veneration, which has come about as the result of a profound misreading of the two corpses.

> And since at such time, miracles are sought,
> I would have that age by this paper taught
> what miracles wee harmelesse lovers wrought. (20–22)

If future readers of both the bones and the lyric describing them look to these bodies as divine objects, he writes, then they must understand the real reason for their holiness. For much of the poem's history, that reason has been identified as the Neoplatonic ascension from physical to spiritual love. In the opening stanza, the two are locked in the state of perpetual penetration described in "The Funerall": The speaker is encircled by his mistress's remains in a grave compared explicitly to a bed, emphasizing the intimacy of the connection. This physical connection is then seemingly abandoned by the final stanzas in the lovers' apotheosis to a purely spiritual union. The speaker there claims that "difference of sex no more wee knew," implying a rejection of embodied affection in favor of the spiritual love akin to that of the angels (25). With the exception of some cursory kissing, he asserts, the lovers never consummated their love. "Our hands ne'er toucht the seales," he declares (29). When read in such a way, "The Relique" seems to suggest that abandoning the body—whether through the act of decaying or the refusal to consummate—leads to a state of purified spiritual existence.

This reading, however, is utterly at odds with the attitudes toward embodiment that define Donne's writing, which is marked by what Schoenfeldt describes as a "profoundly materialist poetics" that rejects the idea that the body is a burden to be laid aside.[17] Targoff concurs that there is not much to suggest that Donne was interested in eschewing the body. "There is little doubt that Donne learned from Neoplatonism," she argues, but "Donne was not a Neoplatonist at heart . . . he rejects the central Neoplatonic tenets that love should move both from particulars to generals and from bodies to souls."[18] The sustained misreading of this final stanza as a Neoplatonic rejection of the body has largely relied on interpreting the stanza's opening word—*first*—as the beginning of a list of reasons why the lovers should be beatified. But this term is not followed by any other cataloging vocabulary. There is no *second* or *next* that follows, extending the sequence further. Instead, this opening finds its counterpart in the *but now* of the poem's antepenultimate line, after which the speaker invokes the mystery of the lovers' miraculousness. Taking both moments together—*first* and *now*—the stanza reveals two contrasting moments in time: *first*, a previous state in which poet and lover were estranged from their physical selves, and *now*, a state in which that estrangement is resolved. Noting that "these miracles wee did" (past tense), the poet hints at the improbability of dematerialized love; love without consumption, in Donne's characteristic wry humor, would be miraculous in that it would be totally outside the realm of human nature (31). "But now," the speaker declares in the present, the lovers' true divinity is revealed. The *now* to which he refers is the present invoked in the first stanza: "When my grave is broke up againe" (1). It is not the absence of a physical union but the persistence of it, the act of perpetual physical consumption achieved by the lovers' mingled bodies, that makes them suitable candidates for veneration. Here, as in "The Funerall," materiality serves as the efficient cause for the lovers' state. Their corpses are buried together as an attempt to secure their future reunion, affirming that the embodied connection fostered by decay holds sway over the state of the eternal self and ultimately determines the theological value of these relics.

The final poem of this short sequence, "The Dissolution," performs a characteristically Donnean shift in scale by reimagining the physical union of the lovers' remains at the microcosmic level. While "The Relique" and "The Funerall" eliminate the "difference of sex" in an act of posthumous intercourse with the joining of arm and bracelet, "The Dissolution" pursues this union even further, examining the lovers' atomic connection.

> Shee'is dead; and all which die
> to their first Elements resolve;
> and wee were mutuall Elements to us,
> and made of one another. (1–4)

The mistress's decomposition into scattered elements enables both lover and speaker to become materially indistinguishable—"made of one another." Like the comparison between sinew and hair in "The Funerall," this description contrasts the insufficiency of individual corporeality with the pleasure and strength afforded by the lovers' union. "Those things whereof I consist" (6) alone, the speaker notes, "nourish not, but smother" (8). Individual materiality is not sustaining but depleting. The speaker expresses a greater sense of stability through his new shared materiality, noting that now, "my body then doth hers involve" (5). Donne's choice of verb here creates an erotic pun on the bodies' connection. As discussed in the previous chapter, the term *involve* had a deeply material significance in the seventeenth century, meaning "to roll or enwrap in anything that is wound round, or surrounds as a case or covering; to enfold, to envelop."[19] This was derived from the Latin *volvo*, meaning "to roll, turn about, turn round."[20] But, importantly for Donne's purposes, that same Latin root also generates *volva* and later *vulva*, meaning "a wrapper [or] covering," a term that, by the time of Donne's writing, had come to refer specifically to genitalia.[21] Donne's word choice echoes the penetrative imagery of both "The Funerall" and "The Relique," marking the blending of decomposed materials as an erotic act of connection. Moreover, *involve* enacts the very eradication of sexual difference to which the speaker of "The Relique" aspires. The poet will both penetrate—will *involve*, be in-*volva*—and be penetrated, enveloping and enfolding the elements of his lover. In this way, the intimacy furnished by decay is the true manifestation of the sexless union—not without bodies but encompassing all bodies in all ways, the individual sexed body transformed into the doubled and unified body that erases all difference between sex.[22] Here, and throughout this first group of poems, the process of decomposition mirrors that of consummation. By joining their remains, Donne expands the act of penetration to an almost infinite degree of time and an atomic degree of scale, allowing him to imagine the most extreme potential for intimacy.

But in the valedictions, Donne must wrestle with a second question: Can this connection persist in the face of physical separation? These lyrics take up the hyperbolic union fostered by decay as a balancing force to the suffering of separation. Faced with the extreme isolation of parting, Donne turns to decay as a refuge. Many critics read decay's prevalence in the valedictions as a symptom of Donne's animosity toward separation. Because of this, some, including Guibbory and Schoenfeldt, argue that decay and love work in opposition in these poems—decay representing all the forces driving the lovers apart, desire working to bring them back together again. "The spherical wholeness that the lovers embody suggests [that] love to some extent counters the fragmenting, degenerative course of history," Guibbory writes, and creates the "hope that intensely mutual love may be able to transcend decay."[23] Schoenfeldt contends that the valedictions' treatment of death is totally contrary to Donne's other works. While in "The Relique" and "The Funerall," "death is the pretext for reunion of body parts and lovers" at the day of resurrection, he writes, in the valedictions, death is "a powerful metaphor for the emotional devastation of parting."[24] For both Schoenfeldt and Guibbory, the valedictions' central goal of reunion and reconnection is incompatible with decay, which can only be seen as a force of dispersal and separation.

But decay does not counteract Donne's desire for wholeness and union, for deep spiritual, emotional, and physical intimacy. Just as the lovers' dissolution creates the potential for new, more intense physical connections in the lyrics already discussed, decay likewise appears in the valedictions as the countervailing force to separation, the eradication of all barriers, bodily as well as geographic, that keep the lovers apart. This is visible, for example, in the opening images of "A Valediction Forbidding Mourning." Critical attention here has historically been focused on the conceits of later stanzas—"gold to ayery thinnesse beate" (24) and the "stiffe twin compasses" (26)—that signal the possibility of continuity over a great distance. The poem's opening metaphor has consequently been read backward from these images as a contrasting example, an opening image of separation that sets up the later stanzas' resolution. Donne begins the poem with an image that would almost certainly remind readers of the exemplary deaths of *ars moriendi* treatises: a quiet bedside, with the dying surrounded by friends and family as they transition peacefully and imperceptibly into death.

> As virtuous men passe mildly'away,
> and whisper to their soules, to goe,
> whilst some of their sad friends doe say,
> the breath goes now, and some say, no.
>
> So let us melt, and make no noise,
> no teare-floods, nor sigh-tempests move,
> t'were prophanation of our joyes
> to tell the layetie our love. (1–8)

The poem opens with decay rather than death. The friends gathered around the bedside are unable to pinpoint the moment of transition but observe as the body slowly but undeniably changes from living to dead. The valediction then seems, initially, to invite readers to equate this quiet transformation with the lovers' separation. That is, as Targoff argues, the parting of poet and mistress appears analogous to the peaceful separation of the virtuous man's body and soul. In such a reading, the next stanza's opening injunction—"So let us melt"—advises the speaker's mistress to approach the death of their union with equal dignity and piety, quietly accepting the injury of their separation.

But melting does not only suggest separation. The speaker urges his mistress to "melt," asking her to replicate not only the action of the first stanza in their parting but also the physical transformation invoked there. For an object to melt, it must undergo a material conversion from solid to liquid state, becoming fluid and mobile. To "melt," Targoff notes, in "common seventeenth-century (as well as modern) usage carries the sense of dissolving or liquefying, so that the image would suggest less the separation of two discrete bodies from each other than the breaking down of a single body."[25] The body's decomposition was often described in precisely these terms, as the process of liquefaction (an image to which Donne returns in his sermons, discussed later in this chapter). We might think, for instance, of the scenes from *The Faerie Queene* discussed in chapter 1, when Amavia and Acrasia's bodies slowly become indistinguishable from the waterscapes around them. There, Spenser allegorizes dissolution, allowing the corpses to flow outward and into the streams and fountains of Faerieland. With the command that opens that second stanza—the imperative *so*—Donne makes it clear here that the dissolution of decay is the means by which the lovers' desire for connection is fulfilled. The speaker's invitation for his lover to "melt" with him—to melt specifically in a way analogous to the deathbed scene of the opening lines—reveals the nature of the transformation he desires.

Rather than imagining their separation, Donne envisions the lovers blurring together as one—a melting not of bonds but of borders. This results in the totalizing intimacy of the poem's sixth stanza: "Our two soules, therefore, which are one" (21). The poem's speaker compares the superior love between himself and his mistress (the result of their melting) to the lesser "dull, sublunary lovers love" (13), a connection that abhors distance because the material "things which elemented it" (16) are absent. Like "The Relique," "A Valediction Forbidding Mourning" seems to present the possibility of a Neoplatonic reading. The speaker and his lover, in one regard, are better than these dull lovers because their connection is spiritual, "so much refin'd" that it "care[s] lesse, eyes, lips, hands to misse" (17, 20). But Donne uses the language of alchemy here to open up more materialist possibilities. That the speaker's love is a "refin'd" love, a term closely associated with processes of purification, suggests that it is itself the product of decay. It has been stripped of dross or impurities, reduced to the core elements that comprise the connection dismissed in the comparison. The individual body parts the speaker mentions—eyes, lips, and hands—are likewise purged, leaving the lovers with a material connection absent of any distinguishable difference. Rather, as the much-discussed images of the final stanzas bear out, the two have become totally physically integrated. Like hammered gold, the lovers have been reduced to a single, purified element that, despite geographic distance, maintains an uninterrupted material connection. And, like the compass leg that "growes erect" at the return of its beloved other half, the connection between the two is grounded in erotic desire. These later images of total intimacy—complete spiritual connection paired with physical pleasure—emerge in the valediction only as a result of previous decay. As the lovers separate, Donne presents a contrapuntal joining characterized through the material transformations of melting and refinement.

Likewise, in "A Valediction of My Name in the Window," Donne counters fears of estrangement with an imagined union brought about by decay, the transition from individual bodies defined by firm physical boundaries to a combined dual existence. The valediction's central image underscores the pain and isolation of individualized existence. The poet's mistress looks out on the world through a window into which the poem's speaker, her absent lover, has scratched his name.

> 'Tis much that Glasse should bee
> as all confessing and through-shine as I,
> 'tis more, that it shewes thee to thee,
> and cleare reflects thee to thine eye. (7–10)

The glass pane functions in much the same way as the living body by delineating the boundary between the self and the world. The glass, with its reflective nature that "shewes thee to thee," allows the mistress to recognize her own image imposed upon the activity of the street beyond. This act of self-recognition requires a solid surface onto which the self can be projected. But in addition to delimiting, the glass encourages permeation. The window is both reflective and transparent, described as an "all confessing and through-shine" pane through which any activity outside can be observed. Because the glass can represent both self and other simultaneously, it can realize the union envisioned by the poem's speaker, joining not only minds but bodies.[26] The mistress looks at her own reflection, overlaid onto her lover's name and the outside world. "Here you see mee," the speaker describes, "and I am you" (11–12).

This palimpsestic image's ability to stand in for the lovers' union with one another relies on their decay. Describing the process of writing the name in the window, Donne repeatedly uses the verb *engrave*. The poet's name on the window is "engrav'd herein," remains "as hard, as that which grav'd it, was," and is composed of "such characters, as graved bee" (1, 4, 35). The words are not just inscribed but in-graved, a figurative burial plot. And, as in "The Funerall," this imagined act of blending is the catalyst for the very intimacy the speaker desires. He instructs his mistress to regard the inscription as a symbol of death.

INTIMACIES OF DECAY 143

> It, as a given deaths head keepe
> lovers mortalie to preach,
> or thinke this ragged bony name to bee
> my ruinous Anatomie. (21–24)

The "rafters of" the poet's "body, bone" are laid bare on the glass before his lover, a skeleton stripped of its flesh (28). The speaker's remains, rendered incomplete and permeable, allow the poet and mistress to form a combined, blended self. The skeleton is then supplemented by the mistress's soft tissue. The "Muscle, Sinew, and Veine" (29) of her reflection fill in the skeletal inscription to create a complete body, that she "this intirenesse better may fulfill" (17). This union is the act by which the speaker can both generate and sustain intimacy. He instructs her not to resist "this names influence" (39). This symbol of their love, manufactured through the image of decay, will, he imagines, prevent any lapse of affection or infidelity, interrupting her wandering eye and truant pen if any other suitors emerge in his absence. Decay becomes the means by which the poet realizes his love in the face of his impending departure, creating an icon of intimacy that will guard their union during their separation.

Donne's use of the specific image of the scratched letters of the lover's name on the windowpane makes clear that it is not just decay that provides the pathway to intimacy but decay through writing—the metaphysical lyric conceit. On the one hand, the poem highlights the limitations of the written word, looking at how language seems to fall short of the full embodied intimacy the lovers desire. The final stanza explores these limits, with a moment exemplifying Christopher Ricks's observation about Donne's attitude toward closure and withdrawal. "The better the best things in his poems," he notes, "the more Donne is driven to rend it with his ending."[27] As the poem's speaker reflects on the union achieved through the conceit of the engraving, the lyric seems to collapse inward.

> But glasse, and lines must bee,
> no meanes our firme substantiall love to keepe;
> neere death inflicts this lethargie,
> and this I murmure in my sleepe;
> impute this idle talke, to that I goe,
> for dying men talke often so. (61–66)

Donne's adjective—*substantial*—indicates not only degree but quality. The word denotes any matter "relating to the tissue of the body, an organ," the quality of "having a corporeal or bodily form."[28] What the speaker craves is a material, bodily connection with his mistress. This physical bond, however, is incompatible with the imagined union created in the "glasse, and lines" of the poem's central image. The total decay of the two bodies into an amalgamated whole, while a compelling conceit, is depicted at this moment to be just that—an idea, not a "substantiall" reality. The lovers are not dead, they are alive and separated, kept apart by their own bodies and the space between them.

But the language of lyric does create something substantial here. The conceit of decay intervenes within the world of the poem to create something unrealized and unrealizable anywhere else. The final lines reinforce the instrumental role that lyric plays in bridging the gap between the two lovers. Here, the poem turns from the failure of the internal act of writing (the engraved name) to the potential success of its own composition (the poem itself). Donne makes this shift through the repeated use of deixis, with an insistent repetition of *this* in three subsequent lines: "this lethargie," "this I murmure," "this idle talk." The *this* of these lines no longer refers only to the lines on the glass but now expands to include the lines on the page: *this*, the object in the reader's hands, the poem itself. "This," the poet writes, is the idle talk of sleeping and dying men—a fantasy, a space outside the rules of conscious reason, an escape from the reality of the lovers' separation. The kind of intimacy the lovers aspire to, the total and complete absorption into one another, is also, fundamentally, impossible. The barriers of material existence prevent this from becoming a reality. However, while those material barriers are impossible hurdles in the real world, they are malleable within the world of the lyric. The reassembled death's head, the infinitely expandable hammered gold, the eternally wound hair bracelet—these conceits stretch beyond material reality to create, through metaphor, a hyperreality of connection that defies possibility. For Donne, it is lyric language that can make possible this miracle of intimacy.

Across his lyrics, Donne frequently refers to the intimacy accomplished by lyric as a theological wonder. The speaker of "The Relique," for instance, stresses at the poem's close that the extent of the lovers' complete physical union is ultimately inexpressible. "All measure, and all language, I should passe," he notes, "should I tell what a miracle shee was" (32–33). "A Valediction Forbidding Mourning" cautions that because the lovers' union is a miracle, it is thus indescribable to those without full theological understanding: "T'were prophanation of our joyes" the speaker declares, "to tell the layetie our love" (7–8). These moments emphasize that lyric's power is, in fact, a metaphysical one. The interlocutor of "The Funerall" is asked not to "question much" the significance of the hair bracelet and told that "the mystery, the signe you must not touch" (2, 4). *Mystery* denotes not only unknowability but, particularly for Donne, a specific spiritual category of knowledge. In its theological sense, a mystery is any aspect of divinity that is incomprehensible by the human mind, "a doctrine of faith involving difficulties which human reason is incapable of solving."[29] Examples included ideas like the relationship among the elements of the trinity—a concept that defied rational explanation but whose truth was nonetheless essential. To compensate for reason's insufficiency in these matters, church doctrine argued, God provides signs: visible and material manifestations that, through extensive interpretive labor, reveal part of the truth of the mystery.[30] By referring to the remains in "The Funerall" as the "signe" of the mystery, Donne suggests that they are the nearest we might come to divine truth. Though the mystery is never fully revealed, the presence of signs ensures the potential for knowledge and, more importantly, a pathway between human understanding and the divine.

For Donne, as these poems suggest, the intimacy created by decay through lyric exceeds the reach of descriptive language, occupying a space beyond communication and associated with divine truth. In the beginning are the words: The act of *poesis*, the joining and intimate work of the metaphysical conceit, is itself an act of divine creation. And as Donne's focus shifts to theological concerns in later works, the claims he makes about lyric's ability to foster this kind of intimacy are also transferred from human to divine love. This is apparent, for example, in Donne's Holy Sonnet "Thou hast made me." While this poem is absent from the Groups I and II manuscripts and the initial 1633 edition of the poems, it serves as the opening poem in the sequence of sonnets in both the Group III manuscripts and the 1635 and 1669 editions.[31] It is clear, from the poem's opening line, that decay seems to create a major barrier between humanity and the divine. The poet describes a relationship marked by division, a fundamental and seemingly irreconcilable disparity between himself and God.

> Thou hast made me, and shall thy work decaye?
> Repaire me nowe, for nowe mine end doth hast,
> I runne to Death, and Death meets me as fast,
> and all my pleasures are like yesterday.
> I dare not moue my dimme eyes any way,
> despaire behind, and Death before doth cast
> such terrour, and my feebled flesh doth wast
> by sinne in it, which it t'wards Hell doth weigh;

> only thou art aboue, and when t'wards thee
> by thy leaue I can looke, I rise againe:
> but our old suttle foe soe tempteth me,
> that not one houre I can my selfe sustaine;
> thy grace may winge me to prevent his Art,
> and thou, like Adamant, drawe mine yron heart.[32]

The poem's opening question suggests that the discrepancy between a perfect creator and an imperfect creation borders on paradox. In particular, he wonders, how can we reconcile an everlasting God with the decay of their creation? Traditionally, the explanation given for this disparity was original sin; decay's presence in the world is a sign of humanity's corruption, a legible trace of Adam's fall in the garden.[33] This explanation seems to fill the sonnet's octave, which frames dissolution as a journey away from God. The poet's "feebled flesh" is wasted by sin, sinking into the ground and into Hell, drawn further and further from the divine light. Here again, Donne offers the temptation of Neoplatonism. Decay, it seems, is the measure of the speaker's distance from the divine: The further he falls, the more the body and its failings (the dim eyes, the feeble flesh) rise to the foreground.

However, with the sonnet's turn, Donne reframes this explanation. Earlier in the octave, Donne employs anadiplosis, a rhetorical figure described by George Puttenham as a "sort of repetition when, with the word by which you finish your verse, ye begin the next verse with the same. . . . I call him the Redouble."[34] Donne establishes this pattern early on; in lines 2 and 3, the repeated terms are *now* and *death*, reinforcing both the centrality and immediacy of the speaker's decay. But while these early examples are relatively concrete, in line 8, Donne uses the more ambiguous *it*. "By sinne in it, which it t'wards Hell doth weigh." The reader is then forced to choose which of the preceding nouns best fits the term. *Death*, in line 6, seems at first the most logical antecedent and has been the one most often chosen by critics. This renders the line, roughly, "my feebled flesh wastes by sin in death, and death weighs me towards hell." Donne's sentiment and structure echo Paul's declaration that "the wages of sin is death; but the gift of God is eternal life."[35]

But while *death* is one option here, it is not the only one. *Terror*, in the beginning of line 7, presents another (closer) candidate for the first *it* of line 8. Additionally, while the anadiplosis of the early lines predisposes readers to choose the same referent for both instances of *it*, that choice is by no means obligatory. We might instead read the line in tandem with the line above it as "my feebled flesh wastes by sin in *terror*, which weighs *my flesh* towards hell." Rather than the body decaying through sin into death (the traditional

Pauline construction), the fear of that demise now becomes the primary threat to salvation.[36] Donne strategically places this ambivalent moment at the *volta*, allowing these two readings of line 8 to be complementary rather than exclusive. The first reading, using *death*, looks back on the octave and its moralized notion of decay where the corruption of the flesh is a mark of sinfulness. The second reading, however, looks forward to the sestet and the sonnet's resolution. It declares that the fault is not in decaying but in the fear of decay, a common sentiment across early modern *artes moriendi*. The poet's damnation is not therefore predestined but instead contingent upon his ability to regard mortality with acceptance rather than fear. This recognition shifts the speaker's momentum, changing the poem's entire direction. While the octave is marked with downcast eyes and downward motion, the sestet directs the reader upward. The poet now "can look, [can] rise again." This shift anticipates his resurrection, transforming earlier anxieties about mortality into a celebration of this new state of existence. By renouncing the fear of death and redirecting his energies toward the adoration of God, poet and poem ascend, a resurrection brought about not by a resistance to decay but by its acceptance.

Dissolution and Resurrection

While the resurrection Donne explores in this sonnet is primarily spiritual—drawing nearer to God, turning away from sinfulness—this moment gestures more broadly at the logical end of this conceit of decay: a theology of bodily resurrection. If lyric has the miraculous power to disassemble the body and explore its potential for intimacy, as these poems suggest, then it is also a useful tool for exploring how that body might be reassembled. Donne's theological writing, particularly his sermons, grapple with the physical reality of decomposition and the real consequences that material destruction might have on one's spiritual future. As discussed in the previous chapter, Donne was among the seventeenth-century metaphysical poets who turned to bodily resurrection as a way of exploring the affordances of lyric. For Donne in particular, this manifests as a markedly embodied perspective on spirituality. Donne's sermons, Carey points out, are deeply concerned with the body's role in achieving spiritual knowledge. "The human body is densely present" in Donne's sermonizing, he writes, "even when it is being disparaged, and even which Donne is supposed to be talking about something quite unphysical. The soul, he tells us, 'hath Bones, as well as the body.'"[37] Gil, in his account of Donne's theology, argues that while Donne sometimes endorsed dualist accounts of the soul's separation from the body, he also continually returned to monist sentiments that centered the material self. "Donne's writing is marked by an inability to turn away from the body," Gil writes, "and Donne values the body for its ability to make him question and rethink the nature of selfhood."[38] This is not just an inability, but a refusal: Donne returns to the body because, for him, the body is what makes spiritual knowledge possible—even in its decay. That is nowhere clearer than on Donne's writing about death and resurrection, subjects that raise these questions to their highest stakes.

In the spring of 1620, Donne preached a sermon on Job 19:26, a verse central to early modern debates about resurrection. In this verse, Job, after raging at God's apparent abandonment, looks to the final judgment and his subsequent resurrection for evidence of God's promise. He declares, "For I know that my redeemer liveth and that he shall stand at the latter day upon the earth: And though after my skin worms destroy this body, yet in my flesh shall I see God: Whom I shall see for myself, and mine eyes shall behold, and not another; though my reins be consumed within me."[39] Job's insistence on seeing for himself suggested to Donne and his contemporaries that the experience of the rapture must be physical. The body lost to death would be reassembled so that the faithful may experience divinity in both body and spirit. "*Ego*, I, I the same body, and the same soul, shall be recompact again," Donne writes in this sermon, echoing line 32 of "A Valediction of My Name in the Window." The resurrected body, he argues, will be "identically, numerically, individually the same man. The same integrity of body, and soul, and the same integrity in the Organs of my body, and in the faculties of my soul too; I shall all be there, my body, and my soul, and all my body, and all my soul."[40] For Donne, to be *all* there—to be fully present with God in eternity—means being there as an embodied self.

But bodily presence at the resurrection means that the utter dissolution of the body in decomposition had to somehow be undone. In this particular sermon, much of Donne's imaginative energies are directed toward the material reality of decay and the details of putrefaction; he wrestles with how those might be reconciled with the possibilities of bodily resurrection. As Bynum argues, one of the central philosophical struggles of early Christianity was how to reconcile the belief in eternal life with the ever-present reality of the body's destruction. More than anything, Bynum notes, early Christians insisted on the persistence of an embodied self. This belief "showed remarkable persistence even where it seemed almost to require philosophical incoherence, theological equivocation, or aesthetic offensiveness. . . . The materialism of this eschatology expressed not body-soul dualism but rather a sense of self as psychosomatic unity. The idea of person, bequeathed by the Middle Ages to the modern world, was not a concept of soul escaping body or soul using body; it was a concept of self in which physicality was integrally bound to sensation, emotion, reasoning, identity—and therefore finally to whatever one means by salvation."[41] While this persistent sense of embodiment offered many benefits—as Bynum points out, the endurance of things like pleasure and affect—the consequence was that the dissolution experienced by the body in the space between death and resurrection was then also an injury to the self as a whole. In this sermon, Donne wrestles with the question of how to reconcile embodied identity with decay. "When of the whole body there is neither eye nor ear, nor any member left, where is the body?" Donne asks. "And what should an eye do there, where there is nothing to be seen but loathsomenesse; or a nose there, where there is nothing to be smelt, but putrefaction; or an ear, where in the grave they doe not praise God?"[42] The whole "skinne and body, beauty and substance must be destroy'd," Donne writes; "destroyed by wormes."[43] For the body Donne so loved in life to be eradicated—the body that formed such a profound part of his identity—opens up the potential for horror, anxiety, and revulsion.

But while potentially horrific, this destruction, Donne suggests, is also an opportunity for generation. Reflecting on Paul's seed metaphor, discussed in the previous chapter, Donne imagines the resurrection following all this dissolution. "If thou hadst seen the bodies of men rise out of the grave, at Christs Resurrection, could that be a stranger thing" he writes, than "to see an Oake that spreads so farre, rise out of an Akorne? Or if Churchyards did vent themselves every spring, and that there were such a Resurrection of bodies every yeare . . . the Resurrection would be no stranger to thee, than the spring is."[44] Like Paul, Donne compares the bodies of the dead to seeds, objects that, through their dissolution and destruction, eventually give rise to new life. But Donne takes this metaphor one step further. If the body is like a seed, he muses, then it is also like its own seed.[45] In one of the sermon's most evocative moments, Donne observes that "between that excrementall jelly that thy body is made of at first, and that jelly which thy body dissolves to at last; there is not so noysome, so putrid a thing in nature. This skinne, (this outward beauty) this body, (this whole constitution) must be destroyed, says Job."[46] Carey notes that Donne's suggestion that "decayed flesh is as runny as human sperm, and that human sperm is as disgusting as decayed flesh" does not shy away from the horror one might feel at the dissolution of the body.[47] Both corpse and sperm are, as Donne describes them, excremental, instances of liminal corporeality that evoke feelings of disgust and horror.[48]

But while both flesh and sperm carry with them a sense of revulsion, for Donne, both also offer a sense of material potentiality. They are the fluid matter from which something greater can be created. In *Deaths Duell*, Donne returns to the comparison between death and the materials of reproduction. There, he compares the space of the womb to a sepulcher: "Our very birth and entrance into this life, is *exitus à morte*, an issue from death," Donne writes, "for in our mothers wombe wee are dead so, as that wee doe not know wee live, not so much as wee doe in our sleepe, neither is there any grave so close, or so putrid a prison, as the wombe would be unto us, if we stayed in it beyond our time, or dyed there before our time."[49] He continues, "Wee have a winding sheete in our Mothers wombe…which growes with us from our conception, and wee come into the world, wound up in that winding sheet, for wee come to seeke a grave."[50] The amniotic sac becomes a type of the funeral shroud to come, a physical manifestation of death at birth. Donne is not the first or only early modern author to link birth and death in this way, of course. As discussed in the previous chapter, many *ars moriendi* texts explicitly compared death with birth to help their readers understand death's relationship with time. Sutton, for instance, in *Disce Mori*, paraphrases Ecclesiastes 3, telling his readers, "As we had a time to be born, so have we a time to die. And our way to enter into life is first to pass the pinching griefs of a momentary death."[51] Even Donne's use of the *womb/tomb* rhyming pair borrows from convention—these two were a frequent combination in verse across schools and style, bordering on the formulaic.[52] He draws on these established associations to reinforce the connection between death and reproduction, between the act of dying and the process of being created again. While death was an unmaking, it also contained the potential for a very real material remaking. The body destroyed was, for Donne, the body reborn.

However, Donne adopts these commonplace comparisons to his own specific ends, arguing that death and reproduction are linked not despite decay but because of it. This is clearest in his treatment of another common anxiety surrounding decay: the problem of cannibalism. Bynum notes that early theologies of bodily resurrection often focused on the logical paradox of cannibalism. If a theory of resurrection relied on the persistence of a unique, materially identical body across time, then the treatment of the dissolved or scattered bodies of the dead caused great concern. Because of this, Bynum writes, many theologians began to focus on the thought experiment of cannibalism: What would happen if the remains of one dead body were eaten, digested, and incorporated into the body of another living person? "If meat and drink do not merely pass through us but become us, there will be too much matter for God to reassemble," she writes; "if people really eat other people, even God may have trouble sorting out the particles."[53] Early church leaders saw this radical material conflation between bodies, facilitated by decomposition, as a threat to individualism. As Bynum notes, this thought experiment forced theologians to evaluate the absolute limits of embodied identity; in order to raise an individual body at the day of resurrection, one must be able to define where one body ends and the next begins. In *Deaths Duell*, Donne adapts this same anxiety to a new, eroticized register. "Miserable riddle," he writes, "when the same worme must bee my mother, and my sister, and my selfe. Miserable incest, when I must bee maried to my own mother and my sister, and bee both father and mother to my owne mother and sister, beget and beare that worme which is all that miserable penury."[54] The worms ingest and intermix the graves' occupants, resulting in a horrific conglomeration. All sense of the individual is lost, and the dead are left in a sexualized and indeterminate mass.

Here, decay's ability to facilitate intimacy blurs into the horrific. Moments such as this have led many to pronounce Donne an ardent individualist. Targoff, for instance, sees in Donne a fervent, almost obsessive desire to remain an individual even after death. He expresses a "desire for absolute continuity between his earthly and his heavenly self," she writes. "Donne worries about how he will remain in his afterlife the person he currently is. He worries that his soul will not locate all the parts of his flesh at the last day, and that he will end up incomplete. He worries that the mere substitution of someone else's knee bone or joint will undo the integrity of the self that he treasures."[55] But while it might be tempting to read this description of the taboo intimacies of decay as genuine horror, it is more likely an example of what Gil describes as Donne's strategic defamiliarization. Donne's preaching would frequently "force his audience to engage with the strangeness of the body," Gil writes, "often in ways that are rhetorically *in excess* of whatever pastoral or theological point Donne might be trying to make."[56] Donne's approach here highlights just such an excessiveness, inviting the listener to imagine the wild possibilities of a dissolving body. And through the performance of his preaching, such moments of excess ultimately reinforce the centrality of the body in his theology. Immediately following his discussion of the dangerous intermingling of decay, Donne reframes the pseudo-incest of vermiculation. "This death of incineration and dispersion, is, to naturall reason, the most irrecoverable death of all," he writes, "and yet . . . by recompacting this dust into the same body, and reanimating the same body with the same soule, [God] shall in a blessed and glorious resurrection give mee such an issue from this death, as shal never passe into any other death, but establish me into a life that shall last as long as the Lord of life himself."[57] The *and yet* of Donne's transition here is telling—even given the most extreme and horrific consequence, the taboo intermingling of bodies, decay's salvific potential greatly outweighs such danger. While Donne does not deny the transgressive potential of decay, he reframes it; his intense and horrific account of the "miserable riddle" of decay provides the rhetorical extreme against which the more likely and significantly more positive outcome can be understood.

That outcome, Donne goes on to explain, is radical intimacy not between individual and individual but between human and divine, with decomposition leading to the body's ultimate regeneration. Like the Pauline seed, the matter of the body remains constant while at the same time being transformed. Resurrection, Donne argues, opens up the body for a state of material interconnectedness with the world. While that risks the danger of mingling with other bodies, it also implies the potential for mingling with the divine. In his sermon on Job, Donne explains that the resurrected bodies of the faithful have in them a new capacity for communion with God made possible by this reformed materiality.

> But, in heaven, it is *Caro mea*, My flesh, my souls flesh, my Saviours flesh. As my meat is assimilated to my flesh, and made one flesh with it; as my soul is assimilated to my God, and *made partaker of the divine nature*, and *Idem spiritus*, the same Spirit with it; so, there my flesh shall be assimilated to the flesh of my Saviour, and made the same flesh with him too. *Verbum caro factum, ut caro resurgeret;* Therefore the Word was made flesh, therefore God was made man, that that union might exalt the flesh of man to the right hand of God. That's spoken of the flesh of Christ; and then to facilitate the passage for us, *Reformat ad immortalitatem suam participes sui;* those who are worthy receivers of his flesh here, are the same flesh with him.[58]

Describing the union between human and divine, Donne echoes the language of the Church of England's marriage rites. Having blessed the couple, the priest reminds the congregants that the ideal marriage is modeled after Christ's union with the Church: earthly marriages "signif[y] and represent[] the spiritual mariage and unitie betwixte Christe and his Churche: Loke mercifully upon these thy servauntes, that both this man may love his wife, according to thy worde (as Christe did love his spouse the Churche, who gave hymselfe for it, lovyng and cherishyng it, even as his owne fleshe)."[59] Donne uses this model of marriage to imagine the connection forged between individual and divine at the moment of resurrection. Like a consummated marriage, the union between God and human is rooted in the body. The spirit of the resurrected individual is joined with God's, and their flesh is made one with the flesh of the divine. That same flesh that throughout these sermons has been marked by its decay becomes the vehicle through which that final union is achieved. Only through its destruction and dissolution can that physical body be remade in this act of holy consummation.

The intimacy and the divinity of this union are so profound, Donne writes, that they are comparable to the hypostatic union between the aspects of Christ's person. "When after my skinne worms shall destroy my body," he writes, "I shall see God, I shall see him in my flesh, which shall be mine as inseparably, (in the effect, though not in the manner) as the Hypostaticall union of God, and man, in Christ, makes our nature and the Godhead one person in him. My flesh shall no more be none of mine, than Christ shall not be man, as well as God."[60] Donne exploits the ambiguity of the phrase from Job—reiterated here as "I shall see him in my flesh"—to underscore the double unity of the resurrected body. First, it is identical to the flesh of the living body; the body from which Donne will view God is Donne's own flesh, the body of his lifetime. Additionally, that same flesh is also linked inextricably with God. Donne will see God realized in God's own flesh, present in Donne's resurrected body. That link, he argues, emulates the connection between Christ's own human and divine selves. The hypostatic union, the theological principle explaining the coexistence of deity and humanity in one person, provides the model for Donne for the unification experienced by the resurrected body.

This state of divine intimacy, as Donne describes it, is the direct result of the body's decay. Only by decomposing and losing its individual material coherency can the body, like Paul's seed, be remade into something new, something unified with divine materiality. However, it is not simply that this destruction allows for the possibility of resurrection. In Donne's account, the dissolution of the body is required to achieve total salvation. In *Deaths Duell*, Donne dwells on another of Paul's writings that served as a touchstone for the church's doctrine on resurrection. In his letter to the Thessalonians, Paul explains to members of the early church what they should expect after their deaths. Early Christians anticipated the day of judgment would occur in their lifetimes, within a generation or two of Christ's resurrection. As the years wore on, however, devotees began to worry what would happen if they died before the second coming occurred. Here, Paul assures them that those who had already died would not be excluded from the kingdom of heaven but would be resurrected in a manner similar to Christ's.

> But I would not have you to be ignorant, brethren, concerning them which are asleep, that ye sorrow not, even as others which have no hope. For if we believe that Jesus died and rose again, even so them also which sleep in Jesus will God bring with him. For this we say unto you

by the word of the Lord, that we which are alive and remain unto the coming of the Lord shall not prevent them which are asleep. For the Lord himself shall descend from heaven with a shout, with the voice of the archangel, and with the trump of God: and the dead in Christ shall rise first: Then we which are alive and remain shall be caught up together with them in the clouds, to meet the Lord in the air: and so shall we ever be with the Lord.[61]

In this account of resurrection, the dead are privileged, allowed to rise first. Only then will the living join them and ascend together into heaven. Paul's account attempts to allay fears about death's permanence, assuring the faithful that dying would not constitute a barrier to salvation.

Donne's exegesis of this passage revises Paul, revealing more of his own resurrection theology in the process. Writing centuries after Paul's death, Donne is not speaking to an audience worried about dying prior to judgment day. Those sitting in the pews of St. Paul's knew that their ends—and, indeed, Donne's own imminent death—would almost inevitably come before Christ's return. Because of this, Donne can shift the focus of Paul's message to explore a more difficult question: What if, perhaps against all odds, those listening faced judgment not as the dead but as the living? How might their resurrections be affected if they had not already gone to be with God?

> (As the Apostle saies, and saies as a secret, as a mystery; behold I shew you a mystery) wee shall not all sleepe, (that is, not continue in the state of the dead in the grave,) but wee shall all be changed. In an instant we shall have a dissolution, and in the same instant a redintegration, a recompacting of body and soule, and that shall be truely a death and truely a resurrection, but no sleeping, no corruption; But for us that dye now and sleepe in the state of the dead, we must al passe this posthume death, this death after death, nay this death after buriall, this dissolution after dissolution, this death of corruption and putrifaction, of vermiculation and incineration, of dissolution in and dispersion from the grave.[62]

Even though those who have not died before the day of judgment will not "sleepe," they, too, will undergo a dissolution similar to that of the grave. While in Paul's account, those living are already suitable for resurrection in their living bodies, Donne adds the need for transformation through decomposition. Those who die prior to the second coming will endure the slow dissolution, the "corruption and putrifaction . . . vermiculation and incineration" of the body within the grave. But those still living are not exempt. In Donne's formulation, those who have not yet died must still endure a "dissolution," albeit an instantaneous one, in order to be prepared for resurrection. Both destruction and reconstruction become an essential step in the process of resurrection, allowing the body to be fully prepared to be "recompact[ed]" and unified with the divine.

Disability Theology

Drawing the metaphysical conceit of his secular lyrics forward into his sermons, Donne creates a theology of bodily resurrection that features, rather than excuses, the body's decay. Just as he imagines the lovers of "The Relique" or "A Valediction of My Name in the Window" finding total intimacy through the dissolution of their individual bodies, he sees the very real decay of his own body and the bodies of all the faithful as preparation for a future bodily union with God. Here, Donne departs from mainstream early modern theologies of embodiment. For many, the reality of the body's tendency toward dissolution was read as a sign of humanity's distance from God. In the Book of Common Prayer's burial orders, for instance, the liturgy called for the priest to recall Paul's letter to the Philippians, reminding those in attendance that they stood "in sure and certein hope of resurrection to eternal lyfe, throughe oure Lorde Jesus Christe, who shall change our vyle body that it may be lyke to his glorious body."[63] For Paul, and for the early modern English Church, that vileness was rooted in the body's materiality and thus in its decay. Death could be endured, then, because it offered the hope of dematerialization, the exchange of vileness for glory. This was both the threat and the promise, discussed in more detail in this book's first chapter, often levied by the memento mori tradition and the temptation toward asceticism and neglect rebuked by early modern *artes moriendi*.

For Donne, however, death and resurrection represented not an exchange but a transformation in and through the realities of decomposition in order to be joined with Christ. And while the role of the body in Donne's theology has been extensively acknowledged, the way he frames decay demands that we also think about this stance on resurrection as informed by disability, by an awareness of the body's openness to decay that does not regard that quality as morally corruptive. That this connection has remained almost entirely undiscussed so far is, in some ways, unsurprising. Theological studies, like many other fields in the humanities, has been slow to embrace disability theory. Deborah Beth Creamer notes, "Lacking an awareness of anything other than the medical model and physical issues of accessibility, theology has failed, for the most part, to engage the emerging field of disability studies either as a topic for examination or as a partner in conversation and theological reflection."[64] While some religious institutional bodies have begun the necessary work of improving access and accommodation, Creamer notes, studies of Protestant theology have been slow to seriously interrogate the aesthetic, theoretical, and theological questions raised by disability.

On the other hand, disability studies, particularly early modern disability studies, has begun to offer some account of the ways that early modern English theological reforms shaped the period's definitions of disability. Row-Heyveld notes that the Reformation's reevaluation of salvation and charity, for instance, had a significant impact on what it meant to be disabled. "Protestant Reformers often included personal almsgiving in their denunciation of Catholic excesses," she writes, "especially almsgiving's vital role in a theology of salvation contingent upon good works rather than upon *sola fide*, 'faith alone.'"[65] Early Protestants, therefore, began to view individuals who begged as potential sources of spiritual corruption, increasing the suspicions of dishonesty that began to accrue around disability. But while Row-Heyveld and others have explored the impact of theology on cultural narratives surrounding disability, comparatively little attention has been paid to disability's impact on early modern theology. Donne's theology of resurrection offers the opportunity to do just this—to explore not an early modern theology *of* disability but early modern disability theology, a model of understanding divinity centered around the decaying and disabled body.[66] The union Donne imagines between decay and resurrection lays out some of the foundational features of what such a theology might look like and provides scholars a framework for thinking about the as-yet-unexplored long history of disability theology.

First, Donne's theology of resurrection insists on the spiritual value of the decaying body, rejecting the notion that physical wholeness or ability is equated with divine perfection. For Donne, the body's decay was not a deviation from the norm but its realization. As Nancy Eiesland argues, a disability-centered theology "necessitates that the body be represented as flesh and blood, bones and braces, and not simply the rationalized realm of activity."[67] Donne foregrounds decay, placing the messy materiality of embodiment—blood, bones, and braces—at the heart of his vision of resurrection. And by insisting on the divinity of the decaying body, Donne crips divinity itself, imagining a God that is themself a reflection of that material existence. In her field-defining study, *The Disabled God*, Eiesland argues that the central and most essential work of disability theology must be arguing for the congruence of disability and divinity. Following the logic that humanity and the divine must be reflections of one another, creations in one another's image, Eiesland contends that the reality of disabled bodies and of disability in the body necessitates constructing a theology that imagines God as disabled. Eiesland argues that since "religious symbols not only prescribe or reproduce social status, but . . . also transform it," adopting a new symbolic language for divinity is essential for disability justice. "Changing the symbol of Christ, from that of suffering servant, model of virtuous suffering, or conquering lord, toward a formulation of Jesus Christ as disabled God," she writes, would necessitate "constitutive change and the creation of new symbols and rituals whereby people with disabilities can affirm our bodies in dignity and reconceive the church as community of justice for people with disabilities."[68] A new symbolic language for the divine, Eiesland argues, makes divinity accessible to marginalized groups and identities. Able-bodied individuals may resist or push back against such a theology, she notes, because to do so means "to become known to themselves as their actually existing bodies." However, "breaking the silence about their real lives as bodies makes possible a 'return to the body'—a positive body awareness that comes not from pursuing an ideal but accepting the reality that bodies evolve, become ill and disabled, and die."[69] Donne's embodied poetics consistently perform this return to the body, always insisting that the physical self is the bedrock upon which all else is built. "Loves mysteries in soules doe grow" (71) Donne writes in "The Extasie," "but yet the body is his booke" (72). Gil notes that "Donne, always, wants to feel God—and find evidence of God—in his bodily experiences, and even in the most unpleasant ones."[70] Perhaps not "even" but "especially"—Donne finds evidence of God *especially* in the pain of aging, sickness, or death. Decay is reimagined as the mark of divinity rather than a sign of its absence.

The next major feature of Donne's disability theology is the central role of interdependence. Donne's insistence that all relationships—erotic, romantic, platonic, and spiritual—thrive on intimacy rejects individualism in favor of radical mutual reliance. The ideal self, defined by decay, is necessarily permeable, open to connection with the world around it. Eiesland argues that disability theology "debunks the myth of individualism and hierarchical orders, in which transcendence means breaking free of encumbrances and needing nobody."[71] Such a theology rejects the notion of independence, instead prioritizing connection with and reliance upon others as the highest realization of the self. This is, in part, an extension of the vision of embodiment at the center of disability theology. John Swinton notes that disability theology helps reframe instances of physical, social, mental, and emotional dependence from being "indicative of lives that are incompatible with being fully in God's image" to illuminating of the "dimensions of God which have been hidden by our culture's preference for such things as power, strength, and intellectual prowess."[72] The need for help and the inability to exist without external support are reframed as the ability to live communally by embracing the social, physical, and emotional entanglement of all beings. For Donne, the body's decay becomes a reminder of the wonderful permeability of selfhood. Whether erotic or spiritual (or erotic and spiritual), Donne's writing seems to relish the notion of an interdependent cosmos where body merges with body and soul with soul. There seems nothing more abhorrent, for Donne, than the idea of being alone; there seems nothing more wonderful, conversely, than the idea of being open to communion with others. The conceit of a body fundamentally fluid and porous invites Donne's readers to think about an interdependent creation in which salvation is equated with the joining of bodies and the divine.

Lastly, Donne is able to imagine disability theology through his deep investment in the work of metaphor, recognizing that literary forms indelibly shape the values and priorities of an ideology. While the reliance on metaphor, particularly the metaphysical conceit, is perhaps unsurprising in the lyric works, Donne is insistent on the important work of metaphor in creating theology. As Sallie McFague argues, the metaphor is the most fundamental, constitutive form of theological language. "Far from being an esoteric or ornamental rhetorical device," McFague writes, "metaphor *is* ordinary language. It is the *way* we think."[73] Because of that, she observes, "religious metaphorical statements are so powerful [because] they are in continuity with the way we think ordinarily. We are not usually conscious of the metaphorical character of our thought, of seeing 'this' in terms of 'that,' of finding the thread of similarity amid dissimilars, but it is the only way a child's world can be constructed or our worlds expanded and transformed."[74] As discussed earlier, Donne often approaches intimacy through the lens of the divine mystery, a theological truth so complex that it cannot be rationally comprehended. The only way of accessing this truth is through signs: the sign of the hair bracelet, wound about the bone, the sign of the lover's name inscribed into the window. Donne affirms that it is sometimes only through metaphor that the most profound theological truths can be accessed. This relationship is, like so many of those at the heart of this book, dependent on the connections between form and content; the theological essence is brought to life in the metaphor, dependent on imagistic and indirect language to bring these truths into being. Mystery shapes metaphor, which in turn shapes the mystery. For a theologian like Eiesland, this means that replacing ableist metaphors for God with disabled ones can fundamentally reshape the nature of divinity. Disability theology, she argues, "must create new images of wholeness" that incorporate the reality of the body; it must, in short, find new metaphors for the mystery of divinity that include, and indeed center, disability.[75]

And nowhere in the history of theology has figurative language played a more central role than in the long debates about bodily resurrection. Bynum notes that explanations of what happened to the body and precisely how it would change after death were always wrapped in the language of metaphor. Theologians have imagined resurrection, Bynum writes, "as the flowering of a dry tree after winter, the donning of new clothes, the rebuilding of a temple, the hatching of an egg, the smelting out of ore from clay, the reforging of a statue that has been melted down, the growth of the fetus from a drop of semen, the return of the phoenix from its own ashes, the reassembling of broken potsherds, [or] the vomiting up of bits of shipwrecked bodies by fishes that have consumed them."[76] Donne's images of decay add to this long catalog: resurrection is the intimacy to be found in the marriage bed or the shared grave, a scene of intense consummation and pleasure. The image born out of the secular lyrics, in which the decomposition of bodies leads to the eradication of the boundaries between them, bleeds over to ultimately shape a theology of resurrection that embraces the dissolution of the body. It is Donne's recognition of the potential of lyric to shape reality—to speak to the embodied self—that allows him, ultimately, to imagine these theological possibilities. Donne's thinking anticipates contemporary disability theology and provides a framework for what it might look like to imagine this work in the early modern period. While Donne certainly would not have had the vocabulary of disability justice, his inclusion of the body's decay in his resurrection theology—and the formal strategies by which he enacts that inclusion—nonetheless offers a glimpse at the wide range of possibilities in the period. Early modern disability studies has, on the whole, taken existing accounts of Reformation theology at face value. But, as Donne's work illustrates, early modern theologies of embodiment merit more sustained exploration and ambitious methodological frameworks and have the potential to reveal a host of new possibilities.

Across Donne's works, decay responds to the limitations of the material world. Lovers kept separate by place, time, or the impermeable spheres of their own bodies are brought together to a degree impossible outside the world of the poems. True intimacy, the eradication of all boundaries, is available only via decay. And lyric, for Donne, is the only thing that can do what decay does. It can create union out of absence, connection out of destruction; it builds an imaginative space in which isolation is transformed into intimacy. Sidney, a few decades before Donne, calls poetry "the maker." "Only the poet," he writes, "disdaining to be tied to any such subjection, lifted up with the vigour of his own invention, doth grow in effect another nature, in making things either better than nature bringeth forth, or, quite anew, forms such as never were in nature, as the Heroes, Demigods, Cyclops, Chimeras, Furies, and such like."[77] Susan Stewart echoes this, noting that lyric's task, above all else, is to create meaning and connection out of nothingness, to give form to the dark void of the space between us. And in doing so, she argues, lyric—like Donne's conceit of decay—allows for connection between individuals. The language of lyric is "not simply intimate," she writes; "it is constitutive of the social, mutual, intersubjective ground of intimacy itself. It is the kind of thing one knows others say when they are face-to-face."[78] Donne, perhaps more than any of his peers, sees in lyric the potential for creating the sense of connectedness he so desires—connection with others, with God, with the world itself. In expostulation 19 of the *Devotions*, as Donne believed himself to be approaching his own death, he cries out to God.

> My god, my God, thou are a direct God, may I not say a literal God, a God that wouldst be understood literally and according to the plain sense of all thou sayest? But thou art also (Lord, I intend it to thy glory, and let no profane misinterpreter abuse it to thy diminution), thou art a figurative, a metaphorical God too; a God in whose words there is such a height of figures, such voyages, such peregrinations to fetch remote and precious metaphors, such extensions, such spreadings, such curtains of allegories, such third heavens of hyperboles, so harmonious elocutions, so retired and so reserved expressions, so commanding persuasions, so persuading commandments, such sinews even in thy milk, and such things in thy words. . . . Neither art thou thus a figurative, a metaphorical God in thy word only, but in thy works too. The style of thy works, the phrase of thine actions, is metaphorical.[79]

Donne's poetics themselves, his views on what lyric can accomplish—nothing short of the miraculous—shape the very heart of his theology. Donne's God is, indeed, a metaphorical god, and the transformations possible through faith are the work of lyric mystery.

Epilogue
Not Alone

> In the time of Plague, Sweat, or such other like contagious times of sickness, or diseases, when none of the Parish or neighbors can be gotten to communicate with the sick in their houses, for fear of the infection, upon special request of the diseased, the Minister may only communicate with him.
>
> —"The Communion of the Sick," Book of Common Prayer (1559)

> You could not come to me
> so instead I set out for you
> these lines. Because the lungs
> and breath and tongue had all
> come under doubt, I wrote
> it down.
>
> —Dave Lucas, "Quarantine" (2020)

The spring of 2020 brought a new generation of readers to Donne's *Devotions*. On March 11 of that year, the World Health Organization officially declared COVID-19 a global pandemic.[1] Much of the United Kingdom and United States moved into lockdown, with residents remaining isolated at home in an attempt to slow the spread of the virus. Suddenly alone and frightened, many found themselves newly drawn to Donne's account of his own illness and isolation, particularly Devotion 17. For Donne, it was the winter of 1623. Bedridden by illness and expecting to die, he lay listening to the parish bells ring in the distance, announcing the death of some other unlucky Londoner. That first spring of the pandemic, those of us living through lockdown found ourselves in a similar situation: hearing the distant echo of ambulance sirens, wondering which of our neighbors those bells might be tolling for. For Donne, the knowledge that someone else had died did not inspire any feelings of relief at being spared. Instead, he began to feel that the death of another was inextricably tied to his own.

> No man is an island, entire of itself; every man is a piece of the continent, a part of the main. If a clod be washed away by the sea, Europe is the less, as well as if a promontory were, as well as if a manor of thy friend's or of thine own were: any man's death diminishes me, because I am involved in mankind, and therefore never send to know for whom the bell tolls; it tolls for thee.[2]

While Donne invokes the logic of the memento mori in the devotion's opening—*"this bell tolling softly for another, says to me: Thou must die"*—the relationship he describes here goes beyond the mnemonic.[3] For Donne, the death of another *was* the death of part of himself, a tear in the fabric of humanity. The intimacy that he so closely associates with decay cuts both ways, offering the potential not only to feel transcendent pleasure but also, as he seems to realize here, to experience profound communal loss.

For Donne and other early modern Christians, this was not merely a philosophical or theoretical belief. Death was, practically speaking, a communal action. The period's many *artes moriendi* imagine the deathbed as an important social and spiritual center where friends and family would gather around the dying. Becon's *Sick Man's Salve*, for instance, is centered around the long dialogue between the dying Epaphroditus and his neighbors, who offer advice, scripture, and comfort. Taylor's *Holy Dying* announces on its title page that it will provide "Prayers and Acts of Virtue to be used by sick and dying persons, or by others standing in their Attendance, to which are added Rules for the visitation of the Sick, and offices proper for that Ministry."[4] Taylor's treatise goes on to provide several chapters of guidance and instruction for how best to support the dying. Sutton—who, like Taylor, offers a number of scripts for communal prayer at the deathbed—argues in *Disce Mori* that gathering around the deathbed was an act of not just physical but spiritual care. "There is nothing which the sick in these extremities do more desire against the natural terrors of death," he writes, "than direction and comfort. For if he may be called a friend that is diligent about a sick person to minister things necessary for his body which shall shortly be dissolved, much more he is called a true and faithful friend that is diligent about a sick person to minister things necessary for his soul, which shall never die but live eternally."[5]

These gatherings are especially significant when we consider what they were not doing. While communal support at the deathbed also featured in the earliest Catholic *artes moriendi*, these gatherings served an instrumental spiritual function in that context: Friends were there to offer intercessory prayer on behalf of the dying. These prayers, early authors argued, could make all the difference in salvation and so were essential to lessen the suffering of the dying, even after death. Post-Reformation, however, such interventions were (at least officially) no longer possible. The advice given by Sutton and others, then, had to walk a fine theological line: Without suggesting that the community gathered was necessary for salvation or that the support offered by witnesses could materially affect God's will or the fate of the dying, these authors nonetheless stressed the absolute importance of dying in community. In part, Vinter notes, these later Protestant treatises flipped the script, focusing on the spiritual benefits experienced not by the dying but by those gathered around the bedside. Vinter writes, "Early modern *artes moriendi* generally assume, or try to simulate, a communal deathbed extending benefits to witnesses as well as the dying person."[6] Being present for a death, particularly a good death, might help those in attendance die well themselves someday, with good deaths inspiring future good deaths.

But these gatherings also offered a benefit that went beyond individual spiritual growth. If, as Donne suggests, every individual death is a loss to the collective, then it is the community itself as a collective that also needs care in these moments. Sociologists of ritual, beginning with Arnold Van Gennep, have argued that our actions surrounding death provide an important script for the community to refashion itself in the wake of a loss. Van Gennep notes that rites of passage—rituals designed to facilitate the movement of an individual from one social role into another—generally reflect three kinds of changes: rites of separation, rites of transition, and rites of incorporation.[7] Death offers a prime example of these transformations—not just for the individual but for the community as a whole. Van Gennep writes, "It is a transitional period for the survivors, and they enter it through rites of separation and emerge from it through rites of reintegration into society."[8] Gathering around the deathbed to bear witness involves the important work of both transitioning the dying out of community and of remaking the community in their absence, "in the same way that a chain which has been broken by the disappearance of one of its links must be rejoined."[9] These deathbed gatherings serve such an instrumental role in communal identity that they have persisted in English culture through to the present day. Glenys Caswell argues that the accounts of dying in community that defined late medieval and early modern *artes moriendi* have, over time, been reinforced and repeated often enough to accrue the weight of a core Anglo-American cultural script. Now, Caswell writes, the good death has come to be defined as "one where the dying person is accompanied by the people who care about them, as well as being at home and free of negative symptoms. The corollary to this is that an unaccompanied death is not a good one and may, indeed, even be a bad one."[10] Even in purely secular settings—cases where there is no definable spiritual benefit for either the dead or the living—the idea that we should not die alone remains fixed.

But for hundreds of thousands of individuals in the early months of the COVID-19 pandemic, dying alone was the only option. A combination of high contagion rates and the absence of a working vaccine, compounded by flagging health care systems and a widespread shortage of personal protective equipment, led hospitals across the United Kingdom and the United States to set strict visitation policies, barring family members from being present at the bedsides of the dying. A team of surgeons at the University of Michigan, reflecting on their experience providing patient care during this time, wrote that families' deep-seated desire to be present with a loved one while they died had now "become an ethical and health care dilemma."[11] The cultural taboo against dying alone runs so deep, in fact, that even in the midst of an overwhelming epidemiological crisis, medical providers still prioritized family presence with the dying. "We have witnessed more death in the past 3 weeks than in all our previous years combined," the surgeons note. "There may be no way for families to hold patients' hands or hug them while they're dying, but with the care and compassion of frontline health care workers, maybe we can harness creative solutions to help them feel some connection, while still keeping everyone safe."[12] Doctors and nurses cobbled together makeshift remote access for families where they could—phones and tablets, propped by hospital bedsides, allowed families to bear witness from a distance. In the absence of physical presence, these caregivers turned to technologies—to *techne*, to tools of whatever sort—to help recreate a sense of communal identity.

The years of the COVID-19 pandemic were in large part shaped by a search for other ways to make connection possible in the face of isolation, ways to die and live together even when many were most alone. Mia Mingus, disability justice activist, argues, "We should be framing this pandemic in terms of interdependence." She continues, "Interdependence acknowledges that our survival is bound up together, that we are interconnected and what you do impacts others. . . . Interdependence is the only way out of most of the most pressing issues we face today."[13] COVID-19 revealed the paradox (one already very familiar to many members of the disabled community) that interdependence is both a danger and an asset, a reliance on one another for worse and, more so, for better. Eve Feder Kittay argues that all individuals, regardless of disability, must abandon "the fiction that as self-determining and self-sufficient agents we can take or leave [a] cooperative arrangement" of existence. Instead, she writes, "to insist on our inextricable interdependence is to say that no matter what social arrangements we enter into on a voluntaristic basis, the fact is that we must be engaged in *some* social arrangements, some forms of dependence; interdependence is not a matter of voluntarism."[14] Importantly, Kittay and others note, mutual dependency is not counter but in fact essential to individual independence. Relying on others for help does not disempower us, she argues; in fact, it is by relying on others that we are most empowered to act as ourselves. During the early months of COVID-19, the need for interdependence was perhaps most tangible and material. The adoption of an interdependent approach to community meant that many more individuals found themselves relying on neighbors and friends, often through grassroots mutual aid efforts, for necessities like food, shelter, or money. But interdependence also goes beyond material needs. As Mingus argues, truly embracing interdependence means fostering a deeper sense of imagined community—the felt and understood entanglement with others, even in their absence.

And while early modern readers might not have had a vocabulary of disability justice or interdependence to describe this value, *ars moriendi* texts bear out these lessons: that the dying and those around them needed to understand themselves as members of a collective and that disability offered the best framework for understanding how one might do that. In Perkins's *A Salve for a Sicke Man*, he tells readers that the dying should look to their neighbors for spiritual and emotional support, a lesson rooted in Luke's account of the paralyzed man being brought to Jesus for healing by his friends.

> When the man that was sick of the dead palsy could not go to Christ himself, he got others to bear him in his bed; & when they could not come near for the multitude, they uncovered the roof of the house, and let the bed down before Christ: even so, when sick men cannot alone by themselves doe the good duties to which they are bound, they must borrow help from their fellow members; who are partly by their counsel to put to their helping hand, & partly by their prayers to present them unto God, and to bring them into the presence of Christ.[15]

Like the friends of the paralytic, the friends of the dying are called to mobilize their spiritual, emotional, and even physical support to help make a good death possible. Donne, too, had the story of the paralyzed man in mind while writing the *Devotions*. In Devotion 4, he argues that seeking medical treatment was not antithetical to having faith in God's healing powers. He writes, "I send for the Physician, but I will hear him enter with these words of Peter, *Jesus Christ maketh thee whole*; I long for his presence, but I look that the power of the Lord should be present to heal me."[16] Donne paraphrases the first verse of Luke's account of the paralyzed man (5:17, "the power of the Lord was present to heal them"), choosing a biblical model for care that foregrounds both miraculous intervention and the instrumental role of community in healing. Like Perkins, Donne emphasizes that though the friends of the dying might not be able to intervene in the act of salvation, they still have an integral role to play in forging a sense of connection—between the dying and the living but also between humanity and the divine.

As Donne's *Devotions* and the other early modern *artes moriendi* emphasize the need for communal consciousness, they also point to the literary form best suited to bring that consciousness into being: prayer.[17] In fact, prayer is so ubiquitous in these works that it has gone mostly unacknowledged, taken as a given. In Donne's *Devotions*, for instance, he ends each with a personal prayer, scripting his cries to God in the face of what feels like imminent death. Other *ars moriendi* treatises offer readers more adaptable or universal forms, providing prayers for common deathbed scenarios. Sutton, for instance, includes "A prayer to be used by the assembly at the time of the Christian man's departure" and "A prayer to be used of any, who finds himself troubled in conscience, or disquieted by evil motions."[18] Taylor gives, among others, a prayer "to be said by or in behalf of people in their danger or near their death" and "A prayer to be said in the case of a sudden surprise by death, as by a mortal wound, or evil accidents in childbirth, when the forms and solemnities of preparation cannot be used."[19] Again, these prayers (at least officially) served no intercessory purpose; these were not charms or petitions designed to change the fate of the dead or sway the mind of God. Instead, they were linguistic frameworks that shaped the reality of death—language scripted for repeated performance, words offered to give shape and structure to the confused mass of emotions and experiences that might emanate from the deathbed. They were, in short, literary forms.

More specifically, prayer is—or, at the very least, can be—a lyric form. Jahan Ramazani notes that while scholars have "shied away from the similarities between poetic apostrophe and the rhetorical structure of prayer," these modes of address share crucial formal features that merit deeper consideration.[20] "Poetry and prayer function simultaneously as acts of address," he writes, "and as forms of meta-address, or images of voicing, because of the decontextualization of address from normal lines of human communication."[21] In both prayer and in lyric, the speaker cries out to those not present and, in return, must wrestle with the echo of their own unanswered voice.

This affinity between lyric and prayer, particularly collective prayer, has not always been acknowledged by literary critics. For many years, early modern scholars argued that private devotional lyric and collective liturgical prayer were antithetical expressions of faith, the one personal and spontaneous (and deeply Protestant), the other conformist and scripted (and suspiciously Catholic). However, as Targoff and others argue, this dichotomy fails to hold up under scrutiny. "Once we remove ourselves from our prejudices against liturgical language as artificial or insincere," Targoff writes, "we can begin to see that what inspired many of the Protestant lyrics we most admire can be traced to the language used in the established church."[22] Poets like Donne and Herbert, she argues, freely move between these modes, allowing the language of communal prayer to shape their lyric imaginations.

And just as lyric draws on the language of prayer, so, too, does prayer learn from lyric, borrowing those features that work to recreate the sense of connection embodied in the community gathered around the deathbed. As I argue throughout this book, lyric offers the promise of alternate relationships with time: the ability to be still, or to be present, or to move outside or against the flow of objective linear time. The collective prayer shares what Roland Greene describes as the ritual dimension of lyric, the ability of a text to invite a reader into "a timeless, infinitely repeatable act" through which they might achieve "an experiential unity with some subset of [their] culture."[23] Reciting the prayers for the dying means entering into an annunciative present—"the 'now' of articulation," in Stewart's description—shared by the many who have read those words in the past and who will read those words again in the future.[24] It is, in fact, the iterability of the form that communicates its comfort. Prayer, like lyric, offers the ability to imagine the many voices spread across history now joined in the great collective that Donne envisions, all folding together into the present moment and reminding the reader that they are not alone.

And through this temporal presence, prayer, like lyric, imagines—might even create—a sense of physical presence, even when that is explicitly impossible. The poets discussed in this book often envision in their works not only a now but a here. Pulter, for instance, imagines her verse, like her death, as a kind of interstellar transport, enabling her to move above and beyond the country estate where she was rooted.

> For I no liberty expect to see
> Until to atoms I dispersèd be;
> Then, being enfranchised, free as my verse,

> I shall surround this spacious universe,
> Until, by other atoms thrust and hurled,
> We give a being to another world.[25]

Free as her verse, Pulter, without leaving her home, moves across the stars.[26] Pulter's vision for lyric here shares much with Herbert's description in "Prayer (1)": "The six-days world transposing in an hour" (7), "church-bells beyond the stars heard" (13). Dubrow, in her study of spatial deixis, notes that lyric often relies on spatial markers—words like *here*, *this*—that we might think of as *"convergers*: words and gestures that . . . point to someone or something, generally with the aim of gathering in and gathering together."[27] These transportive qualities allow prayer, like lyric, to create a space in which those kept apart by distance or disease might come together. Poet and reader, petitioner and God, lover and beloved all meet in the textual gathering place. Donne, hearing the bells tolling from somewhere in the parish, transports himself through prayer to his neighbor's bedside. "I am bold, O Lord, to bend my prayers to thee for his assistance, the voice of whose bell hath called me to this devotion," Donne prays. "Lay hold upon his soul, O God, till that soul have thoroughly considered his account; and how few minutes soever it have to remain in that body, let the power of thy Spirit recompense the shortness of time. . . . breathe inward comforts to his heart, and afford him the power of giving such outward testimonies thereof, as all that are about him may derive comforts from thence, and have this edification, even in this dissolution."[28] Not unlike one of his own valedictions, Donne's prayer transports him across space, finding him at the bedside of the dying; within the world of the text, he is present, spatially and temporally, mourning alongside the friends and family of this unknown neighbor, absorbed in the collective consciousness.

And so, for these early modern readers, the affordances of lyric, brought to life in the act of prayer, amplified and reinforced their place in the interdependent community gathered around the deathbed. And so now, in the wake of a collective mortality crisis like COVID-19, lyric continues to offer the possibility of connection. Ada Limón, reflecting in an interview on the early months of the pandemic, recalls, "I had a hard time in the very beginning like everyone. . . . During that time period, I couldn't write. I've realized I can write from grief and I can write from love. I can even write from anger, but I don't think I can write from fear."[29] But finally, she recounts, out of the fear, anxiety, and isolation of those early months came "The End of Poetry."

Enough of osseous and chickadee and sunflower
and snowshoes, maple and seeds, samara and shoot,
enough chiaroscuro, enough of thus and prophecy
and the stoic farmer and faith and our father and tis
of thee, enough of bosom and bud, skin and god
not forgetting and star bodies and frozen birds,
enough of the will to go on and not go on or how
a certain light does a certain thing, enough
of the kneeling and the rising and the looking
inward and the looking up, enough of the gun,
the drama, and the acquaintance's suicide, the long-lost
letter on the dresser, enough of the longing and
the ego and the obliteration of ego, enough
of the mother and the child and the father and the child
and enough of the pointing to the world, weary
and desperate, enough of the brutal and the border,
enough of can you see me, can you hear me, enough
I am human, enough I am alone and I am desperate,
enough of the animal saving me, enough of the high
water, enough sorrow, enough of the air and its ease,
I am asking you to touch me.[30]

Limón attributes the origins of the poem to the sense of profound loneliness and helplessness that marked those early months of 2020. "I needed to be touched and to be hugged and to be held," she explains, and so the poem emerged first from a sense of frustration with "the uselessness of poetry. . . . I wanted a sharp tool and all I have is soft language, you know?"[31] The poem's echoing *enough* captures the fear and frustration of those months—months when many sought constantly, frantically, for comfort, always to be left wanting. Poetry's limits are revealed in moments like these, the poem seems to suggest; when we are alone and scared, when the world is dying, poetry cannot be enough.

And yet, as Limón's title also suggests, it is precisely moments like this to which poetry is best suited, the end to which lyric intends. "Of course," she jokes, "what does a poet do when all language fails them [but] write a poem?"[32] Poetry must be enough when it remains the only tool, sharp or soft, left to use. The last line of the poem—"I am asking you to touch me"—is, in its own way, another prayer for connection. It is, maybe, even a statement true of all lyric—that all lyric is, in some way, an attempt to get closer to one another. "Poetry sustains and transforms the threshold between individual and social existence," Stewart writes, creating in its articulation the possibility for intersubjectivity.[33] Limón's reader *can* see her, can hear her; kept apart by lockdown, by quarantine, by death, she and the reader brush up against one another in the here and now of the poem, if only briefly.

The argument I make throughout this book is that by paying attention to the many lyric and other nonnarrative forms of early modern literature, we can better understand what dying meant for that period. The pandemic has underscored that this argument still holds true: The way we die and the forms we use to represent death are inextricably linked. And while, especially in a crisis like COVID-19, these lyric forms—these *techne* for community—might not keep us from dying apart from one another, they might help ensure that we are not dying alone.

Notes

Introduction

1. Andrew Marvell, *Andrew Marvell*, ed. Frank Kermode and Keith Walker (Oxford: Oxford University Press, 1990). All citations for Marvell's poetry refer to this edition, except where otherwise indicated.
2. Christopher Marlowe, "The Passionate Shepherd to His Love," *The Complete Poems and Translations*, ed. Stephen Orgel (New York: Penguin, 2007).
3. John Donne, "The Canonization." All citations for Donne's poetry refer to *The Complete Poetry of John Donne*, ed. John T. Shawcross (New York: Anchor, 1967), except where otherwise indicated.
4. In Marlowe, *The Complete Poems and Translations*. Unlike the other examples, Marlowe's proposal and Raleigh's response occur in separate lyrics, first published independently in *Englands Helicon* in 1600. However, the poems appear as a single corrupted hybrid the year before, in 1599's *Passionate Pilgrim*. There, publisher William Jaggard appends a brief version of the nymph's response as the poem's last stanza, suggesting that this logic of promise and refutation is essential to the logic of the carpe diem form.
5. Wendy Beth Hyman, *Impossible Desire and the Limits of Knowledge in Renaissance Poetry* (Oxford: Oxford University Press, 2019), 4.
6. For more on decay as historiographical trope, see Achsah Guibbory, *The Map of Time: Seventeenth-Century English Literature and Ideas of Pattern in History* (Urbana: University of Illinois Press, 1986).
7. *Oxford English Dictionary*, under "decay," n., def. 3a, 4a, 5, accessed April 18, 2025, https://doi.org/10.1093/OED/8255846562.
8. "Concordance of Shakespeare's Complete Works," Open Source Shakespeare, accessed February 24, 2025, https://www.opensourceshakespeare.org/concordance/.
9. All citations from the *Sonnets* refer to *The Oxford Shakespeare: The Complete Sonnets and Poems*, ed. Colin Burrow (Oxford: Oxford University Press, 2002), unless otherwise noted.
10. Frances Dolan, ed., "Made When I Was Not Well," by Hester Pulter (Poem 51, Amplified Edition), in *The Pulter Project: Poet in the Making*, edited by Leah Knight and Wendy Wall (2018), http://pulterproject.northwestern.edu. All quotations from Pulter's poems refer to *The Pulter Project*. Where available, I rely on the amplified edition (the version of the poem edited for scholarly use) and cite the individual editor responsible for that poem.
11. One of the first, and certainly one of the most influential, studies of death as an evolving sociohistorical phenomenon was Phillipe Ariès, *The Hour of Our Death*, 2nd ed., trans. Helen Weaver (New York: Vintage, 2008).

12. Elizabeth Bearden, *Monstrous Kinds: Body, Space, and Narrative in Renaissance Representations of Disability* (Ann Arbor: University of Michigan Press, 2019), 16.

13. Ellen Rooney, "Form and Contentment," *Modern Language Quarterly* 61, no. 1 (2000): 36. For other discussions of form as force, rather than structure, see Ben Burton and Elizabeth Scott-Baumann, "Introduction," *The Work of Form: Poetics and Materiality in Early Modern Culture* (Oxford: Oxford University Press, 2014); Group Phi, "Doing Genre," in *New Formalisms and Literary Theory*, ed. Verena Theile and Linda Tredennick (New York: Palgrave Macmillan, 2013).

14. Rooney, "Form and Contentment," 34.

15. Caroline Levine, *Forms: Whole, Rhythm, Hierarchy, Network* (Princeton, NJ: Princeton University Press, 2015), 5.

16. Levine, *Forms*, 7.

17. Heather Dubrow, *The Challenges of Orpheus* (Baltimore, MD: Johns Hopkins University Press, 2008), 194.

18. In addition to those that focused on the narrative forms of tragedy, many other studies of early modern death turned to tragedy because of the particulars of embodied performance and the many overlaps between theatrical performance and the emerging dissection theaters. For work in this area, see Susan Zimmerman, *The Early Modern Corpse and Shakespeare's Theatre* (Edinburgh: Edinburgh University Press, 2007); Jonathan Sawday, *The Body Emblazoned: Dissection and the Human Body in Renaissance Culture* (New York: Routledge, 1995); and Hillary Nunn, *Staging Anatomies: Dissection and Spectacle in Early Stuart Tragedy* (New York: Routledge, 2005).

19. Michael Neill, *Issues of Death: Mortality and Identity in English Renaissance Tragedy* (Oxford: Oxford University Press, 1997), 3.

20. Neill, *Issues of Death*, 45.

21. David Bevington, *From "Mankind" to Marlowe: Growth of Structure in the Popular Drama of Tudor England* (Cambridge, MA: Harvard University Press, 1962).

22. Maggie Vinter, *Last Acts: The Art of Dying on the Early Modern Stage* (New York: Fordham University Press, 2019).

23. Verena Lobsien, *Transparency and Dissimulation: Configurations of Neoplatonism in Early Modern English Literature* (Berlin: DeGruyter, 2010), 6.

24. Gordon Braden, *Petrarchan Love and the Continental Renaissance* (New Haven, CT: Yale University Press, 1999), 99.

25. This is not, of course, to imply that the *Rime sparse* is only or even primarily narrative in nature. As I discuss in greater detail in chapter 2, the sonnet sequence is a generic space in which the collision between lyric and narrative is perhaps at its most fraught.

26. Baldassare Castiglione, *The Book of the Courtier*, trans. Thomas Hoby (London: 1603), sig. X5v–X6r. Spelling modernized.

27. Castiglione, *The Book of the Courtier*, sig. X8r.

28. Tobin Siebers, *Disability Theory* (Ann Arbor: University of Michigan Press, 2008), 7.

29. Siebers, *Disability Theory*, 7.

30. Alison Kafer, *Feminist, Queer, Crip* (Bloomington: Indiana University Press, 2013), 27.

31. Kafer, *Feminist, Queer, Crip*, 2.

32. Siebers, *Disability Theory*, 27.
33. Lennard Davis, *Enforcing Normalcy: Disability, Deafness, and The Body* (New York: Verso, 1995), 49.
34. Davis, *Enforcing Normalcy*, 48.
35. Bearden, *Monstrous Kinds*, 27.
36. Bearden, *Monstrous Kinds*, 27.
37. Lindsey Row-Heyveld, *Dissembling Disability in Early Modern English Drama* (Cham, Switzerland: Palgrave Macmillan / Springer Nature, 2018), 22.
38. Katherine Schaap Williams, *Unfixable Forms: Disability, Performance, and the Early Modern English Theater* (Ithaca, NY: Cornell University Press, 2021), 6.
39. Williams, *Unfixable Forms*, 9.
40. Genevieve Love, *Early Modern Theatre and the Figure of Disability* (New York: Bloomsbury, 2018).
41. Contemporary poetic theorists have begun to take seriously crip poetics—lyric works produced by and for disabled individuals, often rooted in an activist methodology—as a subfield of lyric studies. For more on contemporary crip poetics, see Susannah B. Mintz, "Lyric Bodies: Poets on Disability and Masculinity," *PMLA* 127, no. 2 (2012): 248–263; David T. Mitchell and Sharon L. Snyder, "Disability Haunting in American Poetics," *Journal of Literary & Cultural Disability Studies* 1, no. 1 (2007): 1–12; and Sheila Black et al., eds., *Beauty Is a Verb—The New Poetry of Disability* (El Paso: Cinco Puntos, 2011).
42. Allison P. Hobgood and David Houston Wood, eds., *Recovering Disability in Early Modern England* (Columbus: Ohio State University Press, 2013).
43. Hobgood and Wood, "Introduction," *Recovering Disability in Early Modern England*, 14.
44. Williams, *Unfixable Forms*, 6.
45. See, for instance, Jonathan Hsy, "Blind Advocacy: Blind Readers, Disability Theory, and Accessing John Gower," *Accessus* 1, no. 1 (2013): 1–38; Julie Singer, *Blindness and Therapy in Late Medieval French and Italian Poetry* (Cambridge, UK: D. S. Brewer, 2011).
46. See Tom Shakespeare, *Disability Rights and Wrongs Revisited* (New York: Routledge, 2014).
47. However, as many medical practitioners, especially hospice care workers, have also indicated, neither are the elderly or the dying welcomed into the social center, particularly now; indeed, early modern England was more inclusive of its aging and dying populations than contemporary British and American culture. Helen Chapple, writing of the failure of hospitals to acknowledge those that are dying as such, writes, "To call a patient *dying* demeans the patient who finds herself in a place designed as a bulwark against death. It is to make her 'other' than 'us,' something that clinicians are usually reluctant to do in the beginning. Furthermore, to do so can erode clinicians' belief not only in their ability to rescue persons from imminent death, but also in the illusion of their own unlimited futures." Chapple, "Bringing Dying Out of the Hospital's Closet," *American Medical Association Journal of Ethics* 22, no. 12 (2020):1063, emphasis in the original).
48. The resistance to this sentiment is made explicit by groups such as Not Dead Yet, a disability activist collective that opposes medically assisted death on the grounds that it strengthens ableist medical ideology.

49. For more on disability gain and disability joy, see Allison Hobgood, *Beholding Disability in Renaissance England* (Ann Arbor: University of Michigan Press, 2021); Rosemarie Garland-Thomson, "Shape Structures Story: Fresh and Feisty Stories About Disability," *Narrative* 15, no. 1 (2007): 113–23.

50. Kafer, *Feminist, Queer, Crip*, 259.

51. Michelle Dowd, "Breaking Form in Early Modern Literary Studies," *English Literary Renaissance* 50, no. 1 (2019): 43.

52. David W. Atkinson, "The English *ars moriendi*: Its Protestant Transformation," *Renaissance and Reformation* 6, no. 1 (1982): 1.

53. Vinter, *Last Acts*, 17.

54. Vinter, *Last Acts*, 7.

55. Vinter, *Last Acts*, 22.

56. William Engel and Grant Williams, "Introduction," *The Shakespearean Death Arts: Hamlet Among the Tombs* (New York: Palgrave Macmillan, 2022), 2.

57. Engel and Williams, "Introduction," *The Shakespearean Death Arts*, 6.

58. Christopher Sutton, *Disce Mori Learn to Die: A Religious Discourse Moving Every Christian Man to Enter into a Serious Remembrance of His End* (London, 1662), sig. A9r. All citations from *Disce Mori* refer to this edition unless otherwise indicated; spelling has been modernized.

59. My thanks to the librarians and staff at the Folger Shakespeare Library and British Library for helping to facilitate a survey of all their copies of Sutton's work. For more on some of the details of the Folger's Sutton holdings, see Eileen Sperry, "The Art of Dying," *The Collation*, September 13, 2022, https://www.folger.edu/blogs/collation/the-art-of-dying/.

60. Mary Hampson Patterson, *Domesticating the Reformation: Protestant Best Sellers, Private Devotion, and the Revolution of English Piety* (Madison, NJ: Farleigh Dickinson University Press, 2007), 24.

61. Nigel Llewelyn, *The Art of Death: Visual Culture in The English Death Ritual c.1500–c.1800* (London: Reaktion, 1997), 19.

62. D. Vance Smith, *Arts of Dying: Literature and Finitude in Medieval England* (Chicago: University of Chicago Press, 2020), 1.

63. Vinter, *Last Acts*, 22, emphasis in the original.

64. Rose Marie San Juan, "The Turn of the Skull: Andreas Vesalius and the Early Modern Memento Mori," *Art History: Journal of the Association of Art Historians* 35, no. 5 (2012): 961.

65. Sutton, *Disce Mori*, sig. B12v.

66. Sutton, *Disce Mori*, sig. B12v–C1r.

67. Sutton, *Disce Mori*, sig. C2r.

68. Robert Herrick, *Seventeenth-Century British Poetry, 1604–1660*, ed. John P. Rumrich and Gregory Chaplin (New York: Norton, 2006).

69. The phrase also indicates Herrick's debt to previous carpe diem poets. It seems to appear first in John Ashmore's 1621 English translation of Horace's *Odes*. There, Ashmore renders the seventh stanza of 2.16 as

> Be Ioviall while time serves (Time will not stay.)
> Hate curiously t' enquire what will betide:

Sowr discontentments with sweet mirth allay.
Entirely good, nothing doth still abide.

70. Cleanth Brooks, *The Well-Wrought Urn* (New York: Harcourt, Brace, & World, 1947), 74.

71. Ramie Targoff, *Posthumous Love: Eros and the Afterlife in Renaissance England* (Chicago: University of Chicago Press, 2014), 185.

72. The victory woodcut first appears in the text's second edition in 1601. On the same page in the previous edition, the 1600 Windet, is instead a comparatively crude woodcut skeleton leaning on a shovel, adapted from one of the engravings of Andreas Vesalius's *De corporis humani fabrica* (1543).

73. "Number of COVID-19 Deaths Reported to WHO," World Health Organization COVID-19 Dashboard, accessed April 1, 2025, https://data.who.int/dashboards/covid19/deaths?n=o.

1. Dying Well

1. For more on the emphasis on lifelong virtue in these texts, see Atkinson, "The English *ars moriendi*: Its Protestant Transformation"; Vinter, *Last Acts*.

2. Sutton, *Disce Mori*, sig. A4v.

3. Sutton, *Disce Mori*, sig. A5r.

4. E. A. Jones, "Anchorites and Hermits in Historical Context," in *Approaching Medieval Anchoritic and Mystical Texts*, ed. Dee Dyas, Valerie Edden, and Roger Ellis (Cambridge, UK: D. S. Brewer, 2005), 12.

5. For more on English mortalist philosophy, see Nicholas McDowell, "Dead Souls and Modern Minds? Mortalism and the Early Modern Imagination, from Marlowe to Milton," *Journal of Medieval and Early Modern Studies* 40, no. 3 (2010).

6. Sami Schalk, *Bodyminds Reimagined: (Dis)Ability, Race, and Gender in Black Women's Speculative Fiction* (Durham, NC: Duke University Press, 2018), 5. See also Margaret Price, "The Bodymind Problem and the Possibilities of Pain," *Hypatia* 30, no. 1 (2014): 268–284.

7. All citations from Spenser's poem refer to *The Faerie Queene*, ed. A. C. Hamilton et al. (London: Pearson Longman, 2007).

8. Jeff Dolven, *Scenes of Instruction in Renaissance Romance* (Chicago: University of Chicago Press, 2008), 17.

9. Michael Schoenfeldt, *Bodies and Selves in Early Modern England: Physiology and Inwardness in Spenser, Shakespeare, Herbert, and Milton* (Cambridge, UK: Cambridge University Press, 1999), 42, emphasis in the original.

10. Kasey Evans, *Colonial Virtue: The Mobility of Temperance in Renaissance England* (Toronto: University of Toronto Press, 2012), 19.

11. William Perkins, *A Salve for a Sicke Man, Or, A Treatise Containing the Nature, Differences, and Kindes of Death as also the Right Manner of Dying Well. and it may Serue for Spirituall Instruction to 1. Mariners when they Goe to Sea. 2. Souldiers when they Goe to Battell. 3. Women when they Trauell of Child* (Cambridge, UK, 1595), sig. E7v. Spelling has been modernized.

12. Sutton, *Disce Mori*, sig. F3r.
13. Evans, *Colonial Virtue*, 20, emphasis in the original.
14. David Quint, *Epic and Empire: Politics and Generic Form from Virgil to Milton* (Princeton, NJ: Princeton University Press, 1993), 9, emphasis in the original.
15. David W. Atkinson, "*A Salve for a Sicke Man*: William Perkins' Contribution to the *ars moriendi*," *Historical Magazine of the Protestant Episcopal Church* 46, no. 4 (1977): 409.
16. Sutton, *Disce Mori*, sig. B4v.
17. Sutton, *Disce Mori*, sig. F1r.
18. Sutton, *Disce Mori*, sig. F1r.
19. Sutton, *Disce Mori*, sig. B12v.
20. Perkins, *Salve for a Sicke Man*, sig. E7r.
21. Perkins, *Salve for a Sicke Man*, sig. E7v.
22. Perkins, *Salve for a Sicke Man*, sig. E7v.
23. Sutton, *Disce Mori*, sig. B7r.
24. Sutton, *Disce Mori*, sig. H12v.
25. Sutton, *Disce Mori*, sig. B7r-v.
26. Perkins, *Salve for a Sicke Man*, sig. C7v.
27. Sutton, *Disce Mori*, sig. B10v.
28. Neill, *Issues of Death*, 36.
29. Sir Thomas Browne, *Religio Medici and Urne-Buriall*, ed. Stephen Greenblatt and Ramie Targoff (New York: New York Review of Books, 2012), 1.44 (49–50).
30. While I am not arguing a direct line of influence between Amavia's words in the *Faerie Queene* and Browne's description, the 1711 catalog detailing the sale of Browne's library does indicate that he owned two copies of Spenser's poem, in both folio and octavo, as well as a wide range of theological works on death. See Thomas Ballard, *A catalogue of the libraries of the learned Sir Thomas Brown, and Dr. Edward Brown, his son . . .* (London, 1711).
31. Browne, *Religio Medici*, 1.44 (49–50).
32. Drew Daniel, *The Joy of the Worm: Suicide and Pleasure in Early Modern English Literature* (Chicago: University of Chicago Press, 2022), 157.
33. Browne, *Religio Medici*, 1.45 (50).
34. Browne, *Religio Medici*, 1.45 (50).
35. Thomas Becon, *The Sick Man's Salve . . .* (London, 1568), sig. A5r-v.
36. Henry E. Jacobs, "Shakespeare, Revenge Tragedy, and the Ideology of the *Memento Mori*," *Shakespeare Studies* 21 (1993): 97–98.
37. San Juan, "The Turn of the Skull," 964.
38. Neill, *Issues of Death*, 204.
39. Dubrow, *Challenges of Orpheus*, 201.
40. For more on late medieval Scholastic debates about the logical paradoxes of being dead, see D. Vance Smith, *Arts of Dying*.
41. *Oxford English Dictionary*, under "corse," n., def. 1 and 2, accessed April 17, 2025, https://doi.org/10.1093/OED/3852551574.
42. Jane Grogan, *Exemplary Spenser: Visual and Poetic Pedagogy in* The Faerie Queene (New York: Routledge, 2016), 5.
43. Grogan, *Exemplary Spenser*, 19.

44. San Juan, "The Turn of the Skull," 960.

45. Dolven, *Scenes of Instruction*, 156.

46. For more on the trope of the unburied corpse in epic, see Andrew McClellan, *Abused Bodies in Roman Epic* (Cambridge, UK: Cambridge University Press, 2019).

47. For more on early modern joint burials, see Ramie Targoff, "Mortal Love: Shakespeare's *Romeo and Juliet* and the Practice of Joint Burial," *Representations* 120, no. 1 (2012): 17–38.

48. Grogan, *Exemplary Spenser*, 16.

49. Spenser's garden is also, of course, modeled around Torquato Tasso's *locus amoenus*. The most thorough catalog of Tasso's influence on the Bower of Bliss is Robert Durling's "The Bower of Bliss and Armida's Palace," *Comparative Literature* 6, no. 4 (Autumn 1954): 335–347.

50. Schoenfeldt, *Bodies and Selves*, 46.

51. As Gail Kern Paster has noted in *The Body Embarrassed: Drama and the Disciplines of Shame in Early Modern England* (Ithaca, NY: Cornell University Press, 1993), the early modern feminized body is always seen as a potentially fluid and overflowing entity. This culture "inscribe[d] women as leaky vessels by isolating one element of the female body's material expressiveness—its production of fluids—as excessive, hence either disturbing or shameful," Kern Paster writes; "the conventional Renaissance association of women and water is used not only to insinuate womanly unreliability but also to define the female body even when it is chaste, even when it is *virgo intacta*, as a crucial problematic in the social formations of capitalism—an instance of corporeal waste of the female body, representing, in Julia Kristeva's phrase, 'the objective frailty of symbolic order'" (*Powers of Horror*, trans. Leon S. Roudiez [New York: Columbia University Press, 1982], 25).

52. For more on the relationship between sleep and death in early modern literature, see Ben Parris, *Vital Strife: Sleep, Insomnia, and the Early Modern Ethics of Care* (Ithaca, NY: Cornell University Press, 2022).

53. Linda Gregerson, *The Reformation of the Subject: Spenser, Milton, and the English Protestant Epic* (Cambridge, UK: Cambridge University Press, 1995), 122.

54. James Nohrnberg, *The Analogy of* The Faerie Queene (Princeton, NJ: Princeton University Press, 1976), 306.

55. Hyman, *Impossible Desire*, 1.

56. Hyman, *Impossible Desire*, 2.

57. Targoff, *Posthumous Love*, 170.

58. William H. Race, *Classical Genres and English Poetry* (New York: Routledge, 1988), 122.

59. Wendy Beth Hyman, "Seizing Flowers in Spenser's Bower and Garden," *English Literary Renaissance* 37, no. 2 (2007): 201.

60. Race, *Classical Genres and English Poetry*, 125.

61. Catullus, *The Poems of Catullus*, trans. Peter Green (Berkeley: University of California Press, 2007).

62. Race, *Classical Genres and English Poetry*, 134.

63. Hyman, in a deft reading in "Seizing Flowers in Spenser's Bower and Garden," notes that this song is not just a carpe diem but, specifically, a *carpe florem* whose urgings to gather are "not just incongruent, but contextually meaningless"

within the context of the bower's "eternal spring," a microclimate in which roses do not, in fact, wither and fade but instead grow ad infinitum (201).

64. Hyman, *Impossible Desire*, 90.

65. Schoenfeldt, *Bodies and Selves*, 68.

66. Angela D. Bullard, "Tempering the Intemperate in Spenser's Bower of Bliss," *Spenser Studies* 31, no. 1 (2018): 168.

67. Paul Alpers, "Bower of Bliss," in *Spenser Encyclopedia*, ed. A. C. Hamilton (Toronto: University of Toronto Press, 1990), 106.

68. Joseph Campana, "Boy Toys and Liquid Joys: Pleasure and Power in the Bower of Bliss," *Modern Philology* 106, no. 3 (2009): 467.

69. Campana, "Boy Toys and Liquid Joys," 478.

70. Hyman, "Seizing Flowers," 206–7.

71. This moment echoes Spenser's reference to "Ægyptian slime" as a space of spontaneous generation in the first canto of *The Faerie Queene*:

As when old father *Nilus* gins to swell
With timely pride aboue the *Ægyptian* vale,
His fattie waues doe fertile slime outwell,
And ouerflow each plaine and lowly dale:
But when his later spring gins to auale,
Huge heapes of mudd he leaues, wherin there breed
Ten thousand kindes of creatures partly male
And partly femall of his fruitful seed;
Such vgly monstrous shapes elswher may no man reed. (1.1.21)

72. Thomas Elyot's 1536 *Castel of Health* embraces this metaphor in much the same way as Spenser. Likewise, 1 Corinthians chapter 3 demonstrates Paul's early use of this metaphor: "Know ye not that ye are the Temple of God, and that the Spirit of God dwelleth in you?" (1 Cor 3:16, Geneva).

73. Sutton, *Disce Mori*, sig. D11v, emphasis in the original. The body as clay substance is not uncommon, nor is it unique to Spenser or Sutton. Isaiah 64:8 declares "But now, O Lord, thou art our Father: we are the clay, and thou art our potter, and we all are the work of thine hands" (Geneva). Appropriately, the clay-as-flesh metaphor occurs most in the book of Job, a narrative preoccupied with death: "Your memories may be compared unto ashes, and your bodies unto bodies of clay" (Job 13:12, Geneva).

74. Schoenfeldt, *Bodies and Selves*, 41.

75. See also Jonathan Goldberg, *Endlesse Work: Spenser and the Structure of Discourse* (Baltimore, MD: Johns Hopkins University Press, 1981).

76. Daniel Vitkus, "The Unfulfilled Form of *The Faerie Queene*: Spenser's Frustrated Fore-Conceit," *Renaissance and Reformation* 35, no. 2 (2012): 84.

77. Paul Alpers, "Narration in *The Faerie Queene*," *English Literary History* 44, no. 1 (Spring 1977): 36.

78. Jeff Dolven, "When to Stop Reading *The Faerie Queene*," in *Never Again Would Birds' Song Be the Same: Essays on Early Modern and Modern Poetry in Honor of John Hollander*, ed. Jennifer Lewin (New Haven, CT: Beinecke Library, 2002), 35.

79. Dolven, "When to Stop Reading," 36.

80. David T. Mitchell and Sharon L. Snyder, *Narrative Prosthesis: Disability and the Dependencies of Discourse* (Ann Arbor: University of Michigan Press, 2001), 53.

81. Mitchell and Snyder, *Narrative Prosthesis*, 49.

2. Lyric Prosthesis

1. While this chapter does not discuss why the fair youth refuses to father a child, the most compelling arguments have been made by the numerous queer readings of *The Sonnets* that highlight the resistance to reproduction as part of the sequence's rejection of heteronormativity. For more, see Valerie Traub, "Sex Without Issue: Sodomy, Reproduction, and Signification in Shakespeare's Sonnets," in *Shakespeare's Sonnets: Critical Essays*, ed. James Schiffer (New York: Garland, 2000), 431–54.

2. For more on the *Sonnets'* engagement with Petrarchism and the Petrarchan tradition, see Heather Dubrow, *Echoes of Desire: English Petrarchism and Its Counterdiscourses* (Ithaca, NY: Cornell University Press, 1995); Gordon Braden, "Shakespeare's Petrarchism," in *Shakespeare's Sonnets: Critical Essays*, ed. Schiffer.

3. Aaron Kunin, "Shakespeare's Preservation Fantasy," *PMLA* 124, no. 1 (2009): 96.

4. For more on the qualities of time in the *Sonnets*, see Dympna Callaghan, "Confounded by Winter: Speeding Time in Shakespeare's Sonnets," in *A Companion to Shakespeare's Sonnets*, ed. Michael Schoenfeldt (Malden, MA: Blackwell, 2007), 104–17.

5. As Stephen Booth points out, line 8 echoes a line from the beginning of the *Book of Common Prayer*'s burial service: "The Lord giveth and the Lord taketh away," a paraphrase of Job 1:21. See *Shakespeare's Sonnets*, ed. Booth (New Haven, CT: Yale University Press, 2000), 240.

6. Shakespeare here inverts the sentiment of a similar phrase from John Florio's translation of Michel Montaigne's *Essaies*. In "That To Philosophize Is To Learn How To Die," Montaigne observes that the movement toward death is tolerable precisely because it occurs gradually and gently.

> Were man all at once to fall into it, I do not think we should be able to bear such a change. But being fair and gently led on by her hand, in a slow and as it were unperceived descent, by little and little, and step by step, she rolls us into that miserable state, and day by day seeks to acquaint us with it. So that when youth fails in us, we feel, nay we perceive, no shaking or transchange at all in ourselves, which in essence and verity is a harder death than that of a languishing and irksome life or that of age. Forsomuch as the leap from an ill being unto a not being is not so dangerous or steepy as it is from a delightful and flourishing being unto a painful and sorrowful condition.

See Montaigne, *Shakespeare's Montaigne: The Florio Translation of the Essays, A Selection*, trans. Florio, ed. Stephen Greenblatt and Peter G. Platt (New York: New York Review of Books, 2014), 26.

7. Kunin, "Shakespeare's Preservation Fantasy," 95, 100.

8. Anne Ferry, *All in War With Time: Love Poetry of Shakespeare, Donne, Jonson, Marvell* (Cambridge, MA: Harvard University Press, 1975), 253.

9. Kunin, "Shakespeare's Preservation Fantasy," 96, 101.

10. Ferry, *All in War With Time*, 253.

11. This strategy is also familiar from the plays; we might consider Marc Anthony's increasingly hollow insistence that "Brutus is an honorable man" or Iago's repeated characterization as "honest" to be moments in which the audience begins to hear, through repeated exposure, the hollowness of the promise offered.

12. Joel Fineman, *Shakespeare's Perjured Eye: The Invention of Poetic Subjectivity in the Sonnets* (Berkeley: University of California Press, 1986), 30–1.

13. Fineman, *Shakespeare's Perjured Eye*, 2.

14. Stephen Guy-Bray, "Notes on the Couplet in the Sonnet," *Shakespeare* 18, no. 3 (2022): 322. My gratitude to Stephen for sharing an early version of this essay with me.

15. Jessica Rosenberg, "The Point of the Couplet: Shakespeare's *Sonnets* and Tusser's *A Hundreth Good Pointes of Husbandrie*," *English Literary History* 83, no. 1 (2016): 7.

16. Rosalie Colie, *Shakespeare's Living Art* (Princeton, NJ: Princeton University Press, 2015), 74.

17. Helen Vendler, *The Art of Shakespeare's Sonnets* (Cambridge, MA: Belknap, 1999), 25.

18. Heather Dubrow, "ShakeSpeare's Undramatic Monologues: Toward a Reading of the Sonnets," *Shakespeare Quarterly* 32, no. 1 (1981): 63.

19. For line 14, I am using the punctuation offered in *Shakespeare's Sonnets*, ed. Katherine Duncan-Jones (London: The Arden Shakespeare, Bloomsbury, 2010), which best conveys the binary patterns that fill this sonnet. Editors have varied widely on the punctuation of this final line. Booth, who includes only a final period, argues that it in fact offers three levels for the young man's survival: "(a) the young man's own lifespan, (b) the lives of his child and his child's children, and (c) his survival as the subject of potentially eternal and infinitely reproducible poems" (*Shakespeare's Sonnets*, 160–161). Burrow includes two commas, one after *it* and one after *twice*, while Duncan-Jones offers the colon and comma structure shown here. Both choices underscore the poem's explicit concern with a future in which the young man's beauty is long absent and deemed the stuff of "a poet's rage," setting aside the concern for the present life of the fair youth.

20. For more on the extent of early modern poem-as-child tropes, see Stephen Guy-Bray, *Against Reproduction: Where Renaissance Texts Come From* (Toronto: University of Toronto Press, 2009).

21. Shakespeare's thinking here may well have been guided by the period's boom in epitaphs and epitaphic writing. For more on this movement, see Scott Newstok, *Quoting Death in Early Modern England: The Poetics of Epitaphs Beyond the Tomb* (New York: Palgrave Macmillan, 2009).

22. David Crystal and Ben Crystal, "Shakespeare: Original Pronunciation," The Open University, October 17, 2011, YouTube, 10 min., 21 sec., https://youtu.be/gPlpphT7n9s.

23. For more on the self-conscious print materiality throughout the *Sonnets*, see Mitchell M. Harris, "The Expense of Ink and Wastes of Shame: Poetic Generation, Black Ink, and Material Waste in Shakespeare's *Sonnets*," in *The Materiality of Color*, ed. Andrea Feeser (New York: Routledge, 2017), 65–80.

24. *Oxford English Dictionary*, under "compound," n., def. 2c and 2a, accessed April 17 2025, https://doi.org/10.1093/OED/5180175891.

25. For more on Shakespeare's grafting metaphors, see Erin Ellerbeck, "Adoption and the Language of Horticulture in *All's Well That Ends Well*," *Studies in English Literature, 1500–1900* 51, no. 2 (2011): 305–26; Vin Nardizzi, "Shakespeare's Penknife: Grafting and Seedless Generation in the Procreation Sonnets," *Renaissance and Reformation* 32, no. 1 (2009): 83–106; and Miranda Wilson, "Bastard Grafts, Crafted Fruits:

Shakespeare's Planted Families," in *The Indistinct Human in Renaissance Literature*, ed. Jean E. Feerick and Vin Nardizzi (New York: Palgrave Macmillan, 2012), 105–6. For more on Shakespeare's use of horticultural language more generally, see Joshua Calhoun, "Ecosystemic Shakespeare: Vegetable Memorabilia in the Sonnets," *Shakespeare Studies* 39 (2011): 64–73; Thomas M. Greene, "Pitiful Thrivers: Failed Husbandry in the Sonnets," in *Shakespeare's Poems: The Scholarly Literature*, ed. Stephen Orgel and Sean Keilen (New York: Routledge, 1999), 50–64.

26. Nardizzi, "Shakespeare's Penknife," 99.

27. Claire Duncan, "'Nature's Bastards': Grafted Generation in Early Modern England," *Renaissance and Reformation* 38, no. 2 (2015): 133.

28. Nardizzi, "Shakespeare's Penknife," 93.

29. Nardizzi, "Shakespeare's Penknife," 98.

30. Shakespeare might have been familiar with the term *prosthesis*, which enters the English language in the early sixteenth century not as a medical term but as a linguistic one—"the addition of a letter or syllable to the beginning of a word" (*Oxford English Dictionary*, under "prosthesis," n., def. 1, accessed April 18 2025, https://doi.org/10.1093/OED/7867201787). It is also possible, though not certain, that Shakespeare would have been familiar with the use of bodily prostheses. Julie Singer notes that the earliest reliable European records suggest that early sixteenth-century surgeon Ambroise Paré proposed prosthetic replacements for missing eyes, ears, noses, and hands. But, she writes, "evidence of premodern prosthesis" before that "is scant, however, and rarely compelling: it is largely limited to ancient Egyptian burials, classical statuary, and depictions on pottery shards and mosaics." See Singer, *Blindness and Therapy in Late Medieval French and Italian Poetry* (Cambridge, UK: D. S. Brewer, 2011), 148. However, as Singer also notes, the history of surgical prosthetics is only a narrow slice of the much longer relationship between the body and technology. The (often-overlooked) prosthetic technology of eyeglasses, for example, was well-established in Europe beginning in the fourteenth century, confirming that Shakespeare and his contemporaries would have been well acquainted with a model of embodiment that included prosthetic intervention and/or technological supplements.

31. Elaine Scarry, "Introduction," in *Literature and The Body: Essays on Populations and Persons*, ed. Scarry (Baltimore, MD: Johns Hopkins University Press, 1988), xi.

32. Scarry, *Literature and The Body*, xxii.

33. David Wills, *Inanimation: Theories of Inorganic Life* (Minneapolis: University of Minnesota Press, 2016), xii, emphasis in the original.

34. Jillian Weise, *Amplitude*, January 3, 2021, https://livingwithamplitude.com/article/cyborg-jillian-weise/.

35. Vivian Sobchack, "A Leg to Stand On: Prosthetics, Metaphor, and Materiality," in *The Prosthetic Impulse: From a Posthuman Present to a Biocultural Future*, ed. Marquard Smith and Joanne Morra (Cambridge, MA: MIT Press, 2006), 26, emphasis in the original.

36. Sobchack, "A Leg to Stand On," 22, emphasis in the original.

37. The question of the prosthetic's animacy has become increasingly complicated by advancements in organ transplantation and xenotransplantation, the practice of transplanting organs grown in animals for human use. For more on this, see Margrit Shildrick, "'Why Should Our Bodies End at the Skin?': Embodiment, Boundaries, and Somatechnics," *Hypatia* 30, no. 1 (2015): 13–29.

38. David Wills, *Prosthesis* (Stanford, CA: Stanford University Press, 1995), 10.
39. Rosenberg, "The Point of the Couplet," 2, emphasis added.
40. Rosenberg, "The Point of the Couplet," 2, emphasis added.
41. Rosenberg, "The Point of the Couplet," 22, emphasis added.
42. Rosenberg, "The Point of the Couplet," 28, emphasis added.
43. Francesco Petrarch, Poem 1, in *Petrarch's Lyric Poems—The Rime Sparse and Other Lyrics*, trans. Robert Durling (Cambridge, MA: Harvard University Press, 1976).
44. Guy-Bray, *Against Reproduction*, 139.
45. Dubrow, *Challenges of Orpheus*, 179.
46. C. S. Lewis, *English Literature in the Sixteenth Century: Excluding Drama* (Oxford: Clarendon, 1954), 327.
47. Michael Spiller, *The Sonnet Sequence: A Study of Its Strategies* (New York: Twayne, 1997), 20.
48. Walter Cohen, Introduction to *The Sonnets*, in *The Norton Shakespeare*, 3rd ed., ed. Greenblatt et al. (New York: Norton, 2016), 2244.
49. Heather Dubrow, "'Incertainties Now Crown Themselves Assur'd': The Politics of Plotting Shakespeare's Sonnets," in *Shakespeare's Sonnets: Critical Essays*, ed. James Schiffer (New York: Garland, 2000), 116.
50. *All the Sonnets of Shakespeare*, ed. Paul Edmonson and Stanley Wells (Cambridge, UK: Cambridge University Press, 2020), 14.
51. Edmonson and Wells, *All the Sonnets of Shakespeare*, 15–16.
52. For more on the organizational structures of early modern miscellanies and the *Sonnets*' relationship with this genre, see Megan Heffernan, *Making the Miscellany: Poetry, Print, and the History of the Book in Early Modern England* (Philadelphia: University of Pennsylvania Press, 2021).
53. Burrow, *The Complete Sonnets and Poems*, 107.
54. Burrow, *The Complete Sonnets and Poems*, 108.
55. Margreta de Grazia, "The Scandal of Shakespeare's Sonnets," in *Shakespeare's Sonnets: Critical Essays*, ed. James Schiffer (New York: Garland, 2000), 89–112; Imtiaz Habib, *Shakespeare and Race: Postcolonial Praxis in the Early Modern Period* (New York: University Press of America, 2000).
56. Mitchell and Snyder, *Narrative Prosthesis*, 53–4.
57. Fineman, *Shakespeare's Perjured Eye*, 132.
58. Hsy, "Blind Advocacy," 25, 24.
59. Singer, *Blindness and Therapy*, 153.
60. Singer, *Blindness and Therapy*, 147, emphasis in the original.

3. Time of Death

1. Joan Didion, *The Year of Magical Thinking* (New York: Vintage International, 2006), 156–17.
2. C. S. Lewis, *A Grief Observed* (New York: Harper Collins, 1994), 33.
3. Lewis, *A Grief Observed*, 33.
4. Roland Barthes, *Mourning Diary*, ed. Nathalie Léger, trans. Richard Howard (New York: Hill and Wang, 2012), 50, emphasis in the original.
5. Didion, *The Year of Magical Thinking*, 147.

6. Didion, *The Year of Magical Thinking*, 25.
7. Elizabeth Kolkovich, "In Defense of Indulgence: Hester Pulter's Maternal Elegies," *Journal of Early Modern Cultural Studies* 20, no. 2 (Spring 2020): 43.
8. Erin Sullivan, "A Disease Unto Death: Sadness in the Time of Shakespeare," in *Emotions and Health, 1200–1700*, ed. Elena Carrera (Boston: Brill, 2013), 159–84.
9. Sullivan, "A Disease Unto Death," 170.
10. Didion, *The Year of Magical Thinking*, 153.
11. Barthes, *Mourning Diary*, 119, emphasis in the original.
12. Frances Dolan, ed., "View But This Tulip," by Hester Pulter (Poem 105, Amplified Edition), in *The Pulter Project: Poet in the Making*, edited by Leah Knight and Wendy Wall (2018), http://pulterproject.northwestern.edu.
13. For more on the complexity of Pulter's use of the term *indivisibles* here, see Alice Eardley, "Hester Pulter's 'Indivisibles' and the Challenges of Annotating Early Modern Women's Poetry," *Studies in English Literature, 1500–1900* 52, no. 1 (2012): 117–41.
14. Levine, *Forms*, 8.
15. Elizabeth Scott-Baumann, "Hester Pulter's Well-Wrought Urns: Early Modern Women, Sonnets, and New Criticism," *Journal of Early Modern Cultural Studies* 20, no. 2 (Spring 2020): 138.
16. Marshelle Woodward, "Formalism Dispossessed: Pulter, Donne, and the Obliviated Urn," in *Feminist Formalism and Early Modern Women's Writing*, ed. Lara Dodds and Michelle M. Dowd (Lincoln: University of Nebraska Press, 2022), 166–84.
17. Elizabeth Scott-Baumann, ed., "The Circle [1]," by Hester Pulter (Poem 17, Amplified Edition), in *The Pulter Project: Poet in the Making*, edited by Leah Knight and Wendy Wall (2018), http://pulterproject.northwestern.edu. I follow *The Pulter Project*'s convention of numbering the Circle poems based on their order of appearance in the manuscript.
18. Scott-Baumann, "Hester Pulter's Well-Wrought Urns," 126.
19. Kolkovich, "In Defense of Indulgence," 65.
20. Jayne Archer, "A 'Perfect Circle'? Alchemy in the Poetry of Hester Pulter," *Literature Compass* 2, no. 1 (2005): 3.
21. Archer, "A 'Perfect Circle'?," 3.
22. Scott-Baumann, "Hester Pulter's Well-Wrought Urns," 139. Though, as both Woodward and Frances Dolan have argued, even Pulter's strictest forms of enclosure are almost always permeable containers. See Dolan, "Hester Pulter's Dunghill Poetics," *Journal of Early Modern Cultural Studies* 20, no. 2 (Spring 2020): 16–42.
23. *Oxford English Dictionary*, under "suspire," v., def. 1, accessed April 17, 2025, https://doi.org/10.1093/OED/4045434391.
24. This desire to sigh oneself away into pure air recalls Ovid's Echo, who is metamorphosed in her grief into pure sound. Petrarch frequently takes up the Echo myth (see, for example, *canzone* 23), which subsequently results in the familiar Petrarchan topos of the bereaved lover sighing themselves into nothingness.
25. *Oxford English Dictionary*, under "involve," v., def. 1, 2a, accessed April 17, 2025, https://doi.org/10.1093/OED/9303879832.
26. Kolkovich, "In Defense of Indulgence," 49.
27. Kolkovich, "In Defense of Indulgence," 57.

28. For more on connections between Donne and Pulter, see Archer, "A 'Perfect Circle'?"; and Woodward, "Formalism Dispossessed: Pulter, Donne, and the Obliviated Urn."

29. *Oxford English Dictionary*, under "emergent," adj., def. 1a and 4, accessed April 17, 2025, https://doi.org/10.1093/OED/2361913777.

30. Browne, *Religio Medici*, sec. 13 (17). While there is no direct evidence to suggest that Pulter and Browne knew one another, it is reasonable to assume that Pulter may have read the popular *Religio Medici*, particularly given the wealth of shared interests and affiliations between the two authors. Both espoused Royalist politics throughout the Civil War. Both had a keen observational eye, especially for the workings of the natural world. And both shared a deep interest in alchemy, natural philosophy, and the new science of the late seventeenth century. Above all, Browne and Pulter shared a common fascination with mortality and the relationship between a person's living body and their spiritual self.

31. Smith, *Arts of Dying*, 23.

32. Taylor is another writer whose work Pulter was likely to have read and with whom she certainly shares key interests and beliefs. *Holy Dying* was one of the most popular *artes moriendi* of the latter half of the century. This was due in large part to the careful prose and inventive metaphor of Taylor's style, a style that often recalls Pulter's. Pulter may well have seen Taylor's life as much like her own, as he was a Royalist sympathizer who managed to find an uneasy peace in life outside London, to his apparent dismay.

33. Vaughan, a prominent Royalist, may well have been part of Pulter's extended social circle. Vaughan's third marriage in 1652 was to Alice Egerton, who performed the lead role of the Lady in Milton's *Comus* at its first performance at Ludlow Castle in 1634. Milton's connection with the Ley/Pulter families is confirmed in his writing.

34. Jeremy Taylor, *The Rule and Exercises of Holy Dying* (London, 1651), sig. A9v–A10r.

35. Dolan, "Hester Pulter's Dunghill Poetics," 21.

36. Dolan, "Hester Pulter's Dunghill Poetics," 21.

37. *Book of Common Prayer*, 1662 version, in *The Book of Common Prayer: The Texts of 1549, 1559, and 1662*, ed. Brian Cummings (Oxford: Oxford University Press, 2011), 455. All citations of *The Book of Common Prayer* refer to this critical edition.

38. Taylor, *Holy Dying*, sig. B2v.

39. See also the discussion of Donne's "Death's Duell" sermon in chapter 4, where he makes this same argument.

40. Elizabeth Scott-Baumann, ed., "The Circle [2]," by Hester Pulter (Poem 21, Amplified Edition), in *The Pulter Project: Poet in the Making*, edited by Leah Knight and Wendy Wall (2018), http://pulterproject.northwestern.edu.

41. Alice Eardley, *Poems, Emblems, and the Unfortunate Florinda* (New York: Iter, 2014), 115.

42. Archer, "A 'Perfect Circle'?," 2.

43. Pulter's poetry often elides mourning and morning; her many dawn and insomnia poems, for instance, juxtapose the arrival of morning and the start of a new day with the end of the poet's grief and suffering. See, for instance, any of the three "Aurora" poems or either of the two "To Aurora" poems of the manuscript for examples of this trope.

44. For more on the subgenre of child loss poems, see Elizabeth Kolkovich, "Child Loss Elegies," *Pulter Project*, accessed November 5, 2024, https://pulterproject.northwestern.edu/#child-loss-elegies; Pamela Hammons, "Despised Creatures: The Illusion of Maternal Self-Effacement in Seventeenth-Century Child Loss Poetry," *ELH* 66, no. 1 (Spring 1999): 25–49; Scott Oldenburg, *A Weaver-Poet and the Plague* (University Park: Pennsylvania State University Press, 2020), 125–8.

45. Scott-Baumann, "The Circle [2]," headnote.

46. Scott-Baumann, "The Circle [2]," headnote.

47. Elizabeth Scott-Baumann, ed., "The Circle [2]," by Hester Pulter (Poem 25, Amplified Edition), in *The Pulter Project: Poet in the Making*, edited by Leah Knight and Wendy Wall (2018), http://pulterproject.northwestern.edu.

48. Taylor, *Holy Dying*, sig. G3v.

49. See Milton's sonnet "To the Lady Margaret Ley," Hester Pulter's sister, in *The Complete Poetry and Essential Prose of John Milton*, ed. William Kerrigan, John Rumrich, and Stephen M. Fallon (New York: Modern Library, 2007). All citations of Milton's works refer to this edition unless otherwise noted.

50. *Oxford English Dictionary*, under "impatient," def. 1a, accessed April 17, 2025, https://doi.org/10.1093/OED/4868424218.

51. Herbert, "Grief," in *George Herbert: The Complete English Poems*, ed. John Tobin (New York: Penguin, 2004). All citations to Herbert's poetry refer to this edition. For more on Herbert and Pulter's connections, see Sarah C. E. Ross, "Hester Pulter's Devotional Complaints," *Journal of Early Modern Cultural Studies* 20, no. 2 (Spring 2020): 99–119.

52. Jack Halberstam, *In A Queer Time and Place* (New York: NYU Press, 2005).

53. Ellen Samuels, "Six Ways of Looking at Crip Time," *Disability Studies Quarterly* 37, no. 3 (2017), https://doi.org/10.18061/dsq.v37i3.5824.

54. Moya Bailey, "The Ethics of Pace," *South Atlantic Quarterly* 120, no. 2 (2021): 286.

55. Petra Kuppers, "Crip Time," *Tikkun* 29, no. 4 (2014): 30.

56. Bailey, "The Ethics of Pace," 286.

57. Ellen Samuels and Elizabeth Freeman, "Introduction: Crip Temporalities," *South Atlantic Quarterly* 120, no. 2 (2021): 249.

58. Kuppers, "Crip Time," 30.

59. Kafer, *Feminist, Queer, Crip*, 28.

60. Samuels, "Six Ways of Looking at Crip Time."

61. Elisabeth Kübler-Ross, *On Death and Dying: What the Dying Have to Teach Doctors, Nurses, Clergy, and Their Own Families* (New York: Scribner, 2014, originally 1969). See also Elisabeth Kübler-Ross, *Questions and Answers on Death and Dying* (New York: Macmillan, 1974) for clarification.

62. Samuels, "Six Ways of Looking at Crip Time."

63. Northrop Frye, "Approaching the Lyric," in *Lyric Theory: Beyond New Criticism*, ed. Chaviva Hošek and Patricia Parker (Ithaca, NY: Cornell University Press, 1985), 31.

64. Frye, "Approaching the Lyric," 32.

65. Jonathan Culler, *Theory of the Lyric* (Cambridge, MA: Harvard University Press, 2015), 213.

66. Culler, *Theory of the Lyric*, 226.

67. Sharon Cameron, *Lyric Time: Dickinson and the Limits of Genre* (Baltimore, MD: Johns Hopkins University Press, 1979), 23.

68. Cameron, *Lyric Time*, 70.

69. Cameron, *Lyric Time*, 70.

70. Dubrow, *Challenges of Orpheus*, 201, 202.

71. Dubrow, *Challenges of Orpheus*, 207.

72. *Book of Common Prayer*, 1662 version, ed. Cummings, 455.

73. Kafer, *Feminist, Queer, Crip*, 8.

74. 1 Corinthians 15:35. All biblical citations in this chapter refer to the 1611 King James Bible, except where otherwise indicated.

75. 1 Corinthians 15:36–39, 42–44.

76. Caroline Walker Bynum, *The Resurrection of the Body in Western Christianity, 200–1336* (New York: Columbia University Press, 1995), 3.

77. *Oxford English Dictionary*, under "never," adv., def. 1a, https://doi.org/10.1093/OED/5533816830

78. Donne explores another theological version of this paradox in *La Corona*, his sonnet cycle mapping the incarnation, death, and resurrection of Christ. There, Donne relies on the dynamic relationship of individual sonnets and the cycle to mirror Christ's place both within and outside of worldly time.

79. Liza Blake, ed., "The [Uncertain] Hope January 1665," by Hester Pulter (Poem 65, Amplified Edition B), in *The Pulter Project: Poet in the Making*, edited by Leah Knight and Wendy Wall (2018), http://pulterproject.northwestern.edu. See also amplified editions C and D, also edited by Blake, as well as amplified edition A, edited by Scott-Baumann.

80. "The [Uncertain] Hope January 1665," amplified edition B, headnote.

81. For more on the ambivalence of this line and the poem's approach to revolutionary action, see Dyani Johns Taff, "Death and Revolution: Thinking with Hester Pulter," *The Sundial*, October 27, 2020, https://medium.com/the-sundial-acmrs/death-and-revolution-thinking-with-hester-pulter-848d5c966b6d.

82. Daniel Juan Gil, *The Fate of the Flesh: Secularization and Resurrection in the Seventeenth Century* (New York: Fordham University Press, 2021), 3.

83. Gil, *The Fate of the Flesh*, 11.

84. Kafer, *Feminist, Queer, Crip*, 27.

85. Kafer, *Feminist, Queer, Crip*, 27.

4. Intimacies of Decay

1. David Novarr called this poem "crudely utilitarian in a genre which is customarily complimentary." See Novarr, "Donne's 'Epithalamion Made at Lincoln's Inn': Context and Date," *Review of English Studies* 7, no. 27 (July 1956): 254. For a response to Novarr's critique and a recuperation of the poem, see Heather Dubrow, "Donne's 'Epithalamion Made at Lincoln's Inn': An Alternative Interpretation," *Studies in English Literature, 1500–1900* 16, no. 1 (Winter 1976): 131–43.

2. Donne, *The Variorum Edition of the Poetry of John Donne*, vol. 8, *The Epigrams, Epithalamions, Epitaphs, Inscriptions, and Miscellaneous Poems*, ed. Gary Stringer et al. (Bloomington: Indiana University Press, 1995).

3. Samuel Johnson, *Samuel Johnson's Lives of the Poets*, ed. Roger Lonsdale (Oxford: Oxford University Press, 2006), 200.

4. Richard Rambuss, "Sacred Subjects and the Aversive Metaphysical Conceit: Crashaw, Serrano, Ofili," *English Literary History* 71, no. 2 (2004): 507.

5. *Intimacy* is not Donne's choice, nor would it have been the first word early modern readers would have turned to for this concept. While Donne demonstrates a sustained interest in erotic and spiritual closeness, his deep affection for linguistic invention means that he uses a wide range of images, terms, and metaphors to access this central idea. I have elected to use the more contemporary *intimacy* because of its ability to efficiently capture a range of experiences that, for Donne, are all interrelated: sexual intercourse, romantic and emotional affection, and the absence of distance, whether literal or figurative. For more on intimacy as a key to Donne's poetics, see Timothy Duffy, "Epistolary Copulation in John Donne's Verse Letters," *Studies in English Literature, 1500–1900*, 59, no. 1 (Winter 2019): 67–90. Other contemporary theorists have used the concept of the erotic to describe these relationships. Audre Lorde offers a theory of the erotic that, like Donne's, extends intersubjective intimacy from the sexual into a wide range of other relationships and experiences. Lorde writes

> The erotic functions for me in several ways, and the first is in providing the power which comes from sharing deeply any pursuit with another person. The sharing of joy, whether physical, emotional, psychic, or intellectual, forms a bridge between the sharers which can be the basis for understanding much of what is not shared between them, and lessens the threat of their difference. Another important way in which the erotic connection functions is the open and fearless underlining of my capacity for joy. In the way my body stretches to music and opens into response, hearkening to its deepest rhythms, so every level upon which I sense also opens to the erotically satisfying experience, whether it is dancing, building a bookcase, writing a poem, examining an idea.

Lorde, "Uses of the Erotic; The Erotic as Power," in *Women in Culture: An Intersectional Anthology for Gender and Women's Studies*, ed. Bonnie Kime Scott et al. (Malden, MA: Wiley Blackwell, 2017), 207.

6. Blaine Greteman, "'All this seed pearl': John Donne and Bodily Presence," *College Literature* 37, no. 3 (Summer 2010): 26.

7. Julie Crawford, *Marvelous Protestantism: Monstrous Births in Post-Reformation England* (Baltimore, MD: Johns Hopkins University Press, 2005).

8. Donald Ramsey Roberts, "The Death Wish of John Donne," *PMLA* 62, no. 4 (December 1947): 959, 961.

9. Ramie Targoff, *John Donne, Body and Soul* (Chicago: University of Chicago Press, 2008), 50.

10. Guibbory, *Map of Time*, 72.

11. John Carey, *John Donne: Life, Mind, and Art* (Oxford: Oxford University Press, 1981), 135, 134.

12. In the St. Paul's and O'Flahertie manuscripts of Donne's works, as well as in the 1633, 1635, and 1669 printed editions, there appears a grouping of lyrics that enact the process of dying and dissolution. In the O'Flahertie manuscript, the sequence is as follows: "The Funeral," "The Relique," "The Curse," "The Blossom," "The Primrose," "The Damp," and "The Dissolution." In the St. Paul's manuscript, "The Will" precedes the group, "The Dissolution" and "The Curse" are absent, and "The Relic"

appears after "The Blossom" and "The Primrose" rather than before. It is then this order, along with the restoration of "The Dissolution" following "The Damp," that appears in the 1633, 1635, and 1669 editions. The continual reappearance of these poems together in the manuscripts suggests the process of death, burial, and dissolution, with the intervening floral poems serving as lyrical memento mori. All information on the manuscripts and publication history of Donne's work sourced from DigitalDonne: The Online *Variorum*, accessed March 2, 2025, https://digitaldonne.tamu.edu.

13. Megan Kathleen Smith, "Reading It Wrong to Get It Right: Sacramental and Excremental Encounters in Early Modern Poems About Hair Jewelry," *Philological Quarterly* 94, no. 4 (Fall 2015): 353.

14. Browne, *Religio Medici and Hydriotaphia, or Urne-Burial*, 122.

15. The kind of joint burial Donne describes here was practiced widely in England during the early modern period. Ramie Targoff, in an essay on this practice—"Mortal Love: Shakespeare's *Romeo and Juliet* and the Practice of Joint Burial," *Representations* 120, no. 1 (Fall 2012): 17–38—notes that shared graves remained common even after the Reformation. "The desire to lie side by side in a single tomb," she writes, "has no rational or justification in a religion that regarded the corpse as something to be dispensed with as soon as it parted from the soul. Until the flesh was retrieved and made new at the resurrection, the corpse served no meaningful purpose within Protestantism.... And yet, in spite of this lack of purpose, Protestants routinely petitioned to be buried alongside their spouses without mentioning any other hopes for the future. What these English couples seem to have craved above all was posthumous intimacy in the grave" (24).

16. For more on the influence of Roman orthodoxy on this lyric, see Helen Wilcox, "Miracles of Love and Wit: John Donne's 'The Relic,'" *GRAAT* 25 (January 2002): 119–37; and Abram Steen, "'remembrest right': Remembering the Dead in John Donne's *Songs and Sonets*," *Renaissance and Reformation* 33, no. 2 (Spring 2010): 93–124. Additionally, Guibbory's work on the links between "The Relique" and the Hebrew lyricism of *The Song of Songs* provides an excellent reading of the wide scope of Donne's theological engagement. See Guibbory, "'The Relique,' *The Song of Songs*, and Donne's *Songs and Sonets*," *John Donne Journal* 15 (1996): 23–44.

17. Schoenfeldt, "Thinking Through the Body: Corporeality and Interiority in Donne," *GRAAT* 25 (January 2002): 28.

18. Targoff, *Body and Soul*, 59. Donne's relationship with Neoplatonism has been the subject of much debate, reflecting the complexity of his engagement with materiality and dualism. Elaine Scarry's assessment perhaps comes closest to unifying Donne's theological understanding of the body with his attitudes toward Neoplatonic thinking. There, she argues that Donne looks to "the willful materialism of the Judeo-Christian God" as the patterning event for all creation; "God, says Donne, has not only repeatedly 'dignified' and 'crowned' the human body, but (invoking the word that becomes nearly electric in his ethical resonance) 'associated' himself with it: he created the body in His own person; he took it as his own in the person of Jesus; he inhabits it in the person of the Holy Ghost" (70). See Scarry, "Donne: 'but yet the body is his booke,'" in *Literature and the Body: Essays on Populations and Persons*, ed. Scarry (Baltimore, MD: Johns Hopkins University Press, 1988). Donne thus inverts traditional Neoplatonic hierarchies of soul or spirit over body as a way of mirroring the

same inversion as demonstrated in God's incarnation; that the word is made flesh, so to speak, indicates that the fleshly aspects of God constitute the highest form of being.

19. *Oxford English Dictionary*, under "involve," v., def. 1, accessed April 17, 2025, https://doi.org/10.1093/OED/9303879832.

20. *Lewis & Short*, under "volvo."

21. *Lewis & Short*, under "volvo."

22. Colby Gordon has noted that "for Donne, death initiates a terrifying and confusing but also pleasurable and desirable process of ungendering," evident in moments like these. See Gordon, *Glorious Bodies: Trans Theology and Renaissance Literature* (Chicago: University of Chicago Press, 2024), 96.

23. Guibbory, *Map of Time*, 85.

24. Schoenfeldt, "Thinking Through the Body," 30.

25. Targoff, *Body and Soul*, 72.

26. Scarry argues this valediction should not just be read as a general description of two separated lovers but as a specific meditation on the parting of Donne and his wife, Ann. Donne's Latinized moniker—Johannes Donne—includes within it the name Ann Donne, allowing for a linguistic realization of the physical union the poem describes.

27. Christopher Ricks, "Donne After Love," in *Literature and the Body*, 39.

28. *Oxford English Dictionary*, under "substantial," def. 8a, 13, accessed April 17, 2025, https://doi.org/10.1093/OED/6036022355.

29. *Oxford English Dictionary*, under "mystery," n., def. 2a, accessed April 17, 2025, https://doi.org/10.1093/OED/8884517462.

30. This interpretive practice is evident, for instance, in the Book of Common Prayer's catechism. When asked to define the term *sacrament*, the parishioner offers a directed response that is "an outward and visible signe of an inward and spiritual grace, given unto us, ordained by Christ himself, as a means whereby we receive the same, and a pledge to assure us thereof." The Eucharist, for example, provides the outward and visible sign of bread and wine through which devotees might contemplate the mystery of divine sacrifice. This section of the catechism on sacraments, Cummings notes, is first added to the liturgy in 1604.

31. Donne, *The Variorum Edition of the Poetry of John Donne: The Holy Sonnets*, vol. 7.1, LXII. While some critics, such as Donald Dickinson in his edition of Donne's poetry, have argued that the 1633 ordering is (at least closest to) authorial, others, such as Angus Fletcher, John Carey, and Louis Martz, adhere to the manuscript ordering.

32. This variation of Holy Sonnet "Thou hast made me" is taken from the *Variorum* "The Original Sequence," which shows only slight textual variance from the Westmoreland sequence.

33. Guibbory traces this rationale for decay in her reading of Donne in *A Map of Time*. There, she argues, Donne crafts a historiographical understanding of the world predicated on its progressive corruption. In Donne's view, she writes, "The Fall provides the paradigm for the pattern of time. Both in the world at large and in human beings there is a force much like gravity that makes them tend downward" (73).

34. George Puttenham, *The Art of English Poesy*, ed. Frank Whigham and Wayne A. Rebhorn (Ithaca, NY: Cornell University Press, 2007), 284.

35. Romans 6:23. All biblical citations in this chapter refer to the 1611 King James Version.

36. This reading is also echoed in Donne's "Hymn To God the Father," in which, at the poem's final stanza, the poet declares "I have a sinne of feare" (13). There, the poet's fear itself of his impending death is also categorized as sinful.

37. Carey, *Life, Mind, and Art*, 135.

38. Gil, *The Fate of the Flesh*, 35.

39. Job 19:25–27.

40. Donne, *Sermons*, ed. George R. Potter and Evelyn M. Simpson, vol. 3 (Berkeley: University of California Press, 1953), 109–110.

41. Bynum, *The Resurrection of the Body*, 11.

42. Donne, *Sermons*, vol. 3, 105.

43. Donne, *Sermons*, vol. 3, 106.

44. Donne, *Sermons*, vol. 3, 97.

45. Donne echoes Jerome here, who, as Bynum notes, largely "rejected the seed metaphor from 1 Corinthians 15 because it expressed too much change between earth and heaven." Jerome instead reframes Paul's metaphor in a tone not unlike Donne's: "Where Jerome does admit that we are seeds[, he] refers to conception not resurrection and souls not bodies. . . . God plants the soul in the uterus of the mother as seeds are sown in soil." Bynum, *The Resurrection of the Body*, 89.

46. Donne, *Sermons*, vol. 3, 105.

47. Carey, *Life, Mind, and Art*, 135.

48. This concept is akin to Julia Kristeva's concept of the abject, in which the materials that stand at the limits of embodiment—hair, excrement, the corpse—throw into relief the contingency of being and thus incite horror in the viewer. See Kristeva, *Powers of Horror*.

49. Donne, *Sermons*, vol. 10, 231–232.

50. Donne, *Sermons*, vol. 10, 233.

51. Sutton, *Disce Mori*, sig. I11r.

52. For more on the womb/tomb associations across genres, see Amy Kenny, *Humoral Wombs on the Shakespearean Stage* (London: Palgrave Macmillan, 2019); G. A. E. Parfitt, "Renaissance Wombs, Renaissance Tombs," *Renaissance and Modern Studies* 15, no. 1 (1971): 23–33.

53. Bynum, *The Resurrection of the Body*, 33.

54. Donne, *Sermons*, vol. 10, 238. This moment is also an intensification of the commonplace fear of death as a social leveler. Donne builds on this in the following lines, where he urges his audience to envision the horror that a "Monarch, who spred over many nations alive, must in his dust lye in a corner of that sheete of lead, and there . . . bee mingled in his dust, with the dust of every high way, and of every dunghill, and swallowed in every puddle and pond."

55. Targoff, *Body and Soul*, 22.

56. Gil, *The Fate of the Flesh*, 42, emphasis in the original.

57. Donne, *Sermons*, vol. 10, 239–40.

58. Donne, *Sermons*, vol. 3, 112-113, emphasis in the original.

59. 1559 Book of Common Prayer.

60. Donne, *Sermons*, vol. 3, 112–13.

61. 1 Thessalonians 4:13–17.

62. Donne, *Sermons*, vol. 10, 238.
63. 1559 Book of Common Prayer.
64. Deborah Beth Creamer, *Disability and Christian Theology: Embodied Limits and Constructive Possibilities* (Oxford: Oxford University Press, 2009), 77.
65. Row-Heyveld, *Dissembling Disability*, 6.
66. Gordon has argued, similarly, that early modern trans studies should pursue "a postsecular turn," reclaiming the language and history of theology as an integral part of the long history of trans identity and wresting sole control of it from transphobic extremists. See Gordon, *Glorious Bodies*, 16.
67. Nancy Eiesland, *The Disabled God: Toward a Liberatory Theology of Disability* (Nashville, TN: Abingdon, 1994), 22.
68. Eiesland, *The Disabled God*, 94.
69. Eiesland, *The Disabled God*, 110–11.
70. Gil, *The Fate of the Flesh*, 45.
71. Eiesland, *The Disabled God*, 103. For more on interdependence in disability theology, see Kathy Black, *A Healing Homiletic: Preaching and Disability* (Nashville, TN: Abingdon), 1996.
72. John Swinton, "The Body of Christ Has Down's Syndrome: Theological Reflections on Vulnerability, Disability, and Graceful Communities," *Journal of Pastoral Theology* 13, no. 2 (2003): 71.
73. Sallie McFague, "Metaphorical Theology," in *Sallie McFague: Collected Readings*, ed. David B. Lott (Minneapolis: Fortress, 2013), 70, emphasis in the original.
74. McFague, "Metaphorical Theology," 71.
75. Eiesland, *The Disabled God*, 92.
76. Bynum, *The Resurrection of the Body*, 6–7.
77. Philip Sidney, "The Defense of Poesy," in *The Major Works*, ed. Katherine Duncan-Jones (Oxford: Oxford University Press, 2002), 216.
78. Susan Stewart, *Poetry and the Fate of the Senses* (Chicago: University of Chicago Press, 2002), 13.
79. John Donne, *Devotions Upon Emergent Occasions together with Deaths Duel* (Ann Arbor: University of Michigan Press, 1975), 124–25.

Epilogue

1. Tedros Adhanom Ghebreyesus, "Opening Remarks at the Media Briefing on COVID-19," World Health Organization, March 11, 2020, https://www.who.int/director-general/speeches/detail/who-director-general-s-opening-remarks-at-the-media-briefing-on-covid-19---11-march-2020.
2. Donne, *Devotions*, 108–9.
3. Donne, *Devotions*, 107, emphasis in the original.
4. Taylor, *Holy Dying*, sig. A2r.
5. Sutton, *Disce Mori*, sig. M4v.
6. Vinter, *Last Acts*, 123.
7. Arnold Van Gennep, *The Rites of Passage*, trans. Monika B. Vizedom and Gabrielle L. Caffee (Chicago: University of Chicago Press, 1960), 11.
8. Van Gennep, *The Rites of Passage*, 147.
9. Van Gennep, *The Rites of Passage*, 165.

10. Glenys Caswell, *Dying Alone: Challenging Assumptions* (London: Palgrave Macmillan, 2022), 83.

11. Glenn K. Wakam, MD, et al., "Not Dying Alone: Modern Compassionate Care in the Covid-19 Pandemic," *New England Journal of Medicine* 382, no. 24 (June 11, 2020).

12. Wakam et al., "Not Dying Alone."

13. Mia Mingus, "You Are Not Entitled to Our Deaths: COVID, Abled Supremacy, and Interdependence," *Leaving Evidence*, January 16, 2022, https://leavingevidence.wordpress.com/2022/01/16/you-are-not-entitled-to-our-deaths-covid-abled-supremacy-interdependence/.

14. Eve Feder Kittay, "Centering Justice on Dependency and Recovering Freedom," in *The Disability Studies Reader*, 5th ed., ed. Lennard Davis (New York: Routledge, 2017), 307.

15. Perkins, *Salve for a Sicke Man*, sig. D5v–D6r.

16. Donne, *Devotions*, 27, emphasis in the original.

17. While Donne's *Devotions* share key features with the *ars moriendi* tradition, some scholars have also identified significant areas of divergence. For a reading of Donne's *Devotions* as resistant to *ars moriendi* generic conventions, see Alexis Butzner, "'I feare the more': Donne's *Devotions* and the Impossibility of Dying Well," *Studies in Philology*, 114, no. 2 (Spring 2017): 331–67.

18. Sutton, *Disce Mori*, sig N5v and P4r.

19. Taylor, *Holy Dying*, sig. O12r and P5r.

20. Jahan Ramazani, *Poetry and Its Others: News, Prayer, Song, and the Dialogue of Genres* (Chicago: University of Chicago Press, 2013), 128.

21. Ramazani, *Poetry and Its Others*, 129.

22. Ramie Targoff, *Common Prayer: The Language of Public Devotion in Early Modern England* (Chicago: University of Chicago Press, 2001), 87.

23. Roland Greene, "Sir Philip Sidney's *Psalms*, the Sixteenth-Century Psalter, and the Nature of Lyric," *Studies in English Literature* 30 (1990): 20.

24. Stewart, *Poetry and the Fate of the Senses*, 150.

25. Leah Knight and Wendy Wall, ed., "Why Must I Thus Forever Be Confined?," by Hester Pulter (Poem 25, Elemental Edition), *The Pulter Project: Poet in the Making*, edited by Leah Knight and Wendy Wall (2018), http://pulterproject.northwestern.edu.

26. For more on Pulter's stellar poetics, see Victoria Burke, "Playing Football with the Stars: Hester Pulter Rethinks the Metaphysical Astronomy Poem," *Journal for Early Modern Cultural Studies* 20, no. 2 (2020): 169–91.

27. Heather Dubrow, *Deixis in the Early Modern English Lyric* (New York: Palgrave Macmillan, 2015), 37, emphasis in the original.

28. Donne, *Devotions*, 113.

29. Lauren Leblanc, "'All Writing Is Basically Failure': Ada Limón Reckons with Poetry in Today's World," *Vanity Fair*, May 9, 2022, https://www.vanityfair.com/style/2022/05/ada-limon-reckons-with-poetry-in-todays-world.

30. Ada Limón, "The End of Poetry," in *Together in a Sudden Strangeness*.

31. Leblanc, "All Writing is Basically Failure."

32. Leblanc, "All Writing is Basically Failure."

33. Stewart, *Poetry and the Fate of the Senses*, 2.

Bibliography

Alpers, Paul. "Bower of Bliss." In *Spenser Encyclopedia*, edited by A. C. Hamilton. Toronto: University of Toronto Press, 1990.

Alpers, Paul. "Narration in *The Faerie Queene*." *English Literary History* 44, no. 1 (Spring 1977): 19–39.

Archer, Jayne. "A 'Perfect Circle'? Alchemy in the Poetry of Hester Pulter." *Literature Compass* 2, no. 1 (2005): 1–14.

Ariès, Phillipe. *The Hour of Our Death*. 2nd ed. Translated by Helen Weaver. New York: Vintage, 2008.

Ashmore, John. *Certain selected odes of Horace, Englished; and their arguments annexed. With poems (antient and modern) of divers subjects, translated. Whereunto are added, both in Latin and English, sundry new epigrams, anagrams, epitaphs.* Printed by H[umphrey] L[ownes] for Richard Moore. London, 1621.

Atkinson, David W. "The English *ars moriendi*: Its Protestant Transformation." *Renaissance and Reformation* 6, no. 1 (1982): 1–10.

Atkinson, David W. "*A Salve for a Sicke Man:* William Perkins' Contribution to the *ars moriendi*." *Historical Magazine of the Protestant Episcopal Church* 46, no. 4 (1977): 409–18.

Bailey, Moya. "The Ethics of Pace." *South Atlantic Quarterly* 120, no. 2 (2021): 285–99.

Ballard, Thomas. *A catalogue of the libraries of the learned Sir Thomas Brown, and Dr. Edward Brown, his son . . . Which will begin to be sold by auction, at the Black-boy coffee-house, in Ave-Mary-Lane, near Ludgate, on Monday the 8th day of January, 1710/11, beginning every evening at four of the clock, till the sale is finish'd.* London, 1711. Facsimile edition, University Microfilms, 1969. https://hdl.handle.net/2027/uiug.30112113407982.

Barthes, Roland. *Mourning Diary*. Edited by Nathalie Léger. Translated by Richard Howard. New York: Hill and Wang, 2012.

Bataille, Georges. *Eroticism*. Translated by Mary Dalwood. London: Marion Boyers, 1987.

Bearden, Elizabeth. *Monstrous Kinds: Body, Space, and Narrative in Renaissance Representations of Disability*. Ann Arbor: University of Michigan Press, 2019.

Becon, Thomas. *The Sick Man's Salve, wherein the faithful Christian may learn both how to behave themselves patiently and thankfully in the time of sickness, and also virtuously to dispose their temporal goods, and finally to prepare themselves gladly and godly to die.* London, 1568.

Bevington, David. *From "Mankind" to Marlowe: Growth of Structure in the Popular Drama of Tudor England*. Cambridge, MA: Harvard University Press, 1962.

Black, Kathy. *A Healing Homiletic: Preaching and Disability*. Nashville, TN: Abingdon, 1996.

Black, Sheila et al., ed. *Beauty Is a Verb: The New Poetry of Disability*. El Paso: Cinco Puntos, 2011.

Blake, Liza, ed. "The [Uncertain] Hope January 1665," by Hester Pulter (Poem 65, Amplified Edition B). In *The Pulter Project: Poet in the Making*, edited by Leah Knight and Wendy Wall (2018). http://pulterproject.northwestern.edu.

Braden, Gordon. *Petrarchan Love and the Continental Renaissance*. New Haven, CT: Yale University Press, 1999.

Braden, Gordon. "Shakespeare's Petrarchism." In *Shakespeare's Sonnets: Critical Essays*, edited by James Schiffer. New York: Garland, 2000.

Brooks, Cleanth. *The Well-Wrought Urn*. New York: Harcourt, Brace, & World, 1947.

Browne, Sir Thomas. *Religio Medici and Urne-Buriall*. Edited by Stephen Greenblatt and Ramie Targoff. New York: New York Review of Books, 2012.

Bullard, Angela D. "Tempering the Intemperate in Spenser's Bower of Bliss." *Spenser Studies* 31, no. 1 (2018): 167–87.

Burke, Victoria. "Playing Football with the Stars: Hester Pulter Rethinks the Metaphysical Astronomy Poem." *Journal for Early Modern Cultural Studies* 20, no. 2 (2020): 169–91.

Burton, Ben, and Elizabeth Scott-Baumann, eds. *The Work of Form: Poetics and Materiality in Early Modern Culture*. Oxford: Oxford University Press, 2014.

Butzner, Alexis. "'I feare the more': Donne's *Devotions* and the Impossibility of Dying Well." *Studies in Philology* 114, no. 2 (Spring 2017): 331–67.

Bynum, Caroline Walker. *The Resurrection of the Body in Western Christianity, 200–1336*. New York: Columbia University Press, 1995.

Calhoun, Joshua. "Ecosystemic Shakespeare: Vegetable Memorabilia in the Sonnets." *Shakespeare Studies* 39 (2011): 64–73.

Callaghan, Dympna. "Confounded by Winter: Speeding Time in Shakespeare's Sonnets." In *A Companion to Shakespeare's Sonnets*, edited by Michael Schoenfeldt. Malden, MA: Blackwell, 2007.

Cameron, Sharon. *Lyric Time: Dickinson and the Limits of Genre*. Baltimore, MD: Johns Hopkins University Press, 1979.

Campana, Joseph. "Boy Toys and Liquid Joys: Pleasure and Power in the Bower of Bliss." *Modern Philology* 106, no. 3 (2009): 465–96.

Carey, John. *John Donne: Life, Mind, and Art*. Oxford: Oxford University Press, 1981.

Castiglione, Baldassare. *The Book of the Courtier*. Translated by Thomas Hoby. London, 1603.

Caswell, Glenys. *Dying Alone: Challenging Assumptions*. London: Palgrave Macmillan, 2022.

Catullus. *The Poems of Catullus*. Translated by Peter Green. Berkeley: University of California Press, 2007.

Chapple, Helen. "Bringing Dying Out of the Hospital's Closet." *American Medical Association Journal of Ethics* 22, no. 12 (2020): E1062–66.

Colie, Rosalie. *Shakespeare's Living Art*. Princeton, NJ: Princeton University Press, 2015.

Crawford, Julie. *Marvelous Protestantism: Monstrous Births in Post-Reformation England*. Baltimore, MD: Johns Hopkins University Press, 2005.

Creamer, Deborah Beth. *Disability and Christian Theology: Embodied Limits and Constructive Possibilities*. Oxford: Oxford University Press, 2009.
Crystal, David, and Ben Crystal. "Shakespeare: Original Pronunciation." The Open University, October 17, 2011. YouTube. 10 min., 21 sec. https://youtu.be/gPlpphT7n9s.
Culler, Jonathan. *Theory of the Lyric*. Cambridge, MA: Harvard University Press, 2015.
Cummings, Brian, ed. *The Book of Common Prayer: Texts of 1549, 1559, and 1662*. Oxford: Oxford University Press, 2011.
Daniel, Drew. *The Joy of the Worm: Suicide and Pleasure in Early Modern English Literature*. Chicago: University of Chicago Press, 2022.
Davis, Lennard. *Enforcing Normalcy: Disability, Deafness, and The Body*. New York: Verso, 1995.
de Grazia, Margreta. "The Scandal of Shakespeare's Sonnets." In *Shakespeare's Sonnets: Critical Essays*, edited by James Schiffer. New York: Garland, 2000.
Didion, Joan. *The Year of Magical Thinking*. New York: Vintage International, 2006.
Dolan, Frances. "Hester Pulter's Dunghill Poetics." *Journal of Early Modern Cultural Studies* 20, no. 2 (Spring 2020): 16–42.
Dolan, Frances, ed. "Made When I Was Not Well," by Hester Pulter (Poem 51, Amplified Edition). In *The Pulter Project: Poet in the Making*, edited by Leah Knight and Wendy Wall (2018). http://pulterproject.northwestern.edu.
Dolan, Frances, ed. "View But This Tulip," by Hester Pulter (Poem 105, Amplified Edition). In *The Pulter Project: Poet in the Making*, edited by Leah Knight and Wendy Wall (2018). http://pulterproject.northwestern.edu.
Dolven, Jeff. *Scenes of Instruction in Renaissance Romance*. Chicago: University of Chicago Press, 2008.
Dolven, Jeff. "When to Stop Reading *The Faerie Queene*." In *Never Again Would Birds' Song Be the Same: Essays on Early Modern and Modern Poetry in Honor of John Hollander*, edited by Jennifer Lewin. New Haven, CT: Beinecke Library, 2002.
Donne, John. *The Complete Poetry of John Donne*. Edited by John T. Shawcross. New York: Anchor, 1967.
Donne, John. *Devotions Upon Emergent Occasions together with Deaths Duel*. Ann Arbor: University of Michigan Press, 1975.
Donne, John. *Sermons*. Edited by George R. Potter and Evelyn M. Simpson. Berkeley: University of California Press, 1953.
Donne, John. *The Variorum Edition of the Poetry of John Donne*. Vol. 7.1, *The Holy Sonnets*. Edited by Gary Stringer and Paul A. Parrish. Bloomington: Indiana University Press, 2005.
Donne, John. *The Variorum Edition of the Poetry of John Donne*. Vol. 8, *The Epigrams, Epithalamions, Epitaphs, Inscriptions, and Miscellaneous Poems*. Edited by Gary Stringer, Ted-Larry Pebworth, Ernest W. Sullivan, II, William A. McClung, and Jeffrey Johnson. Bloomington: Indiana University Press, 1995.
Dowd, Michelle. "Breaking Form in Early Modern Literary Studies." *English Literary Renaissance* 50, no. 1 (2019): 40–46.
Dubrow, Heather. *The Challenges of Orpheus*. Baltimore, MD: Johns Hopkins University Press, 2008.
Dubrow, Heather. *Deixis in the Early Modern English Lyric*. New York: Palgrave Macmillan, 2015.

Dubrow, Heather. "Donne's 'Epithalamion Made at Lincoln's Inn': An Alternative Interpretation." *Studies in English Literature, 1500–1900* 16, no. 1 (Winter 1976): 131–43.

Dubrow, Heather. *Echoes of Desire: English Petrarchism and Its Counterdiscourses.* Ithaca, NY: Cornell University Press, 1995.

Dubrow, Heather. "'Incertainties Now Crown Themselves Assur'd': The Politics of Plotting Shakespeare's Sonnets." In *Shakespeare's Sonnets—Critical Essays*, edited by James Schiffer. New York: Garland, 2000.

Dubrow, Heather. "ShakeSpeare's Undramatic Monologues: Toward a Reading of the Sonnets." *Shakespeare Quarterly* 32, no. 1 (1981): 55–68.

Duffy, Timothy. "Epistolary Copulation in John Donne's Verse Letters." *Studies in English Literature, 1500–1900* 59, no. 1 (Winter 2019): 67–90.

Duncan, Claire. "'Nature's Bastards': Grafted Generation in Early Modern England." *Renaissance and Reformation* 38, no. 2 (2015): 121–47.

Durling, Robert. "The Bower of Bliss and Armida's Palace." *Comparative Literature* 6, no. 4 (Autumn 1954): 335–347.

Eardley, Alice. "Hester Pulter's 'Indivisibles' and the Challenges of Annotating Early Modern Women's Poetry." *Studies in English Literature, 1500–1900* 52, no. 1 (2012): 117–41.

Eiesland, Nancy. *The Disabled God: Toward a Liberatory Theology of Disability.* Nashville, TN: Abingdon, 1994.

Ellerbeck, Erin. "Adoption and the Language of Horticulture in *All's Well That Ends Well.*" *Studies in English Literature, 1500–1900* 51, no. 2 (2011): 305–26.

Engel, William, and Grant Williams, eds. *The Shakespearean Death Arts: Hamlet among the Tombs.* New York: Palgrave Macmillan, 2022.

Evans, Kasey. *Colonial Virtue: The Mobility of Temperance in Renaissance England.* Toronto: University of Toronto Press, 2012.

Ferry, Anne. *All in War With Time: Love Poetry of Shakespeare, Donne, Jonson, Marvell.* Cambridge, MA: Harvard University Press, 1975.

Fineman, Joel. *Shakespeare's Perjured Eye: The Invention of Poetic Subjectivity in the Sonnets.* Berkeley: University of California Press, 1986.

Frye, Northrop. "Approaching the Lyric." In *Lyric Theory: Beyond New Criticism*, edited by Chaviva Hošek and Patricia Parker. Ithaca, NY: Cornell University Press, 1985.

Garland-Thomson, Rosemarie. "Shape Structures Story: Fresh and Feisty Stories About Disability." *Narrative* 15, no. 1 (2007): 113–23.

Ghebreyesus, Tedros Adhanom. "Opening Remarks at the Media Briefing on COVID-19." World Health Organization, March 11, 2020. https://www.who.int/director-general/speeches/detail/who-director-general-s-opening-remarks-at-the-media-briefing-on-covid-19---11-march-2020.

Gil, Daniel Juan. *The Fate of the Flesh: Secularization and Resurrection in the Seventeenth Century.* New York: Fordham University Press, 2021.

Goldberg, Jonathan. *Endlesse Work: Spenser and the Structure of Discourse.* Baltimore, MD: Johns Hopkins University Press, 1981.

Gordon, Colby. *Glorious Bodies: Trans Theology and Renaissance Literature.* Chicago: University of Chicago Press, 2024.

Greene, Roland. "Sir Philip Sidney's *Psalms*, the Sixteenth-Century Psalter, and the Nature of Lyric." *Studies in English Literature* 30 (1990): 19–40.

Greene, Thomas M. "Pitiful Thrivers: Failed Husbandry in the Sonnets." In *Shakespeare's Poems: The Scholarly Literature*, edited by Stephen Orgel and Sean Keilen. New York: Routledge, 1999.

Gregerson, Linda. *The Reformation of the Subject: Spenser, Milton, and the English Protestant Epic*. Cambridge, UK: Cambridge University Press, 1995.

Greteman, Blaine. "'All this seed pearl': John Donne and Bodily Presence." *College Literature* 37, no. 3 (Summer 2010): 26–42.

Grogan, Jane. *Exemplary Spenser: Visual and Poetic Pedagogy in* The Faerie Queene. New York: Routledge, 2016.

Group Phi. "Doing Genre." In *New Formalisms and Literary Theory*, edited by Verena Theile and Linda Tredennick. New York: Palgrave Macmillan, 2013.

Guibbory, Achsah. *The Map of Time: Seventeenth-Century English Literature and Ideas of Pattern in History*. Urbana: University of Illinois Press, 1986.

Guibbory, Achsah. "'The Relique,' *The Song of Songs*, and Donne's *Songs and Sonnets*." *John Donne Journal* 15 (1996): 23–44.

Guy-Bray, Stephen. *Against Reproduction: Where Renaissance Texts Come From*. Toronto: University of Toronto Press, 2009.

Guy-Bray, Stephen. "Notes on the Couplet in the Sonnet." *Shakespeare* 18, no. 3 (2022): 322–31.

Habib, Imtiaz. *Shakespeare and Race: Postcolonial Praxis in the Early Modern Period*. New York: University Press of America, 2000.

Halberstam, Jack. *In A Queer Time and Place*. New York: NYU Press, 2005.

Hammons, Pamela. "Despised Creatures: The Illusion of Maternal Self-Effacement in Seventeenth-Century Child Loss Poetry." *ELH* 66, no. 1 (Spring 1999): 25–49.

Harris, Mitchell M. "The Expense of Ink and Wastes of Shame: Poetic Generation, Black Ink, and Material Waste in Shakespeare's *Sonnets*." In *The Materiality of Color*, edited by Andrea Feeser. New York: Routledge 2017.

Heffernan, Megan. *Making the Miscellany: Poetry, Print, and the History of the Book in Early Modern England*. Philadelphia: University of Pennsylvania Press, 2021.

Herbert, George. *George Herbert: The Complete English Poems*. Edited by John Tobin. New York: Penguin, 2004.

Herrick, Robert. *Seventeenth-Century British Poetry, 1604–1660*. Edited by John P. Rumrich and Gregory Chaplin. New York: Norton, 2006.

Hobgood, Allison. *Beholding Disability in Renaissance England*. Ann Arbor: University of Michigan Press, 2021.

Hsy, Jonathan. "Blind Advocacy: Blind Readers, Disability Theory, and Accessing John Gower." *Accessus* 1, no. 1 (2013): 1–38.

Hyman, Wendy Beth. *Impossible Desire and the Limits of Knowledge in Renaissance Poetry*. Oxford: Oxford University Press, 2019.

Hyman, Wendy Beth. "Seizing Flowers in Spenser's Bower and Garden." *English Literary Renaissance* 37, no. 2 (2007): 193–214.

Jacobs, Henry E. "Shakespeare, Revenge Tragedy, and the Ideology of the *Memento Mori*." *Shakespeare Studies* 21 (1993): 96–108.

Johnson, Samuel. *Samuel Johnson's Lives of the Poets*. Edited by Roger Lonsdale. Oxford: Oxford University Press, 2006.

Jones, E. A. "Anchorites and Hermits in Historical Context." In *Approaching Medieval Anchoritic and Mystical Texts*, edited by Dee Dyas, Valerie Edden, and Roger Ellis. Cambridge, UK: D. S. Brewer, 2005.

Kafer, Alison. *Feminist, Queer, Crip*. Bloomington: Indiana University Press, 2013.

Kaske, Carol. "'Religious Reuerence Doth Buriall Teene': Christian and Pagan in *The Faerie Queene*, II. i–ii." *Review of English Studies* 30, no. 118 (1979): 129–43.

Kenny, Amy. *Humoral Wombs on the Shakespearean Stage*. London: Palgrave Macmillan, 2019.

Kittay, Eve Feder. "Centering Justice on Dependency and Recovering Freedom." In *The Disability Studies Reader*, 5th ed., edited by Lennard Davis. New York: Routledge, 2017.

Knight, Leah, and Wendy Wall, ed. "Why Must I Thus Forever Be Confined?," by Hester Pulter (Poem 25, Elemental Edition). In *The Pulter Project: Poet in the Making*, edited by Leah Knight and Wendy Wall (2018). http://pulterproject.northwestern.edu.

Kolkovich, Elizabeth. "Child Loss Elegies." *Pulter Project*. Accessed November 5, 2024, https://pulterproject.northwestern.edu/#child-loss-elegies.

Kolkovich, Elizabeth. "In Defense of Indulgence: Hester Pulter's Maternal Elegies." *Journal of Early Modern Cultural Studies* 20, no. 2 (Spring 2020): 43–70.

Kristeva, Julia. *Powers of Horror*. Translated by Leon S. Roudiez. New York: Columbia University Press, 1982.

Kübler-Ross, Elisabeth. *On Death and Dying: What the Dying Have to Teach Doctors, Nurses, Clergy, and Their Own Families*. New York: Scribner, 2014, originally 1969.

Kübler-Ross, Elisabeth. *Questions and Answers on Death and Dying*. New York: Macmillan, 1974.

Kunin, Aaron. "Shakespeare's Preservation Fantasy." *PMLA* 124, no. 1 (2009): 92–106.

Kuppers, Petra. "Crip Time." *Tikkun* 29, no. 4 (2014): 29–30.

Leblanc, Lauren. "'All Writing Is Basically Failure': Ada Limón Reckons with Poetry in Today's World." *Vanity Fair*, May 9, 2022. https://www.vanityfair.com/style/2022/05/ada-limon-reckons-with-poetry-in-todays-world.

Levine, Caroline. *Forms: Whole, Rhythm, Hierarchy, Network*. Princeton, NJ: Princeton University Press, 2015.

Lewis, C. S. *English Literature in the Sixteenth Century: Excluding Drama*. Oxford: Clarendon, 1954.

Lewis, C. S. *A Grief Observed*. New York: Harper Collins, 1994.

Limón, Ada. "The End of Poetry." In *Together in a Sudden Strangeness*, edited by Alice Quinn. New York: Alfred A. Knopf, 2020.

Llewelyn, Nigel. *The Art of Death: Visual Culture in The English Death Ritual c.1500–c.1800*. London: Reaktion, 1997.

Lobsien, Verena. *Transparency and Dissimulation: Configurations of Neoplatonism in Early Modern English Literature*. Berlin: DeGruyter, 2010.

Lorde, Audre. "Uses of the Erotic; The Erotic as Power." In *Women in Culture: An Intersectional Anthology for Gender and Women's Studies*, edited by Bonnie Kime Scott, Susan E. Cayleff, Anne Donadey, and Irene Lara. Malden, MA: Wiley Blackwell, 2017.

Love, Genevieve. *Early Modern Theatre and the Figure of Disability*. New York: Bloomsbury, 2018.

Lucas, Dave. "Quarantine." In *Together in a Sudden Strangeness*, edited by Alice Quinn. New York: Alfred A. Knopf, 2020.

Marlowe, Christopher. *The Complete Poems and Translations*. Edited by Stephen Orgel. New York: Penguin, 2007.

Marvell, Andrew. *Andrew Marvell*. Edited by Frank Kermode and Keith Walker. Oxford: Oxford University Press, 1990.

McClellan, Andrew. *Abused Bodies in Roman Epic*. Cambridge, UK: Cambridge University Press, 2019.

McDowell, Nicholas. "Dead Souls and Modern Minds?: Mortalism and the Early Modern Imagination, from Marlowe to Milton." *Journal of Medieval and Early Modern Studies* 40, no. 3 (2010): 559–92.

McFague, Sallie. "Metaphorical Theology." In *Sallie McFague: Collected Readings*, edited by David B. Lott. Minneapolis: Fortress, 2013.

Milton, John. *The Complete Poetry and Essential Prose of John Milton*. Edited by William Kerrigan, John Rumrich, and Stephen M. Fallon. New York: Modern Library, 2007.

Mingus, Mia. "You Are Not Entitled to Our Deaths: COVID, Abled Supremacy, and Interdependence." *Leaving Evidence*, January 16, 2022. https://leavingevidence.wordpress.com/2022/01/16/you-are-not-entitled-to-our-deaths-covid-abled-supremacy-interdependence/.

Mintz, Susannah B. "Lyric Bodies: Poets on Disability and Masculinity." *PMLA* 127, no. 2 (2012): 248–63.

Mitchell, David T., and Sharon L. Snyder. "Disability Haunting in American Poetics." *Journal of Literary & Cultural Disability Studies* 1, no. 1 (2007): 1–12.

Mitchell, David T., and Sharon L. Snyder. *Narrative Prosthesis: Disability and the Dependencies of Discourse*. Ann Arbor: University of Michigan Press, 2001.

Montaigne, Michel. *Shakespeare's Montaigne: The Florio Translation of the Essays, A Selection*. Translated by John Florio. Edited by Stephen Greenblatt and Peter G. Platt. New York: New York Review of Books, 2014.

Nardizzi, Vin. "Shakespeare's Penknife: Grafting and Seedless Generation in the Procreation Sonnets." *Renaissance and Reformation* 32, no. 1 (2009): 83–106.

Neill, Michael. *Issues of Death: Mortality and Identity in English Renaissance Tragedy*. Oxford: Oxford University Press, 1997.

Newstok, Scott. *Quoting Death in Early Modern England: The Poetics of Epitaphs Beyond the Tomb*. New York: Palgrave Macmillan, 2009.

Nohrnberg, James. *The Analogy of* The Faerie Queene. Princeton, NJ: Princeton University Press, 1976.

Novarr, David. "Donne's 'Epithalamion Made at Lincoln's Inn': Context and Date." *Review of English Studies* 7, no. 27 (July 1956): 250–63.

Nunn, Hillary. *Staging Anatomies: Dissection and Spectacle in Early Stuart Tragedy*. New York: Routledge, 2005.

Oldenburg, Scott. *A Weaver-Poet and the Plague*. University Park: Pennsylvania State University Press, 2020.

Parfitt, G. A. E. "Renaissance Wombs, Renaissance Tombs." *Renaissance and Modern Studies* 15, no. 1 (1971): 23–33.

BIBLIOGRAPHY

Parris, Ben. *Vital Strife: Sleep, Insomnia, and the Early Modern Ethics of Care*. Ithaca, NY: Cornell University Press, 2022.

Paster, Gail Kern. *The Body Embarrassed: Drama and the Disciplines of Shame in Early Modern England*. Ithaca, NY: Cornell University Press, 1993.

Patterson, Mary Hampson. *Domesticating the Reformation: Protestant Best Sellers, Private Devotion, and the Revolution of English Piety*. Madison, NJ: Farleigh Dickinson University Press, 2007.

Perkins, William. *A Salve for a Sicke Man, Or, A Treatise Containing the Nature, Differences, and Kindes of Death as also the Right Manner of Dying Well. and it may Serue for Spirituall Instruction to 1. Mariners when they Goe to Sea. 2. Souldiers when they Goe to Battell. 3. Women when they Trauell of Child*. Cambridge, UK, 1595.

Petrarch, Francesco. *Petrarch's Lyric Poems: The Rime Sparse and Other Lyrics*. Translated by Robert Durling. Cambridge, MA: Harvard University Press, 1976.

Price, Margaret. "The Bodymind Problem and the Possibilities of Pain." *Hypatia* 30, no. 1 (2014): 268–84.

Pulter, Hester. *Poems, Emblems, and the Unfortunate Florinda*. Edited by Alice Eardley. New York: Iter, 2014.

Pulter, Hester. *The Pulter Project*. Edited by Leah Knight and Wendy Wall. Accessed March 4, 2025. https://pulterproject.northwestern.edu.

Puttenham, George. *The Art of English Poesy: A Critical Edition*. Edited by Frank Whigham and Wayne A. Rebhorn. Ithaca, NY: Cornell University Press, 2007.

Quint, David. *Epic and Empire: Politics and Generic Form from Virgil to Milton*. Princeton, NJ: Princeton University Press, 1993.

Race, William H. *Classical Genres and English Poetry*. New York: Routledge, 1988.

Ramazani, Jahan. *Poetry and Its Others: News, Prayer, Song, and the Dialogue of Genres*. Chicago: University of Chicago Press, 2013.

Rambuss, Richard. "Sacred Subjects and the Aversive Metaphysical Conceit: Crashaw, Serrano, Ofili." *English Literary History* 71, no. 2 (2004): 497–530.

Recovering Disability in Early Modern England. Edited by Allison P. Hobgood and David Houston Wood. Columbus: Ohio State University Press, 2013.

Ricks, Christopher. "Donne After Love." In *Literature and the Body: Essays on Populations and Persons*, edited by Elaine Scarry. Baltimore, MD: Johns Hopkins University Press, 1988.

Roberts, Donald Ramsey. "The Death Wish of John Donne." *PMLA* 62, no. 4 (December 1947): 958–76.

Rooney, Ellen. "Form and Contentment." *Modern Language Quarterly* 61, no. 1 (2000): 17–40.

Rosenberg, Jessica. "The Point of the Couplet: Shakespeare's *Sonnets* and Tusser's *A Hundreth Good Pointes of Husbandrie*." *English Literary History* 83, no. 1 (2016): 1–41.

Ross, Sarah C. E. "Hester Pulter's Devotional Complaints." *Journal of Early Modern Cultural Studies* 20, no. 2 (Spring 2020): 99–119.

Row-Heyveld, Lindsey. *Dissembling Disability in Early Modern English Drama*. Cham, Switzerland: Palgrave Macmillan / Springer Nature, 2018.

Samuels, Ellen. "Six Ways of Looking at Crip Time." *Disability Studies Quarterly* 37, no. 3 (2017). https://doi.org/10.18061/dsq.v37i3.5824.

Samuels, Ellen, and Elizabeth Freeman. "Introduction: Crip Temporalities." *South Atlantic Quarterly* 120, no. 2 (2021): 245–54.

San Juan, Rose Marie. "The Turn of the Skull: Andreas Vesalius and the Early Modern Memento Mori." *Art History: Journal of the Association of Art Historians* 35, no. 5 (2012): 958–75.

Sawday, Jonathan. *The Body Emblazoned: Dissection and the Human Body in Renaissance Culture*. New York: Routledge, 1995.

Scarry, Elaine. "Donne: 'but yet the body is his booke.'" In *Literature and the Body: Essays on Populations and Persons*, edited by Elaine Scarry. Baltimore, MD: Johns Hopkins University Press, 1988.

Scarry, Elaine. "Introduction." In *Literature and the Body: Essays on Populations and Persons*, edited by Elaine Scarry. Baltimore, MD: Johns Hopkins University Press, 1988.

Schalk, Sami. *Bodyminds Reimagined: (Dis)Ability, Race, and Gender in Black Women's Speculative Fiction*. Durham, NC: Duke University Press, 2018.

Schoenfeldt, Michael. *Bodies and Selves in Early Modern England: Physiology and Inwardness in Spenser, Shakespeare, Herbert, and Milton*. Cambridge, UK: Cambridge University Press, 1999.

Schoenfeldt, Michael. "Thinking Through the Body: Corporeality and Interiority in Donne." *GRAAT* 25 (January 2002): 22–8.

Scott-Baumann, Elizabeth, ed. "The Circle [1]," by Hester Pulter (Poem 17, Amplified Edition). In *The Pulter Project: Poet in the Making*, edited by Leah Knight and Wendy Wall (2018). http://pulterproject.northwestern.edu.

Scott-Baumann, Elizabeth, ed. "The Circle [2]," by Hester Pulter (Poem 21, Amplified Edition). In *The Pulter Project: Poet in the Making*, edited by Leah Knight and Wendy Wall (2018). http://pulterproject.northwestern.edu.

Scott-Baumann, Elizabeth, ed. "The Circle [3]," by Hester Pulter (Poem 25, Amplified Edition). In *The Pulter Project: Poet in the Making*, edited by Leah Knight and Wendy Wall (2018). http://pulterproject.northwestern.edu.

Scott-Baumann, Elizabeth. "Hester Pulter's Well-Wrought Urns: Early Modern Women, Sonnets, and New Criticism." *Journal of Early Modern Cultural Studies* 20, no. 2 (Spring 2020): 120–43.

Shakespeare, Tom. *Disability Rights and Wrongs Revisited*. New York: Routledge, 2014.

Shakespeare, William. *All the Sonnets of Shakespeare*. Edited by Paul Edmonson and Stanley Wells. Cambridge, UK: Cambridge University Press, 2020.

Shakespeare, William. *The Oxford Shakespeare: The Complete Sonnets and Poems*. Edited by Colin Burrow. Oxford: Oxford University Press, 2002.

Shakespeare, William. *Shakespeare's Sonnets*. Edited by Stephen Booth. New Haven, CT: Yale University Press, 2000.

Shakespeare, William. *Shakespeare's Sonnets*. 3rd ed. Edited by Katherine Duncan-Jones. London: The Arden Shakespeare, Bloomsbury, 2010.

Shakespeare, William. *The Sonnets*. Edited by Walter Cohen. In *The Norton Shakespeare*, 3rd ed., edited by Stephen Greenblatt, Walter Cohen, Susanne Gossett, Jean E. Howard, Katharine Eisaman Maus, and Gordon McMullan. New York: Norton, 2016.

Shildrick, Margrit. "'Why Should Our Bodies End at the Skin?': Embodiment, Boundaries, and Somatechnics." *Hypatia* 30, no. 1 (2015): 13–29.

Sidney, Philip. "The Defense of Poesy." In *The Major Works*, edited by Katherine Duncan-Jones. Oxford: Oxford University Press, 2002.

Siebers, Tobin. *Disability Theory*. Ann Arbor: University of Michigan Press, 2008.

Singer, Julie. *Blindness and Therapy in Late Medieval French and Italian Poetry*. Cambridge, UK: D. S. Brewer, 2011.

Smith, D. Vance. *Arts of Dying: Literature and Finitude in Medieval England*. Chicago: University of Chicago Press, 2020.

Smith, Megan Kathleen. "Reading It Wrong to Get It Right: Sacramental and Excremental Encounters in Early Modern Poems About Hair Jewelry." *Philological Quarterly* 94, no. 4 (Fall 2015): 353–75.

Sobchack, Vivian. "A Leg to Stand On: Prosthetics, Metaphor, and Materiality." In *The Prosthetic Impulse: From a Posthuman Present to a Biocultural Future*, edited by Marquard Smith and Joanne Morra. Cambridge, MA: MIT Press, 2006.

Spenser, Edmund. *The Faerie Queene*. Edited by A. C. Hamilton, Hiroshi Yamashita, and Toshiyuki Suzuki. London: Pearson Longman, 2007.

Sperry, Eileen. "The Art of Dying." *The Collation*, September 13, 2022. Folger Shakespeare Library. https://www.folger.edu/blogs/collation/the-art-of-dying/.

Spiller, Michael. *The Sonnet Sequence: A Study of Its Strategies*. New York: Twayne, 1997.

Steen, Abram. "'remembrest right': Remembering the Dead in John Donne's *Songs and Sonnets*." *Renaissance and Reformation* 33, no. 2 (Spring 2010): 93–124.

Stewart, Susan. *Poetry and the Fate of the Senses*. Chicago: University of Chicago Press, 2002.

Sullivan, Erin. "A Disease Unto Death: Sadness in the Time of Shakespeare." In *Emotions and Health, 1200–1700*, edited by Elena Carrera. Boston: Brill, 2013.

Sutton, Christopher. *Disce Mori Learn to Die: A Religious Discourse Moving Every Christian Man to Enter into a Serious Remembrance of His End*. London, 1662.

Swinton, John. "The Body of Christ Has Down's Syndrome: Theological Reflections on Vulnerability, Disability, and Graceful Communities." *Journal of Pastoral Theology* 13, no. 2 (2003): 71.

Taff, Dyani Johns. "Death and Revolution: Thinking with Hester Pulter." *The Sundial*, October 27, 2020. https://medium.com/the-sundial-acmrs/death-and-revolution-thinking-with-hester-pulter-848d5c966b6d.

Targoff, Ramie. *Common Prayer: The Language of Public Devotion in Early Modern England*. Chicago: University of Chicago Press, 2001.

Targoff, Ramie. *John Donne, Body and Soul*. Chicago: University of Chicago Press, 2008.

Targoff, Ramie. "Mortal Love: Shakespeare's *Romeo and Juliet* and the Practice of Joint Burial." *Representations* 120, no. 1 (2012): 17–38.

Targoff, Ramie. *Posthumous Love: Eros and the Afterlife in Renaissance England*. Chicago: University of Chicago Press, 2014.

Taylor, Jeremy. *The Rule and Exercises of Holy Dying*. London, 1651.

Traub, Valerie. "Sex Without Issue: Sodomy, Reproduction, and Signification in Shakespeare's Sonnets." In *Shakespeare's Sonnets: Critical Essays*, edited by James Schiffer. New York: Garland, 2000.

Van Gennep, Arnold. *The Rites of Passage*. Translated by Monika B. Vizedom and Gabrielle L. Caffee. Chicago: University of Chicago Press, 1960.

Vendler, Helen. *The Art of Shakespeare's Sonnets*. Cambridge, MA: Belknap, 1999.
Vinter, Maggie. *Last Acts: The Art of Dying on the Early Modern Stage*. New York: Fordham University Press, 2019.
Vitkus, Daniel. "The Unfulfilled Form of *The Faerie Queene*: Spenser's Frustrated Fore-Conceit." *Renaissance and Reformation* 35, no. 2 (2012): 83–112.
Wakam, Glenn K., MD, John R. Montgomery, MD, Ben E. Biesterveld, MD, and Craig S. Brown, MD. "Not Dying Alone: Modern Compassionate Care in the Covid-19 Pandemic." *New England Journal of Medicine* 382, no. 24 (June 11, 2020): e88.
Weise, Jillian. "Cyborg: Jillian Weise." *Amplitude*, January 3, 2021. https://livingwithamplitude.com/article/cyborg-jillian-weise/.
Wilcox, Helen. "Miracles of Love and Wit: John Donne's 'The Relic.'" *GRAAT* 25 (January 2002): 119–37.
Williams, Katherine Schaap. *Unfixable Forms: Disability, Performance, and the Early Modern Theater*. Ithaca, NY: Cornell University Press, 2021.
Wills, David. *Inanimation: Theories of Inorganic Life*. Minneapolis: University of Minnesota Press, 2016.
Wills, David. *Prosthesis*. Stanford, CA: Stanford University Press, 1995.
Wilson, Miranda. "Bastard Grafts, Crafted Fruits: Shakespeare's Planted Families." In *The Indistinct Human in Renaissance Literature*, edited by Jean E. Feerick and Vin Nardizzi. New York: Palgrave Macmillan, 2012.
Woodward, Marshelle. "Formalism Dispossessed: Pulter, Donne, and the Obliviated Urn." In *Feminist Formalism and Early Modern Women's Writing*, edited by Lara Dodds and Michelle M. Dowd. Lincoln: University of Nebraska Press, 2022.
World Health Organization. "Number of COVID-19 Deaths Reported to WHO." World Health Organization COVID-19 Dashboard. Accessed October 11, 2024. https://data.who.int/dashboards/covid19/deaths?n=o.
Zimmerman, Susan. *The Early Modern Corpse and Shakespeare's Theatre*. Edinburgh: Edinburgh University Press, 2007.

Index

ability
    see ideology of ability, cure
aging, 14–15, 68–69, 173n47
    wrinkles, 66–69
alchemy, 103, 109–112, 138, 141
Alpers, Paul, 54, 58
Archer, Jayne, 103, 110
Ariés, Phillipe, 171n11
artes moriendi
    cultural legacy of, 8–9, 16–17, 140, 162–163
    formal features of, 18
    lessons in, 30–31, 33–38, 55, 59, 147, 155, 165–166
    time in, 33, 36–37, 107–109, 113, 150
    see also Becon, Thomas; Perkins, William; Sutton, Christopher; Taylor, Jeremy.
asceticism, 30–31
Ashmore, John, 174n69
Atkinson, David W., 16

Bailey, Moya, 115
Barthes, Roland, 97–99
Bearden, Elizabeth, 6, 12
beauty, 4–5, 10, 53, 61–62, 67–70, 73–74, 76, 82
Becon, Thomas
    Sick Mans Salve, 17, 34, 40–41, 162
Bevington, David, 8
The Book of Common Prayer
    burial orders, 109, 120, 155, 179n5
    catechism, 189n30
    marriage rites, 152
Booth, Stephen, 179n5, 180n19
Braden, Gordon, 9
Brooks, Cleanth, 22, 86
Browne, Thomas, 176n30, 184n30
    Religio Medici, 39–41, 47, 106
    Hydriotaphia, or Urne-Buriall, 135
Bullard, Angela D., 54
burial, 46–47, 136–137, 188n15
    see also The Book of Common Prayer
Bynum, Caroline Walker, 122, 148–151, 159, 190n45

Cameron, Sharon, 118–119
Campana, Joseph, 54
cannibalism, 150
Carey, John, 134, 147, 149
carpe diem lyric
    decay in, 51–53, 59–60, 130, 177n63
    literary history of, 171n4, 174n69
    time in, 1–4, 21–23, 51–53, 62, 119
Castiglione, Baldasarre, 9–10
Caswell, Glenys, 163–164
Catullus, 52–53
Chapple, Helen, 173n47
Cohen, Walter, 89
Colie, Rosalie, 72
collision
    between lyric and narrative, 17, 24–27, 57, 64–65, 88–89, 91, 94–95
    between models of time, 100, 107, 115, 120–121, 127–128
    as methodology, 7–8, 100, 132
corpse, 43–44, 75–76, 135–139, 149–152, 154–155
    in art, *see* iconography; memento mori
couplet, 71–73, 78, 86–87, 92, 95–96
COVID-19
    death and dying during, 28, 164
    and community, 161, 164–165, 168–170
Crawford, Julie, 133
Creamer, Deborah Beth, 155–156
crip time, 11–12, 15, 27, 100–101, 115–118, 120–121, 129
Crystal, Ben, 77
Crystal, David, 77
Culler, Jonathan, 118–119
Cummings, Brian, 189n30
cure, 11, 116–117
    see also ideology of ability

Daniel, Drew, 40
Davis, Lennard, 11–12
dead body
    see corpse
death
    the good death, 29–30, 163–164

INDEX

and literary form, 5, 17
as leveler, 190n54
see also time: and mortality
deathbed, 18, 149, 162–164, 166, 168
decomposition, 4, 108–109, 131–132, 134–135, 138–139, 141, 148–152, 154–155
de Grazia, Margreta, 90
Didion, Joan, 97–99
disability
   crip poetics, 173n41
   and death, 14
   disability theology, 133, 155–160
   and literary form, 11–13
   models of, 14, 121
Dolan, Frances, 108, 123, 183n22
Dolven, Jeff, 31, 45, 58–59
Donne, Ann, 189n26
Donne, John
   "The Blossom," 187n12
   "The Canonization," 2
   La Corona, 186n78
   "The Damp," 187n12
   Deaths Duell, 150–151, 153–155
   Devotions on Emergent Occasions, 160–162, 165–166, 168
   "The Dissolution," 134, 138–139, 187n12
   "Epithalamion Made at Lincoln's Inn," 130–131
   "The Extasie," 157
   "The Flea," 136
   "The Funerall," 134–139, 144, 187n12
   Holy Sonnet "Thou Hast Made Me," 145–147
   "Hymn to God the Father," 190n36
   "The Primrose," 187n12
   "The Relique," 134, 136–139, 144
   Sermon on Job 19:26, 148–149, 152–153
   "A Valediction Forbidding Mourning," 140–142, 144
   "A Valediction of My Name in the Window," 142–144
Dowd, Michelle, 16
Dubrow, Heather, 8, 42, 72, 88–91, 119, 168
Duncan, Claire, 80
Duncan-Jones, Katherine, 89, 180n19
Durling, Robert, 177n49

Eardley, Alice, 110
Eiesland, Nancy, 156–159
Elyot, Thomas, 178n72
Engel, William, 17
epic, 33–34
Evans, Kasey, 32

Ferry, Anne, 69–70
Fineman, Joel, 70–71, 91, 94
Florio, John, 179n6
form
   in disability theory, 10–15, 58–59
   formal unity, 86–87, 93–94, 103, 127
   as hermeneutic, 25–27, 32, 48, 57–58, 62–64, 88–89, 95–96, 99–101, 128–129, 132, 158–159, 166–167
   and mortality, 8–9, 17, 33–34, 41–42, 55, 59–60, 90, 114–115
   new formalism, 7–8, 15–16, 101
   see also collision
Freeman, Elizabeth, 116, 120
Frye, Northrop, 118–119
future
   see cure; ideology of ability; resurrection

Gil, Daniel Juan, 127–128, 147–148, 151, 157
Gordan, Colby, 189n22, 191n66
grafting, 79–81
Greene, Roland, 167
Greteman, Blaine, 132
grief
   and embodiment, 98–99
   five stage model of, 117
   and time, 97–100, 102–107, 109, 11, 128–129
   and literary form, 114–115, 120–121
Grogan, Jane, 44, 48
Guibbory, Achsah, 134, 139, 189n33
Guy-Bray, Stephen, 71, 88

Habib, Imtiaz, 90–91
Halberstam, Jack, 115
Herbert, George, 127
   "Grief," 114–115
   "Prayer," 168
Herrick, Robert
   "Corinna's Going A-Maying," 21–23
Horace, 52, 174n69
Hsy, Jonathan, 95–96
Hyman, Wendy Beth, 2, 51–55, 177n63
hypostatic union, 153

iconography, 18, 23
   as reading method, 44–47
   see also memento mori
ideology of ability, 10–11, 118
immortality
   see memorial model; prosthesis, lyric; resurrection.
interdependence, 157–158, 164–166

INDEX

Jacobs, Henry E., 41
Jerome, 190n45
Johnson, Samuel, 131

Kafer, Alison, 11–12, 15, 116–117, 121, 129
Kittay, Eve Feder, 164–165
Kolkovich, Elizabeth, 98, 103–105
Kristeva, Julia, 177n51, 190n48
Kübler-Ross, Elisabeth, 117
Kunin, Aaron, 64–65, 69–70
Kuppers, Petra, 116

Levine, Caroline, 7–8, 100
Lewis, C.S., 88–89, 97
Limón, Ada, 168–170
Llewelyn, Nigel, 18
Lobsien, Verena, 9
Lorde, Audre, 187n5
Love, Genevieve, 13

Marlowe, Christopher
  "The Passionate Shepherd to His Love," 1–2
Marvell, Andrew
  "To His Coy Mistress," 1–2, 119
McFague, Sallie, 158
memento mori
  as literary form, 59–60, 187n12
  moral function of, 39–42, 47–48, 51–53
  role of identification within, 20, 44, 122
  time in, 21–25, 41–42, 48
  tu fui form of, 18–21
memorial model, 62–63, 68–71, 73–79
metaphor
  metaphysical conceit, 131, 143–44
  and theology, 158–160
Milton, John
  Comus, 1884n33
  Paradise Lost, 113
  "To The Lady Margaret Ley," 185n49
Mingus, Mia, 164–165
miracle, 73, 144
miscellany, 89
Mitchell, David T., 12, 58–59, 90–91
Montaigne, Michel, 179n6
mourning
  see grief
mystery, 145, 154, 158–160, 189n30

Nardizzi, Vin, 79–80, 94
narrative, 57–60, 90–91
  and memento mori, 41
  see also time; death
Neill, Michael, 8, 39, 41

Neoplatonism
  body and soul hierarchy, 131–132, 137–138, 141–142, 146, 188n18
  as narrative form, 9–11, 90–91, 94
  in Petrarchan literature, 62–64
Norhnberg, James, 51
Novarr, David, 186n1

Ovid, 183n24

Paster, Gail Kern, 177n51
Perkins, William
  A Salve for a Sicke Man, 34–38, 165–166
Petrarch, Francesco, 87, 172n4
Petrarchan mode, 77–78, 183n24
prayer
  for the dead and dying, 30, 162–163, 166
  and lyric, 166–169
prosthetics, 83–86, 181n30, 181n37
prosthesis, lyric, 63–64, 79, 81–86, 91, 93–96
prosthesis, narrative, 12, 90–91, 94
Pulter, Hester
  "The Circle [1]," 102–109
  "The Circle [2]," 109–112
  "The Circle [3]," 112–114
  "The Eclipse," 114
  "The Hope," 124–127
  "Made When I Was Not Well," 4–5
  "A Solitary Discourse," 114
  "View But This Tulip," 100, 122–124, 126–127
  "Why Must I Thus Forever Be Confined?" 167–168
Puttenham, George, 146

Quint, David, 33

Race, William H., 52
Raleigh, Walter
  "The Nymph's Reply to the Shepherd," 2
Ramazani, Jahan, 166
Rambuss, Richard, 131
resurrection,
  bodily, 121–124, 147–155, 159
  seed metaphor of, 121–123, 149, 152–153, 190n45
  and early modern poetics, 127–128
  see also scripture
Ricks, Christopher, 143
Roberts, Donald Ramsey, 133
Rooney, Ellen, 7
Rosenberg, Jessica, 71–72, 86–87
Row-Heyveld, Lindsey, 12, 156

INDEX

Samuels, Ellen, 115–117, 120
San Juan, Rose Marie, 20, 41, 44
Scarry, Elaine, 81, 188n18, 189n26
Schalk, Sami, 30
Schoenfeldt, Michael, 32, 49, 54, 56–57, 137, 139
Scott-Baumann, Elizabeth, 100–105, 110–113, 124–127
scripture
    1 Corinthians, 121–122, 178n72, 190n45
    1 Thessalonians, 153–155
    Ecclesiastes, 150
    Isaiah, 178n73
    Job, 148–149, 152–153, 178n73, 179n5
    Luke, 165–166
    Numbers, 35
    Philippians, 155
    Romans, 146–147
Shakespeare, Tom, 14
Shakespeare, William
    Julius Caesar, 179n11
    Othello, 179n11
    sonnet 1, 61–62
    sonnet 3, 69
    sonnet 11, 70
    sonnet 15, 79–81
    sonnet 16, 74–76, 82–83
    sonnet 17, 74–76, 82, 96
    sonnet 18, 83–84
    sonnet 19, 65–66, 68–69, 71–73
    sonnet 55, 62, 69
    sonnet 60, 66–69, 71–73
    sonnet 63, 67–69, 71–73
    sonnet 65, 67–69, 71–73
    sonnet 71, 69
    sonnet 74, 69
    sonnet 76, 74, 76–79
    sonnet 81, 69, 84
    sonnet 83, 74
    sonnet 126, 91–96
Sidney, Philip, 80, 160
Siebers, Tobin, 10–11, 30, 34, 57, 118
Singer, Julie, 95–96, 181n30
Smith, D. Vance, 18–19, 107
Smith, Megan Kathleen, 134
Snyder, Sharon L., 12, 58–59, 90–91
Sobchack, Vivian, 84–85
sonnet, 111–112, 145–146
    English, 71–72
    sonnet-like forms, 124, 126
    see also couplets
sonnet sequence, 87–91, 172n25
Spenser, Edmund

The Faerie Queene, 30–32, 57–60
The Faerie Queene Book 2 Canto 1, 38–48
The Faerie Queene Book 2 Canto 9, 55–57
The Faerie Queene Book 2 Canto 12, 49–55
Letter to Raleigh, 31
Spiller, Michael, 88–89
suicide, 37–40, 113
Sullivan, Erin, 98
Sutton, Christopher
    Disce Mori, 17–25, 35–38, 56–57, 150, 162–163, 166
Stewart, Susan, 160, 167, 170
Swinton, John, 157–158

Targoff, Ramie, 22, 51, 133, 137, 140–141, 151, 167, 188n15
Tasso, Torquato, 177n49
Taylor, Jeremy
    The Rule and Exercises of Holy Dying, 107–109, 113, 162, 166, 184n32
temperance, 30–38, 40–41, 46–48, 54–55, 58–59
temporarily able body, 15
time
    as cycle, 103–106, 108–109, 113–114
    as destroyer, 65–68, 74–75, 92
    in lyric, 3–4, 22–23, 27, 42, 62–63, 69–70, 77–78, 92–93, 101, 118–120, 128–129, 167
    and materiality, 68–69, 76–77
    and mortality, 1, 4–6, 19–20, 33, 100, 106–108, 123–129
    in narrative, 21–25, 57–58
    see also artes moriendi; carpe diem lyric, crip time; grief; memento mori
tragedy, 8–9, 39, 172n18

Van Gennep, Arnold, 163
Vaughan, Henry, 127
Vaughan, Richard, 107, 184n33
Vendler, Helen, 72
Vesalius, Andreas, 175n72
Vinter, Maggie, 8–9, 16–17, 163
Vitkus, Daniel, 57–58

Weise, Jillian, 84
Williams, Grant, 17
Williams, Katherine Schaap, 12–13
Wills, David, 83, 85–86
World Health Organization, 28, 161
Woodward, Marshelle, 101, 127, 183n22

xenotransplantation, 181n37

www.ingramcontent.com/pod-product-compliance
Lightning Source LLC
Chambersburg PA
CBHW031359230426
43670CB00006B/591